Fifty Lectures
American Invitational Mathematics Examination (AIME)

Volume 1

http://www.mymathcounts.com/index.php

ACKNOWLEDGEMENTS

We wish to thank the following reviewers for their invaluable solutions, insightful comments, and suggestions for improvements to this book:

Anthony Cheng (UT), William Sun (VA), Kevin Wang (CO), Stephan Xie (TX), Cindy Ye (AR); Christopher Chang (CA), Jessica Chen (NC), Jin Cheng (CA), Felix Cui (NE), Dr. Maria Du (OH), Dr. Changyong Feng (NY), Linda Gong (CA), Deepak Haldiya (FL), Dr. Ziying Han (NY), Yanli Huang (NJ), Tommy Hu (MA), Dr. Li Yong (I L), L. Lin (CA), Latha Philip (Ontario, Canada), Aditya Sharma (IL), Huili Shao (MA), Yiqing Shen (TN), Dr. Yang Wei (TX), Yihan Zhong (CT), and Guihua Zhou (CT).

We would also like to thank the following math contests for their mathematical ideas. Many problems in this book are modified or inspired from these tests. We also cited very few problems directly from these tests for the purpose of comparisons with our own solutions.

The AIME (American Invitational Mathematics Examination).
The ARML (American Regions Mathematics League).
The China High School Math Competition.
USAMO
IMO

Yongcheng Chen, Ph.D., Author.
Guiling Chen, Owner, mymathcounts.com, Typesetter, Editor.

Copyright © 2014 by mymathcounts.com. All rights reserved. Printed in the United States of America. Reproduction of any portion of this book without the written permission of the authors is strictly prohibited, except as may be expressly permitted by the U.S. Copyright Act.

ISBN-13: 978-1499298536
ISBN-10: 1499298536

Please contact mymathcounts@gmail.com for suggestions, corrections, or clarifications.

Table of Contents

Chapter 1 Solid Geometry – Cube and Prism 1

Chapter 2 Solid Geometry - Tetrahedron 19

Chapter 3 Counting with Solid Geometry 43

Chapter 4 Plane Geometry Similar Triangles 64

Chapter 5 Plane Geometry Area and Area Method 94

Chapter 6 Plane Geometry Menelaus and Ceva 126

Chapter 7 Algebraic Manipulations 155

Chapter 8 Logarithms 179

Chapter 9 Solving Equations 202

Chapter 10 Cauchy Inequalities 228

Index 256

This page is intentionally left blank.

BASIC KNOWLEDGE

A prism is a polyhedron bounded by lateral faces and two parallel planes.

Bases, Lateral Surface, Edges.
The two parallel cross-sections which bound a prism are its bases and the other faces form its lateral surface. The edges are the lines in which its lateral faces meet.

The two parallel faces are congruent polygons.
$ABCD = A'B'C'D'$. $ABCD \parallel A'B'C'D'$.

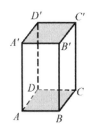

The lateral edges of a prism are equal and parallel.
$AA' = BB'$. $AA' \parallel BB'$.

The lateral faces of a prism are parallelograms.
$ABCD$ is a parallelogram.

An oblique prism is a prism whose lateral edges are oblique to the bases.

A right prism is a prism whose lateral edges are perpendicular to the bases.

A regular prism is a prism whose bases are regular polygons.

The lateral faces are rectangles in a right prism.

A parallelepiped is a prism whose bases, as well as lateral faces, are parallelograms.

A rectangular prism has its bases and all its faces rectangles.

A cube is a parallelepiped whose bases and faces are all squares.

A cross section of a geometric solid is the intersection of a plane and the solid. The cross-sections of a prism made by parallel planes are equal polygons.

Given a prism cut by two parallel planes forming the polygons *ABCDE* and *A'B'C'D'E'*. *ABCDE* = *A'B'C'D'E'*.

 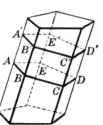

Altitude: The altitude of a prism is the perpendicular distance between the planes of its bases. The altitude of a right prism is equal to its edge.

Area: The lateral area of a prism is the sum of the areas of its lateral faces. The total area is the sum of its lateral area and the areas of its bases.

Volume, *V* The volume of any prism is equal to the product of its base and altitude.

$V = Bh$
B = base area, h = altitude.

Volume of a rectangular Prism:
$V = abc$
a: length of the base of the solid
b: width of the base of the solid
c: height of the solid
d: space diagonal of the solid, $d^2 = a^2 + b^2 + c^2$.

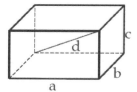

Surface area of a rectangular Prism, *S*
$S = 2(ab + bc + ca)$
Note: For a cube, $a = b = c$.

Example 1. The side, front, and bottom faces of a rectangular solid have areas of 32, 24, and 48 square units respectively. What is the number of cubic units in the volume of the solid?

Solution: 192 (units^2).
Let the dimensions of the solid be a, b, and c.
$a \times b = 32$ (1)
$b \times c = 24$ (2)
$c \times a = 48$ (3)
(1) × (2) × (3):
$(a \times b \times c)^2 = 32 \times 24 \times 48 \Rightarrow a \times b \times c = \sqrt{32 \times 24 \times 48} = 192$.

Example 2. A unit cube has the vertices $ABCD - A'B'C'D'$. Points L, M, N, are on the same plan and are the midpoints of BC, CC', and CD, respectively. The ratio of the surface area of cube to the surface area of the tetrahedron $C-LMN$ can be expressed in simplest radical form as $m(s - \sqrt{n})$, where m, s, and n are positive integers. Find the sum of m, s, and n.

Solution: 014.
The surface area of the cube is $6 \times 1^2 = 6$.
The base of the tetrahedron $C-LMN$ is an equilateral triangle with the side length of $\sqrt{(\frac{BC}{2})^2 + (\frac{CD}{2})^2} = \frac{\sqrt{2}}{2}$. Its area is $\frac{\sqrt{3}}{4}a^2 = \frac{\sqrt{3}}{4} \times (\frac{\sqrt{2}}{2})^2 = \frac{\sqrt{3}}{8}$.

The surface area of the tetrahedron $C-LMN$ is $\frac{\sqrt{3}}{8} + \frac{1}{8} \times 3 = \frac{\sqrt{3}+3}{8}$.

The ratio is $6 \div \frac{\sqrt{3}+3}{8} = \frac{48}{3+\sqrt{3}} = \frac{48(3-\sqrt{3})}{6} = 8(3-\sqrt{3})$. The answer is $8 + 3 + 3 = 14$.

Example 3. The sum of all edges of a rectangular prism is 60. Find the maximum value of the volume.

Solution: 125.
Let x, y, and z be the side lengths of the rectangular prism.

$4(x+y+z) = 60 \implies x+y+z = 15$.

The volume is $V = xyz$.

By $AM-GM$, $V = xyz \leq (\frac{x+y+z}{3})^3 = 5^3 = 125$.

The equality holds when $x = y = z = 5$. The answer is 125.

Example 4. A unit cube has the vertices $ABCD - A'B'C'D'$. Points L, M, N, L', M', N' are the midpoints of $BC, CD, DD', D'A', A'B', B'B$, respectively. The areas of hexagon $LMNL'M'N'$ can be expressed as $\frac{a\sqrt{b}}{c}$, where a, b, c are positive integers. Find the sum of a, b, and c. a and c are relatively prime.

Solution: 010.
Since $M'L' // B'D'$, and $NN' // B'D'$, M', L', N, N' are on the same plane.

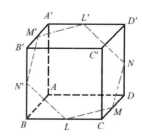

Since $M'M // A'D$, and $L'N // A'D$, M', L', N, M are on the same plane.

Since $NM // D'C$, and $L'L // D'C$, N, M, L, L' are on the same plane.

We see that these three planes share the same three points, so they are the same plane.

Therefore, points L, M, N, L', M', N' are on the same plane.

Let the diagonal of each face of the cube be d.
$M'N' = NL = LM = MN = NL' = L'M' = M'N' = N'L$
$= \frac{1}{2}A'B = \frac{1}{2}d = \frac{\sqrt{2}}{2}$.

So hexagon $LMNL'M'N'$ is a regular hexagon.

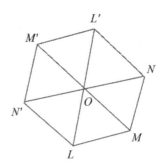

The area is $6 \times \frac{\sqrt{3}}{4}a^2 = 6 \times \frac{\sqrt{3}}{4} \times (\frac{\sqrt{2}}{2})^2 = \frac{3\sqrt{3}}{4}$. the sum is $3 + 3 + 4 = 010$.

Example 5. Given a unit cube $ABCD - EFGH$. From one of the vertices, as A, draw the three surface diagonals meeting at that point. Join the other extremities of these diagonals. These lines are the edges of a new solid $ACFH$, called a regular tetrahedron, or 4-faced solid. The area of the base CFH of the tetrahedron is $\dfrac{\sqrt{a}}{b}$ and the height is $\dfrac{c\sqrt{d}}{e}$ in simplest radical form. Find the product of a, b, c, d, and e.

Solution: 108.
The side length of tetrahedron $A-CFH$ is $\sqrt{2}$. The base CFH is an equilateral triangle with the area $\dfrac{\sqrt{3}}{4} \times (\sqrt{2})^2 = \dfrac{\sqrt{3}}{2}$.

Let the centroid of equilateral triangle CFH be O.

$CO = \dfrac{\sqrt{3}}{4}(\sqrt{2}) \times \dfrac{2}{3} = \sqrt{\dfrac{2}{3}}$.

The height $AO = \sqrt{AC^2 - OC^2} = \sqrt{2 - \dfrac{2}{3}} = \dfrac{2\sqrt{3}}{3}$.

The answer is $3 \times 2 \times 2 \times 3 \times 3 = 108$.

Example 6. As shown in the figure, the cube has the side length of $100\sqrt{3}$. Find the distance from the plane DEG to the plane ACF.

Solution: 100.
We know that BF is $\perp$ to the plane ABC. So $BF \perp AC$.

We know that $BD \perp AC$. Thus AC is $\perp$ to the plane $BDHF$. Line BH is in the plane $BDHF$. So $AC \perp BH$.

Similarly, $CF \perp BH$. Then we know that BH is $\perp$ to the plane ACF.

Similarly, $BH \perp DE$, $BH \perp DG$. Then we know that BH is $\perp$ to the plane DEG.

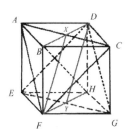

5

Connect *BD*. *BD* meets *AC* at *X*.
Connect *FH*. *FH* meets *EG* at *Y*.

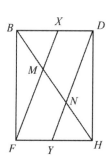

X and *Y* are midpoints of sides *BD* and *FH* of the rectangle *BFHD*, respectively.

Connect *FX*. *FX* meets *BH* at *M*.

Connect *DY*. *DY* meets *BH* at *N*.
M and *N* trisect *BH*.

Since *M* and *N* are the interesting points of *BH* with the planes *ACF* and *DEG*, *MN* is the distance from the plane *DEG* to the plane *ACF*.

So $MN = \frac{1}{3}BH = \frac{\sqrt{3}}{3}a = \frac{\sqrt{3}}{3} \times 100\sqrt{3} = 100$.

Example 7. An octahedron is formed by joining the centers of adjoining faces of a 10 cm × 15 cm × 20 cm rectangular prism. Find the volume of the octahedron.

Solution: 500.
P, Q, R, S, V, V' are the center of faces *ABCD, ABB'A', A'B'C'D', CC'D'D, ADD'A', BCC'B'*, respectively.
Let *AB = a, BC = b,* and *BB' = c*.

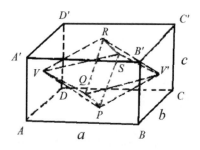

Since the plane *PQRS* ⊥ *VV'*, its area is $\frac{1}{2}bc$.

We know that *VV' = a*, The volume of the octahedron is
$\frac{1}{3} \times (\frac{1}{2}bc) \times a = \frac{1}{6}abc = \frac{1}{6} \times 10 \times 15 \times 20 = 500$.

☆**Example 8.** Three of the vertices of a cube are *P* = (6, 11, 10), *Q* = (7, 7, 1) and *R* = (10, 2, 9) are three vertices of a cube. Find the volume of the cube.

Solution: 343.
Δ*PQR* is an equilateral triangle.
$PQ = \sqrt{(7-6)^2 + (7-11)^2 + (1-10)^2} = \sqrt{1+16+81} = 7\sqrt{2}$.

The side length of the cube is then $x = 7$. The volume of the cube is $7^3 = 343$.

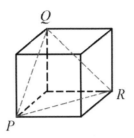
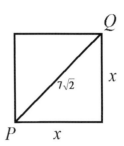

Example 9. (1988 IMO Longlist) Suppose that *ABCD* and *EFGH* are opposite faces of a rectangular solid, with $\angle DHC = 45°$ and $\angle FHB = 60°$. Find the cosine of $\angle BHD$.

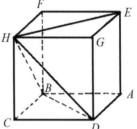

Solution: $\dfrac{\sqrt{6}}{4}$.

Let $AB = 1$.
We know that $\angle DHC$ is 45°. So *CDGH* is also a square with $DH = \sqrt{2}$.

We are given that $\angle FHB = 60°$. We see that $FB = HC = CD = AB = 1$. So $HB = \dfrac{2}{\sqrt{3}}$.

Since $HC = CD$, $DB = HB = \dfrac{2}{\sqrt{3}}$.

Applying the law of cosine to triangle *HBD*, $\cos \angle BHD = \dfrac{(\sqrt{2})^2 + (\dfrac{2}{\sqrt{3}})^2 - (\dfrac{2}{\sqrt{3}})^2}{2 \times \sqrt{2} \times \dfrac{2}{\sqrt{3}}} = \dfrac{\sqrt{6}}{4}$.

☆**Example 10.** A 12 cm × 12 cm square is divided into two pieces by joining to adjacent side midpoints, as shown in the first figure. Copies of the triangular piece are placed on alternate edges of a regular hexagon with the side length of $6\sqrt{2}$ and copies of the other piece are placed on the other edges, as shown in the first figure. The resulting figure is then folded to give a polyhedron with 7 faces. What is the volume of the polyhedron?

(1)   (2)

7

Solution: 864.

Method 1:
The original solid is a cube with the side length 10 cm. The volume of the 7-faces polyhedron is half of the volume of the cube.
The answer is $12^3 /2 = 864$ cm^3.

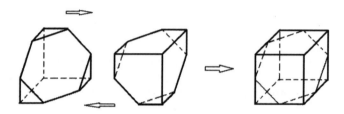

Method 2:
The original solid is a tetrahedron with the side length 18 cm. The volume of the 7-faces polyhedron is $V = \dfrac{1}{3} \times \dfrac{1}{2} \times 18^3 - 3 \times \dfrac{1}{3} \times \dfrac{1}{2} \times 6^3 = 864$.

PROBLEMS

Problem 1. The side, front, and bottom faces of a rectangular solid have areas of $\sqrt{3}$, $\sqrt{5}$, and $\sqrt{15}$ square units, respectively. What is the number of units in the length of the space diagonal of the solid?

Problem 2. For one vertex of a solid cube with the side length of 2, consider the tetrahedron formed by the vertex and the midpoints of three edges that meet at that vertex. The surface area of the portion of the cube that remains when the tetrahedron is cut away can be expressed as $\dfrac{a+\sqrt{b}}{c}$ in simplest radical form. Find the value of $a + b + c$.

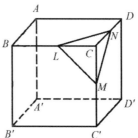

Problem 3. The sum of all edges of a rectangular prism is 60. Find the maximum value of the surface area of the rectangular prism.

Problem 4. The ratio of the length to width to height of a rectangular prism is 4:3:2. The space diagonal of the rectangular prism is the same as the space diagonal of a cube. The ratio of the surface areas of the rectangular prism to the surface area of the cube is $a:b$, where a and b are positive integers relatively prime. Find the sum of a and b.

Problem 5. A rectangular box is 5 inches long, 4 inches wide, and 2 inches high. The vertices are $ABCD - A'B'C'D'$. Points L, M, N, L', M', N' are on the same plane and are the midpoints of $BC, CD, DD', D'A', A'B', B'B$, respectively. The ratio of the area of the hexagon $LMNL'M'N'$ to the area of the triangle $A'BD$ can be expressed as $\dfrac{a}{b}$, where a and b are positive integers relatively prime. Find the sum of a and b.

Problem 6. A rectangular prism with volume 32 cm³ and height 2 cm has the vertices *ABCD-EFGH*. Connect the vertices of *BEG* to form a tetrahedron *FBEG* with the base *BEG*. The maximum distance from *F* to the base *BEG* can be expressed as $\frac{a\sqrt{b}}{c}$ in simplest radical form. Find the product of *a, b,* and *c*.

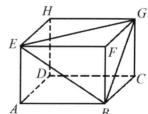

Problem 7. A rectangular prism has the side lengths *a, b,* and *c*. A tetrahedron *P–A'B'C'* is formed as shown in the figure with the base *A'B'C'*. Find *PH*, the distance from *P* to the base *A'B'C'*.

Problem 8. As shown in the figure, the rectangular prism has the dimensions $AA' = 4$, $A'B' = 8$, and $A'D' = 16$. Points *M, N, P, Q* are the midpoints of *A'B', D'A', BC, CD*, respectively. Find the distance between the centroids of △*AMN* and △*C'PQ*.

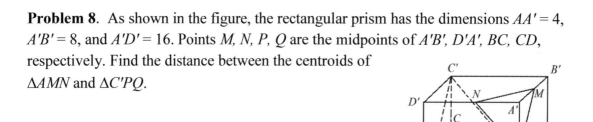

Problem 9. A tetrahedron *D–ACH* is formed by joining the vertices of *ACH* of a rectangular prism with the square base. The surface area of the tetrahedron *DACH* is $\sqrt{3}+3$. $\angle AHC = 60°$. Find the surface area of the rectangular prism.

Problem 10. Given a cube $ABCD-A'B'C'D'$. E is the midpoint of the edge BB'. F is a point on BC. Find $\angle D'EF$ if $C'E \perp EF$.

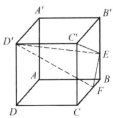

Problem 11. Given a rectangular prism $ABCD-A'B'C'D'$. $AA' = 2AB$. The cosine of the angle formed by $A'B$ and AD' can be expressed as $\dfrac{a}{b}$. Find the sum of a and b if a and b are relatively prime.

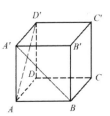

☆**Problem 12 (1986 AIME)** The shortest distances between an interior diagonal of a rectangular parallelepiped (box), P, and the edges it does not meet are $2\sqrt{5}$, $\dfrac{30}{\sqrt{13}}$, and $\dfrac{15}{\sqrt{10}}$. Determine the volume of P.

Problem 13. The space diagonal of a rectangular box is $8\sqrt{2}$. The angle formed by the space diagonal and the base of the rectangular box is $30°$. The angle formed by the two diagonal of the base is 45. Find the volume of the rectangular box.

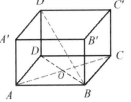

Problem 14. The space diagonal of a rectangular box is l. The angle formed by the space diagonal and the base of the rectangular box is α. The angle formed by the two diagonal of the base is β. Find the volume of the rectangular box.

SOLUTIONS

Problem 1. Solution: 003.
Let the dimensions of the solid be a, b, and c, and the length of the space diagonal is l.
$$a \times b = \sqrt{3} \tag{1}$$
$$b \times c = \sqrt{5} \tag{2}$$
$$c \times a = \sqrt{15} \tag{3}$$

Method 1:
$(1) \times (2) \times (3)$:
$$(a \times b \times c)^2 = \sqrt{3} \times \sqrt{5} \times \sqrt{15} \quad \Rightarrow \quad a \times b \times c = \sqrt{15} \tag{4}$$
$(4) \div (1)$: $c = \sqrt{5}$.
$(4) \div (2)$: $a = \sqrt{3}$.
$(4) \div (3)$: $b = 1$.
$l = \sqrt{a^2 + b^2 + c^2} = \sqrt{3+1+5} = \sqrt{9} = 3$.

Method 2 (by Cindy Ye):
$(1) \times (2)$: $a \times b^2 \times c = \sqrt{3} \times \sqrt{5} = \sqrt{15}$ \hfill (4)
Substituting (3) into (4): $a \times b^2 \times c = a \times c \quad \Rightarrow \quad b^2 = 1$.
So $b = 1$. We then get $a = \sqrt{3}$ and $c = \sqrt{5}$.
$l = \sqrt{a^2 + b^2 + c^2} = \sqrt{3+1+5} = \sqrt{9} = 3$.

Problem 2. Solution: 050.
As shown in the figure, the cube is $ABCD - A'B'C'D'$. Points L, M, N are the midpoints of BC, CC', and CD, respectively.

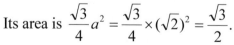

The tetrahedron $C-LMN$ is a regular tetrahedron. Its base is an equilateral triangle with the side length of $\sqrt{(\frac{BC}{2})^2 + (\frac{CD}{2})^2} = \sqrt{2}$.

Its area is $\frac{\sqrt{3}}{4}a^2 = \frac{\sqrt{3}}{4} \times (\sqrt{2})^2 = \frac{\sqrt{3}}{2}$.

The lateral surface area of the tetrahedron $C-LMN$ is $\frac{1}{2} \times 3 = \frac{3}{2}$.

The surface area of the portion of the cube that remains is
$6 \times 4 - \frac{3}{2} + \frac{\sqrt{3}}{2} = \frac{45 + \sqrt{3}}{2}$.
The answer is $45 + 3 + 2 = 50$.

Problem 3. Solution: 150.
Let x, y, and z be the side lengths of the rectangular prism.
$4(x + y + z) = 60 \implies x + y + z = 15$.
The surface area is $S = 2(xy + yz + zx)$
We know that $(x + y + z)^2 = x^2 + y^2 + z^2 + 2(xy + yz + zx)$.
$2(xy + yz + zx) = (x + y + z)^2 - (x^2 + y^2 + z^2)$.
By Cauchy, $x^2 + y^2 + z^2 \geq \frac{(x + y + z)^2}{3} = 75$.
The smallest value of is 75 when $x = y = z = 5$.
When $x^2 + y^2 + z^2$ has the smallest value, $2(xy + yz + zx)$ has the maximum value, which is $15^2 - 75 = 150$.

Problem 4. Solution: 055.
Let the length, width, and height of the rectangular prism be $4x$, $3x$, and $2x$, respectively.
The space diagonal is $d_1 = \sqrt{(4x)^2 + (3x)^2 + (2x)^2} = \sqrt{29}x$.
The space diagonal of the cube is $d_2 = \sqrt{3}y = \sqrt{29}x$. y is the side of the cube. $y = \frac{\sqrt{29}}{\sqrt{3}}x$.
The surface area of the rectangular prism is $2(4x \times 3x + 3x \times 2x + 2x \times 4x) = 52x^2$.
The surface area of the cube is $6y^2 = 6 \times (\frac{\sqrt{29}}{\sqrt{3}})^2 = 58x^2$.
The ratio is $52:58 = 26:29$. The answer is $26 + 29 = 55$.

Problem 5. Solution: 005.
$M'N' = NM = \frac{1}{2}A'B$, $N'L = L'N = \frac{1}{2}A'D$,

$LM = L'M = \frac{1}{2}BD$.

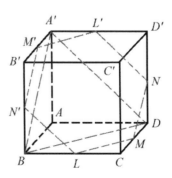

$$S_{M'N'OL'} = S_{N'LMO} = S_{MNL'O} = \frac{1}{2}S_{\triangle A'BD}.$$

The ratio of the areas of hexagon
$LMNL'M'N'$ and triangle $A'BD$ is:
$$\frac{3S_{MNL'O}}{S_{\triangle A'BD}} = \frac{3}{2}.$$
The sum is $2 + 3 = 005$.

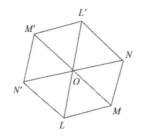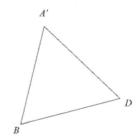

Problem 6. Solution: 036.

Draw $FM \perp EG$ at M in the plane $EFGH$. Connect BM. Let d be the distance from F to the base BEG.

Let $AB = x$ and $BC = y$.

We know that the edge BF is $\perp$ to the plane $EFGH$. We also know that $FM \perp EG$. Thus $BM \perp EG$.

The volume of the tetrahedron $FBEG$ can be expressed in the following two ways:

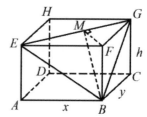

$$\frac{1}{3}S_{\triangle BEG} \cdot d = \frac{1}{3}S_{\triangle EFG} \cdot BF \quad \Rightarrow \quad d = \frac{\frac{1}{3}S_{\triangle EFG} \cdot BF}{\frac{1}{3}S_{\triangle BEG}} = \frac{S_{\triangle EFG} \cdot h}{S_{\triangle BEG}} \text{ or}$$

$$d = \frac{\frac{1}{2}EG \cdot MF}{\frac{1}{2}EG \cdot BM} \cdot h = \frac{MF}{BM} \cdot h = \frac{MF}{\sqrt{BF^2 + MF^2}} \cdot h = \frac{MF \cdot h}{\sqrt{h^2 + MF^2}}.$$

Squaring both sides: $d^2 = \frac{MF^2 \cdot h^2}{h^2 + MF^2} \Rightarrow \quad \frac{1}{d^2} = \frac{h^2 + MF^2}{h^2 \cdot MF^2} = \frac{1}{MF^2} + \frac{1}{h^2}$ (1)

The area of the right triangle EFG can be expressed in the following two ways:
$$\frac{1}{2}EG \cdot MF = \frac{1}{2}EF \cdot FG \quad \Rightarrow \quad MF = \frac{EF \cdot FG}{EG} \text{ or}$$

$MF = \dfrac{xy}{\sqrt{x^2 + y^2}} = \dfrac{xyh}{h\sqrt{x^2+y^2}} = \dfrac{V}{h\sqrt{x^2+y^2}}$. Thus $\dfrac{1}{MF^2} = \dfrac{h^2(x^2+y^2)}{V^2}$.

We know that $x^2 + y^2 \geq 2xy$. The equality holds when $x = y$.

Thus $\dfrac{1}{MF^2} \geq \dfrac{h^2 2xy}{V^2} = \dfrac{2h}{V}$ \hfill (2)

The equality holds when $x = y$.

From (1) and (2), we get: $\dfrac{1}{d^2} \geq \dfrac{2h}{V} + \dfrac{1}{h^2} = \dfrac{2h^3 + V}{Vh^2} \Rightarrow d \leq h\sqrt{\dfrac{V}{2h^3 + V}}$.

When $ABCD$ is a square, the maximum distance from F to the base BEG can be expressed $d = h\sqrt{\dfrac{V}{2h^3 + V}}$, or $d = 2 \times \sqrt{\dfrac{32}{2 \times 2^3 + 32}} = \dfrac{2\sqrt{6}}{3}$. The answer is $2 \times 6 \times 3 = 36$.

Problem 7. Solution:
Applying the law of cosine to triangle $A'B'C'$:

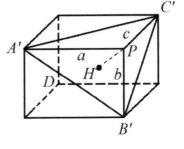

$\cos \angle A'C'B' = \dfrac{C'A'^2 + C'B'^2 - A'B'^2}{2C'A' \cdot C'B'} =$

$\dfrac{(c^2 + a^2) + (c^2 + b^2) - (a^2 + b^2)}{2\sqrt{(c^2 + a^2)(c^2 + b^2)}} = \dfrac{c^2}{\sqrt{(c^2 + a^2)(c^2 + b^2)}}$.

So $\sin \angle A'C'B' = \dfrac{\sqrt{a^2 b^2 + b^2 c^2 + c^2 a^2}}{\sqrt{(c^2 + a^2)(c^2 + b^2)}}$.

So $S_{\triangle A'B'C'} = \dfrac{1}{2} C'A' \times C'B' \sin \angle A'C'B' = \dfrac{1}{2}\sqrt{a^2 b^2 + b^2 c^2 + c^2 a^2}$.

We know that $V_{P-A'B'C'} = \dfrac{1}{6} abc$.

Therefore $\dfrac{1}{3} S_{\triangle A'B'C'} \times PH = \dfrac{1}{6} abc \Rightarrow PH = \dfrac{\frac{1}{6}abc}{\frac{1}{3}S_{\triangle A'B'C'}} = \dfrac{abc}{2 S_{\triangle A'B'C'}} = \dfrac{abc}{\sqrt{a^2 b^2 + b^2 c^2 + c^2 a^2}}$.

Problem 8. Solution: 012.
Let rectangle $A'C'CA$ meet the plane AMN at AX and the plane $C'PQ$ at $C'Y$. Then AX is the median of $\triangle AMN$ and $C'Y$ is the median of $\triangle C'PQ$.

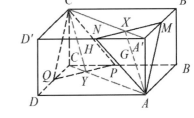

Let the centroids of $\triangle AMN$ and $\triangle C'PQ$ be G and H. The projections of them are G_x, H_x, and G_y, H_y on AC, CC', respectively.

So $G_y H_y = \dfrac{4}{3}$.

Then $G_y H_y = \dfrac{4}{3}$. $G_x H_x = (1 - 2\dfrac{2}{3} \times \dfrac{1}{4})\sqrt{8^2 + 16^2} = \dfrac{2}{3}\sqrt{320}$.

$GH = \sqrt{(\dfrac{4}{3})^2 + (\dfrac{2}{3}\sqrt{320})^2} = \sqrt{\dfrac{16}{9} + \dfrac{4 \times 320}{9}}$

$= \sqrt{\dfrac{1296}{9}} = \sqrt{144} = 12$.

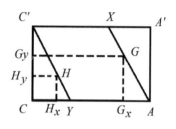

Problem 9. Solution: 012.

Let a be the side length of the rectangle $ABCD$. $AC = \sqrt{2}a$.

We see that $AH = HC$, $\angle AHC = 60°$. Thus $\triangle AHC$ is an equilateral triangle. So $AH = HC$
$AC = \sqrt{2}a$. $DH = a$. So this rectangular prism is a cube. The surface area is $6a^2$.
Let the surface area of the tetrahedron $D-ACH$ be S.

$S = S_{\triangle AHC} + 3 \times \dfrac{a^2}{2} = \dfrac{\sqrt{3}}{4} \times (\sqrt{2}a)^2 + 3 \times \dfrac{a^2}{2} = \dfrac{1}{2}a^2(3 + \sqrt{3})$.

Therefore $\dfrac{1}{2}a^2(3 + \sqrt{3}) = \sqrt{3} + 3$ $\Rightarrow$ $a^2 = 2$.

The surface area of the rectangular prism is $6a^2 = 6 \times 2 = 12$.

Problem 10. Solution: 090.

Since $\angle C'EF = 90°$, $\triangle C'B'E \sim \triangle EBF$. So $\dfrac{C'E}{EF} = \dfrac{B'E}{BF} = \dfrac{C'B'}{EB}$.

Let the side length of the cube be 1. Then $C'B' = 1$. $B'E = \dfrac{1}{2}$.

$C'E = \dfrac{\sqrt{5}}{2}$. $EB = \dfrac{1}{2}$.

Thus $BF = \dfrac{1}{4}$. $EF = \dfrac{\sqrt{5}}{4}$. $CF = \dfrac{3}{4}$.

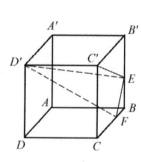

In right triangle $D'C'E$, $D'E = \sqrt{1^2 + (\dfrac{\sqrt{5}}{2})^2} = \dfrac{3}{2}$.

In right triangle $D'C'F$, $D'F = \sqrt{(\sqrt{2})^2 + (\dfrac{3}{4})^2} = \dfrac{\sqrt{41}}{4}$.

$$\cos \angle D'EF = \frac{(\frac{3}{2})^2 + (\frac{\sqrt{5}}{4})^2 - (\frac{\sqrt{41}}{4})^2}{2 \times \frac{3}{2} \times \frac{\sqrt{5}}{4}} = 0 \quad \Rightarrow \quad \angle D'EF = 90°.$$

Problem 11. Solution: 009.
Connect $D'C$ and AC. We know that $A'B // D'C$.
The solution is to find $\cos AD'C$.
Let $AB = 1$. Then $AA' = 2$. $AD' = D'C = \sqrt{5}$. $AC = \sqrt{2}$.
Applying the law of cosine to triangle $AD'C$,

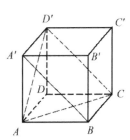

$$\cos \angle AD'C = \frac{(\sqrt{5})^2 + (\sqrt{5})^2 - (\sqrt{2})^2}{2 \times \sqrt{5} \times \sqrt{5}} = \frac{4}{5}.$$

The answer is $4 + 5 = 9$.

☆Problem 12 (1986 AIME) Solution: 750.
The space diagonal is $D'B$.
Let the three edges of the rectangular box be $A'D' = a$, $A'A = b$, $AB = c$.

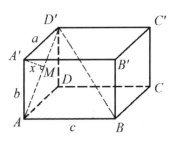

We first find the shortest distance from edges $A'A$ that does not meet $D'B$ to $A'B'$.

Connect AD'. Draw the height from A' to $A'D$ to meet AD' at M. We see that the height $A'M$ is exactly the distance from $A'B'$ to $D'B$. We write the area of triangle $A'AD'$ in two ways: $\frac{1}{2} A'A \times A'D' = \frac{1}{2} AD' \times x \quad \Rightarrow$

$$b \times a = (\sqrt{a^2 + b^2}) \times x.$$

Solving for x: $x = \frac{ab}{\sqrt{a^2 + b^2}}$. Similarly we get:

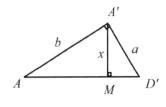

$y = \frac{bc}{\sqrt{b^2 + c^2}}$ and $z = \frac{ca}{\sqrt{c^2 + a^2}}$.

Solving the system of equations:
$$\frac{ab}{\sqrt{a^2 + b^2}} = 2\sqrt{5} \Rightarrow \frac{a^2 b^2}{a^2 + b^2} = 20 \Rightarrow \frac{a^2 + b^2}{a^2 b^2} = \frac{1}{20} \Rightarrow \frac{1}{a^2} + \frac{1}{b^2} = \frac{1}{20} \quad (1)$$

$$\frac{bc}{\sqrt{b^2+c^2}} = \frac{30}{\sqrt{13}} \quad \Rightarrow \quad \frac{b^2c^2}{b^2+c^2} = \frac{900}{13} \quad \Rightarrow \quad \frac{1}{b^2}+\frac{1}{c^2} = \frac{13}{900} \quad (2)$$

$$\frac{ca}{\sqrt{c^2+a^2}} = \frac{15}{\sqrt{10}} \quad \Rightarrow \quad \frac{c^2a^2}{c^2+a^2} = \frac{45}{2} \quad \Rightarrow \quad \frac{1}{c^2}+\frac{1}{a^2} = \frac{2}{45} \quad (3)$$

Solving we get $a = 5$, $b = 10$, and $c = 15$. The volume is 750.

Problem 13. Solution: 192.
Let O be the intersection of base diagonals AC and BD.
$\angle AOD = 45°$. $\angle D'BD = 30°$.
In right triangle $D'DB$, $D'D = D'B \times \sin 30° = \frac{1}{2} \times 8\sqrt{2} = 4\sqrt{2}$.

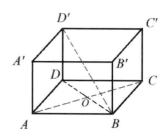

$BD = D'B \times \cos 30° = \frac{\sqrt{3}}{2} \times 8\sqrt{2} = 4\sqrt{6}$.

So $AO = DO = \frac{1}{2}BD = \frac{\sqrt{3}}{4} \times 8\sqrt{2} = 2\sqrt{6}$.

$S_{ABCD} = 4S_{\triangle AOD} = 4 \times \frac{1}{2} AO \times DO \times \sin 45° = 4 \times \frac{1}{2} \times (2\sqrt{6})^2 \times \frac{\sqrt{2}}{2} = 24\sqrt{2}$.

the volume of the rectangular box is $V = S_{ABCD} \times D'D = 24\sqrt{2} \times 4\sqrt{2} = 192$.

Problem 14. Solution:
Let O be the intersection of base diagonals AC and BD.
$\angle AOD = \beta$. $\angle ECA = \alpha$.
In right triangle ECA, $EA = l \sin \alpha$. $AC = l \cos \alpha$.

So $AO = BO = CO = DO = \frac{1}{2} l \cos \alpha$.

The area of rectangle $ABCD$

$$S_{ABCD} = 2S_{\triangle ADC} = 4S_{\triangle AOD} = 4 \times \frac{1}{2} AO \times DO \times \sin \beta = 2 \times (\frac{1}{2} l \cos \alpha)^2 \times \sin \beta$$

$$= \frac{1}{2} l^2 \times \cos^2 \alpha \times \sin \beta.$$

The volume of the rectangular box is $V = S_{ABCD} \times EA = \frac{1}{2} l^2 \times \cos^2 \alpha \times \sin \beta \times l \sin \alpha$

$$= \frac{1}{2} l^3 \times \cos^2 \alpha \times \sin \alpha \times \sin \beta.$$

Chapter 2 Tetrahedron

BASIC KNOWLEDGE

Polyhedron: A polyhedron is a geometric solid whose boundary consists of plane polygons.

Faces, Vertices, Edges: The polygons which bound the polyhedron are its faces; the sides of these faces are the edges and their vertices are the vertices of the polyhedron.

Tetrahedron: A polyhedron of four triangular faces is a tetrahedron.

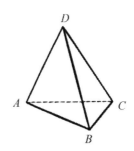

Base and lateral edges: For a tetrahedron, if the four vertices are $DABC$ and the base is $\triangle ABC$, the tetrahedron can be written as D–ABC. DA, DB, and DC are called the lateral edges.

Regular tetrahedron: A tetrahedron whose four faces are equilateral triangles is a regular tetrahedron.

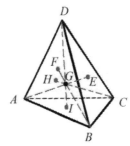

The four medians of a regular tetrahedron concur in a point which divides each tetrahedron median in the ratio 1:3, the longer segment being on the side of the vertex of the tetrahedron. For example, G is the center of the regular tetrahedron D–ABC. $DG \perp$ to the plane D–ABC. $\dfrac{DG}{DI} = \dfrac{2}{3}$.

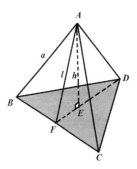

Volume of a tetrahedron, V

$$V = \frac{1}{3} S_{\triangle BCD} \times h \qquad (2.1)$$

$S_{\triangle BCD}$ is the area of the triangle BCD. h is the height.

Volume of a regular tetrahedron, V

$$V = \frac{\sqrt{2}}{12} a^3 \qquad (2.2)$$

a: the edge length.

l: the slant height (the height of the equilateral triangle ABC)
$$l = \frac{\sqrt{3}}{2}a \qquad (2.3)$$
h: the height of the regular tetrahedron.
$$h = \frac{\sqrt{6}}{3}a \qquad (2.4)$$
The surface area of the tetrahedron is simply four times the area of a single equilateral triangle face:
$$S = \sqrt{3}a^2 \qquad (2.5)$$

The radius of the sphere inscribed in a regular tetrahedron:
$$r = \frac{\sqrt{6}}{12}a \qquad (2.6)$$
The radius of the sphere circumscribed about a regular tetrahedron:
$$R = \frac{\sqrt{6}}{4}a \qquad (2.7)$$

Example 1. The volume of a tetrahedron each of whose edges is a can be written as $\frac{\sqrt{m}}{n}a^3$ in simplest radical form, where m and n are positive integers. Find $m + n$.

Solution: 014.
Let the tetrahedron be $P-ABC$.
Since $AB = BC = CA = a$, $\triangle ABC$ is an equilateral triangle. Draw $PO \perp$ to the plane ABC at O.

Since $PA = PB = PC = a$, O is the centroid of $\triangle ABC$. OA is the radius of the circumscribed circle of the equilateral triangle $\triangle ABC$.

So $AB = \sqrt{3}OA \quad \Rightarrow \quad OA = \frac{AB}{\sqrt{3}} = \frac{\sqrt{3}}{3}a$.

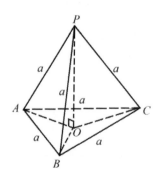

Applying Pythagorean Theorem to right triangle POA:
$$PO = \sqrt{PA^2 - OA^2} = \sqrt{a^2 - (\frac{\sqrt{3}}{3}a)^2} = \frac{\sqrt{6}}{3}a.$$

The area of $\triangle ABC$ is $S = \frac{\sqrt{3}}{4}a^2$.
The volume of the tetrahedron be $P-ABC$ is

$$V = \frac{1}{3}S \times PO = \frac{1}{3} \times \frac{\sqrt{3}}{4}a^2 \times \frac{\sqrt{6}}{3}a = \frac{\sqrt{2}}{12}a^3.$$
So $m + n = 2 + 12 = 14$.

Example 2. The volume of the tetrahedron $D{-}ABC$ can be written as a common fraction $\frac{m}{n}$ in simplest form, where m and n are positive integers. Find $m + n$ if $AB = CD = 4$ and $AC = BC = BD = 3$.

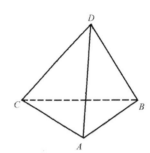

Solution: 011.
Let M and N be the midpoints of AB and CD, respectively.
Connect CM, DM, and MN.
In $\triangle CAB$, $CA = CB$. M is the midpoint of AB. So $CM \perp AB$.

In $\triangle DAB$, $DA = DB$. M is the midpoint of AB. So $DM \perp AB$.

Thus we know that AB is $\perp$ to the plane CDM.
So AM is the height of tetrahedron $A{-}CDM$. BM is the height of tetrahedron $B{-}CDM$.
$AM = BM = AB/2 = 2$.

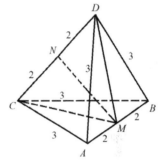

Applying Pythagorean Theorem to triangle ACM:
$CM = \sqrt{AC^2 - AM^2} = \sqrt{3^2 - 2^2} = \sqrt{5}$.
Applying Pythagorean Theorem to triangle ADM:
$DM = \sqrt{AD^2 - AM^2} = \sqrt{3^2 - 2^2} = \sqrt{5}$.
Thus we see that triangle MCD is an isosceles triangle. MN is the median on CD.
So $MN \perp CD$.

Applying Pythagorean Theorem to triangle MND:
$MN = \sqrt{MD^2 - ND^2} = \sqrt{(\sqrt{5})^2 - 2^2} = 1$.
The area of the triangle MCD is $S = \frac{1}{2}CD \times MN = \frac{1}{2} \times 4 \times 1 = 2 1 \times 2 = 2$.

The volume of the tetrahedron $D{-}ABC$ is $2 \times V_{A\text{-}MCD} = 2 \times \frac{1}{3}S \times AM = 2 \times \frac{1}{3} \times 2 \times 2 = \frac{8}{3}$.

So $m + n = 8 + 3 = 11$.

Example 3. Find the volume of the tetrahedron $P-ABC$ if three lateral faces of the tetrahedron are mutually perpendicular. The areas of three lateral faces are 3 cm^2, 4 cm^2, and 6 cm^2.

Solution: 004.
Since three lateral faces of the tetrahedron are mutually perpendicular, PA, PB, and PC are mutually perpendicular.

Let $PA = a$, $PB = b$, and $PC = c$.

$$\frac{1}{2}ab = 3 \quad (1)$$

$$\frac{1}{2}bc = 4 \quad (2)$$

$$\frac{1}{2}ca = 6 \quad (3)$$

$(1) \times (2) \times (3)$: $(abc)^2 = 576 \Rightarrow abc = 24 \quad (4)$

$$V_{A-PBC} = \frac{1}{3}S_{PBC} \times PA = \frac{1}{3} \times \frac{1}{2} \times a \times b \times c = \frac{1}{6} \times 24 = 4.$$

Example 4. Find the sum of the lateral areas of the tetrahedron $P-ABC$ if three lateral edges of the tetrahedron have the equal lengths and mutually perpendicular. The area of equilateral triangle ABC is $123\sqrt{3}$.

Solution: 369.
In tetrahedron $P-ABC$, let $PA = PB = PC = a$, $AB = AC = BC = x$。 $S_{\triangle ABC} = Q$

Then $Q = \frac{\sqrt{3}}{4}x^2 \Rightarrow x^2 = \frac{4\sqrt{3}}{3}Q$.

Let E be the midpoint of BC. Connect AE and PE.
Since $AB = AC$, $AE \perp BC$.
Since $PB = PC$, $PE \perp BC$.
Then $AP \perp PE$.

The area of triangle PBC is $\dfrac{PE \times BC}{2}$

Since $PB \perp BC$, the area of triangle PBC can also be written as $\dfrac{PB \times PC}{2}$.

Thus we have $PE = \dfrac{PB \times PC}{BC} = \dfrac{a^2}{x}$

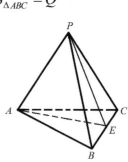

Since AE is the height of $\triangle ABC$, $AE = \dfrac{\sqrt{3}}{2}x$.

Applying Pythagorean Theorem to right $\triangle PAC$: $PA^2 + PE^2 = AE^2 \Rightarrow a^2 + \dfrac{a^4}{x^2} = \dfrac{3}{4}x^2$

$\Rightarrow 4a^2 + 4a^2x^2 - 3x^4 = 0 \Rightarrow (2a^2 + 3x^2)(2a^2 - x^2) = 0$.

$a^2 = \dfrac{x^2}{2}$.

The sum of the lateral areas is $3 \times \dfrac{1}{2} \times a^2 = 3 \times \dfrac{1}{2} \times \dfrac{x^2}{2} = \sqrt{3}Q = \sqrt{3} \times 123\sqrt{3} = 369$.

☆**Example 5.** The tetrahedron $D-ABC$ has $AB = 3$. The area of $\triangle ABC = 15$. The area of $\triangle ABD = 12$. The angle between the faces ABC and ABD is $30°$. Find the volume of the tetrahedron.

Solution: 020.

Draw DH, the height of the tetrahedron $D-ABC$ to meet the plane ABC at H. Draw DK, the height of $\triangle ABD$ to meet AB at K. Connect KH. Since the angle between the faces ABC and ABD is $30°$, $\angle DKH = 30°$.

$S_{\triangle ABD} = \dfrac{1}{2} AB \times DK = \dfrac{1}{2} \times 3 \times DK = 12 \quad \Rightarrow \quad DK = 8$.

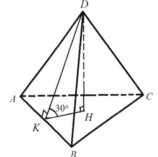

Note that $\triangle DHK$ is a $30°-60°-90°$ right triangle and

$DH = \dfrac{1}{2}DK = 4$.

The volume is then $V_{D-ABC} = \dfrac{1}{3} S_{\triangle ABC} \times DH = \dfrac{1}{3} \times 15 \times 4 = 20$.

Example 6. In a regular tetrahedron with the edge length of $18\sqrt{2}$, the centers of four faces are the vertices of a smaller tetrahedron. Find the volume of this smaller tetrahedron.

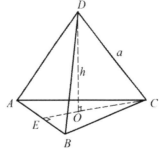

Solution: 072.

Let $a = 18\sqrt{2}$.

The area of the equilateral triangle is $S = \dfrac{\sqrt{3}}{4}a^2$.

Draw CE, the height of the equilateral triangle ABC: $\frac{\sqrt{3}}{2}a$.

Draw PO, h, the height of the regular tetrahedron.

$h = \sqrt{DC^2 - OC^2}$

$OC = \frac{2}{3} \times \frac{\sqrt{3}}{2}a$.

So $h = \sqrt{DC^2 - OC^2} = \sqrt{a^2 - (\frac{\sqrt{3}}{4}a \times \frac{2}{3})^2} = \sqrt{\frac{2}{3}}a$

The volume of the original tetrahedron is

$V_O = \frac{1}{3}Sh = \frac{1}{3}\frac{\sqrt{3}}{4}a^2 \times \sqrt{\frac{2}{3}}a = \frac{\sqrt{2}}{12}a^3$.

Connect DE. We see that the length of each edge of the smaller tetrahedron is OP. $\triangle DCE \sim \triangle OPE$.

So $OP = \frac{1}{3}DC = \frac{a}{3}$.

Since the original tetrahedron and the new tetrahedron (V_n) are similar, we have

$\frac{V_N}{V_O} = (\frac{OP}{DC})^3 = \frac{1}{27} \quad \Rightarrow \quad V_N = \frac{1}{27}V_O = \frac{1}{27} \times \frac{\sqrt{2}}{12}a^3 = \frac{\sqrt{2}}{324}a^3 = \frac{\sqrt{2}}{324} \times (18\sqrt{2})^3 = 72$

Example 7. In a regular tetrahedron, the centers of four faces are the vertices of a smaller tetrahedron. The ratio of the surface area of the original tetrahedron to that of the resulting tetrahedron is m/n, where m and n are relatively prime. What is the value of $m + n$?

Solution: 010.
Let the length of each edge be a.
Let the centers be O, P, Q, and R. Connecting them we get the resulting tetrahedron.

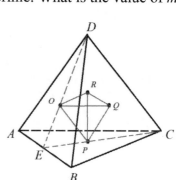

Draw DOE, the heights of equilateral triangle ABD.
Draw CPE, the heights of equilateral triangle ABC.
We see that the length of one edge of the smaller tetrahedron is OP. Since $\triangle DCE \sim \triangle OPE$, $OP = \frac{1}{3}DC = \frac{a}{3}$.

Since the original tetrahedron and the resulting tetrahedron are similar, the ratio of the surface area of the original tetrahedron to that of the resulting tetrahedron is
$$\frac{S_N}{S_O} = (\frac{OP}{DC})^2 = \frac{1}{9}.$$
The answer is $1 + 9 = 10$.

Example 8. Find the height of the regular tetrahedron $D–ABC$. M and N are the centers of $\triangle ABC$ and $\triangle ACD$, respectively and $MN = 1$.

Solution: $\sqrt{6}$.

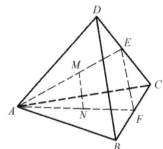

Connect AM and extend it to meet CD at E. E is the midpoint of CD.
Connect AN and extend it to meet BC at F. F is the midpoint of BC.

Thus $EF = \frac{1}{2}a \quad \Rightarrow \quad a = 2EF$.

$\triangle AEF \sim \triangle AMN$. $\quad \frac{AE}{AM} = \frac{EF}{MN} = \frac{3}{2} \quad \Rightarrow \quad EF = \frac{3}{2}. \quad a = 3$.

By (2.4), $h = \frac{\sqrt{6}}{3}a = \sqrt{6}$.

Example 9. Let $ABCD$ be a tetrahedron with P, Q, R on the edges BC, CD, and DA, respectively such that $BP = 2PC$, $CQ = 2QD$, and $DR = RA$, as shown in the figure. The distance from A to the plane PQR is h_A and the distance from B to the plane PQR is h_B. The ratio of h_A to h_B can be written as a common fraction m/n, where m and n are positive integers. Find $m + n$.

Solution: 005.
Method 1:
The distance from C to the plane PQR is h_C and the distance from D to the plane PQR is h_D.
We know that P, Q, R are the intersections of the lines BC, CD, and DA with the plane PQR. We also know that $BP = 2PC$, $CQ = 2QD$, and $DR = RA$.

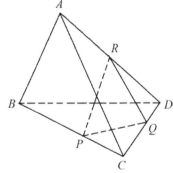

So $\frac{h_C}{h_B} = \frac{PC}{BP} = \frac{1}{2}$ \quad (1)

$$\frac{h_D}{h_C} = \frac{QD}{QC} = \frac{1}{2} \qquad (2)$$

$$\frac{h_A}{h_D} = \frac{RA}{DR} = 1 \qquad (3)$$

Solving (1), (2), and (3): $\frac{h_A}{h_B} = \frac{1}{4}$. The answer is $1 + 4 = 5$.

Method 2:
Extend PQ to meet the extension of BD at S.
Let M be the midpoint of CQ. Connect PM.
$PM \parallel BD$ and $PM = \frac{1}{3}BD$. ΔPMQ is congruent to ΔSDQ.
Thus $PM = DS$.
Let the distance from D to the plane PQR is h_D.

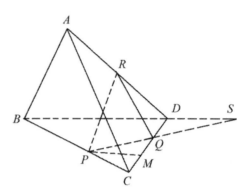

We know that R and S are the intersections of the lines DA and BD with the plane PQR.

So $\frac{h_A}{h_D} = \frac{RA}{DR} = 1 \quad \Rightarrow \quad h_A = h_D.$

$\frac{h_D}{h_B} = \frac{DS}{BS} = \frac{DS}{BD + DS} = \frac{PM}{3PM + PM} = \frac{1}{4}$. Thus $\frac{h_A}{h_B} = \frac{1}{4}$.

The answer is $1 + 4 = 5$.

Method 3:
Connect BQ and PD.
We know that $BP = 2PC$, $CQ = 2QD$.
So $S_{\Delta PCQ} = \frac{1}{2} S_{\Delta BPQ}$ and $S_{\Delta PDQ} = \frac{1}{2} S_{\Delta PCQ}$

$S_{\Delta PDQ} = \frac{1}{4} S_{\Delta BPQ}$.

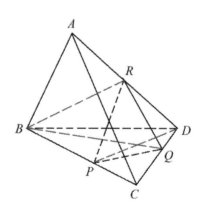

Note that the tetrahedron R–PDQ and R–BPQ have the same height.

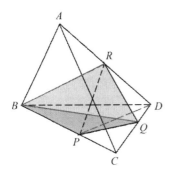

R–BPQ   R–PDQ

Thus $\dfrac{V_{R-PDQ}}{V_{R-BPQ}} = \dfrac{S_{\triangle PDQ}}{S_{\triangle BPQ}} = \dfrac{1}{4}$.

Let the distance from D to the plane PQR be h_D.

$\dfrac{V_{D-PQR}}{V_{B-PQR}} = \dfrac{h_D}{h_B} = \dfrac{V_{R-PDQ}}{V_{R-BPQ}} = \dfrac{1}{4} \quad \Rightarrow \quad \dfrac{h_D}{h_B} = \dfrac{1}{4}$.

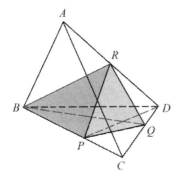 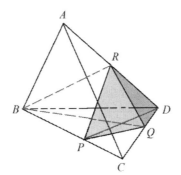

B–PQR   D–PQR

We know that $h_A = h_D$. So $\dfrac{h_A}{h_B} = \dfrac{1}{4}$.

The answer is $1 + 4 = 5$.

Method 4:
Draw $AM \parallel RQ$ to meet CD at M.
Draw $MN \parallel PQ$ to meet BC at N.
Then AM is $\parallel$ to the plane PQR and MN is $\parallel$ to the plane PQR.
Thus the plane AMN is $\parallel$ to the plane PQR. So the

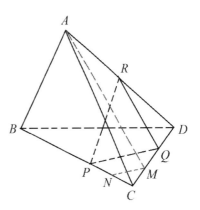

distance from *A* to the plane *PQR* is the same as the distance from *N* to the plane *PQR*. *N* is the midpoint of *PC*.
Let the distance from *N* to the plane *PQR* be h_N.

$$\frac{h_A}{h_B} = \frac{h_N}{h_B} = \frac{PN}{BP} = \frac{\frac{1}{2}PC}{2PC} = \frac{1}{4}.$$ The answer is $1 + 4 = 5$.

Example 10. The shaded regions are cut and removed from a square. The figure is then folded to form a tetrahedron. The three lateral faces of the tetrahedron are all isosceles triangles and the base is an equilateral triangle. Find the volume of this tetrahedron.

Solution:
$b^2 = 2a^2 - 2a^2 \cos 30° = (2 - \sqrt{3})a^2$
$b = \sqrt{2 - \sqrt{3}}a = \frac{1}{2}(\sqrt{6} - \sqrt{2})a^2$

Draw $AF \perp$ to the plane *BCD* at *F*.

Since $\triangle ABC$, $\triangle ACD$, and $\triangle ABD$ are congruent and $\triangle BCD$ is equilateral, *AF* is the height of the tetrahedron and *F* is also the centroid of $\triangle BCD$.

$AF = \sqrt{a^2 - (\frac{\sqrt{3}}{2}b \times \frac{2}{3})^2} = \sqrt{a^2 - \frac{4 - 2\sqrt{3}}{6}a^2}$
$= \frac{1}{3}\sqrt{3 + 3\sqrt{3}}\,a.$

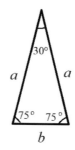
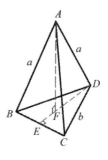

The volume is $V = \frac{1}{3} \times \frac{\sqrt{3}}{4}b^2 \times AF = \frac{1}{12}(2 - \sqrt{3})(\sqrt{1 + \sqrt{3}})a^3$.

Example 11. The tetrahedron *D–ABC* has $AB = 13$, $AC = 15$, and $BC = 14$. The four faces are congruent. The volume of the tetrahedron can be expressed as $a\sqrt{b}$ in simplest radical form. Fond $a + b$.

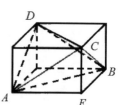

Solution: 097.
We draw a rectangular prism that

28

contains the tetrahedron as shown in the figure. The volume of the tetrahedron is the same as the volume of the rectangular prism − 4 × the volume of the tetrahedron $C-AEB$.

Let the sides be x, y, and z of the rectangular prism.
$$\begin{cases} x^2 + y^2 = 13^2 \\ x^2 + z^2 = 14^2 \\ y^2 + z^2 = 15^2 \end{cases}$$

Solving we get: $x = \sqrt{99}$, $y = \sqrt{70}$, and $z = \sqrt{126}$.

The volume of the rectangular prism is $xyz = \sqrt{99} \times \sqrt{70} \times \sqrt{126} = 126\sqrt{55}$.

The volume of the tetrahedron $C-AEB$ is $\dfrac{xyz}{3} \times \dfrac{1}{2} = \dfrac{1}{6}\sqrt{99} \times \sqrt{70} \times \sqrt{126} = 21\sqrt{55}$

The volume of the tetrahedron $D-ABC$ is $126\sqrt{55} - 4 \times 21\sqrt{55} = 42\sqrt{55}$.

The answer is $42 + 55 = 97$.

Example 12. $ABCD$ is a unit square. E and F are the midpoints of BC and CD. The figure is folded along AE, EF, and AF to form a tetrahedron so that the points C, B, and D are met at one point M. The volume of this tetrahedron can be expressed as $\dfrac{a}{b}$ in simplest fraction form. What is $a + b$?

Solution: 025.
We draw the tetrahedron as shown in the figure.
The base of the tetrahedron is CEF with $EC \perp FC$.
$EC = FC = \dfrac{1}{2}$. $AM = 1$.

The area of $\triangle CEF = \dfrac{1}{2} \times \dfrac{1}{2} \times \dfrac{1}{2} = \dfrac{1}{8}$.

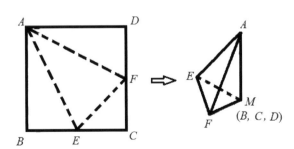

The volume of this tetrahedron is
$\dfrac{1}{3} \times (\dfrac{1}{8}) \times 1 = \dfrac{1}{24}$.

The answer is $1 + 24 = 25$.

PROBLEMS

Problem 1. Find the volume of the tetrahedron $P-ABC$. $\triangle ABC$ is an equilateral triangle. $AB = BC = CA = a$, and $PA = PB = PC = b$.

Problem 2. The volume of the tetrahedron $D-ABC$ can be expressed as $m\sqrt{n}$ in simplest radical form, where m and n are positive integers. Find $m + n$ if $AB = AC = 17$, $DB = DC = 10$, $BC = 16$, and $AD = 3\sqrt{21}$.

Problem 3. The volume of the tetrahedron $A-BCD$ can be expressed as $\dfrac{\sqrt{m}}{n}$ in simplest radical form, where m and n are positive integers. Find $m + n$ if $AB = BC = CD = DA = BD = 2$ and $AC = 3$.

Problem 4. Find the volume of the tetrahedron $P-ABC$ if three lateral faces of the tetrahedron are mutually perpendicular. The areas of three lateral faces are x^2, y^2, and z^2.

Problem 5. The area of the base triangle ABC in the tetrahedron $S-ABC$ can be expressed as m/n, where m and n are relatively prime. Find $m + n$ if three lateral faces of the tetrahedron are mutually perpendicular. The three lateral areas are $S_{\triangle SAB} = \dfrac{3}{2}$, $S_{\triangle SBC} = 2$, and $S_{\triangle SAC} = 6$, respectively.

Problem 6. Find the volume of the tetrahedron $S-ABC$ if ABC is an equilateral triangle with $AB = 6$. Three lateral edges of the tetrahedron have the equal length of $\sqrt{15}$.

☆**Problem 7.** $D-ABC$ is a tetrahedron. Area $ABC = 120$, area $BCD = 80$. $BC = 10$ and the faces ABC and BCD meet at an angle of $30°$. What is the volume of $D-ABC$?

Problem 8. The tetrahedron $A-BCD$ has $AB = 1$ and $CD = \sqrt{3}$. The distance between the lines AB and CD is 2. The angle between the lines AB and CD is 60°. The volume of the tetrahedron can be expressed as a common fraction m/n. Find $m + n$.

☆**Problem 9.** T is a regular tetrahedron. T' is the tetrahedron whose vertices are the centers of the faces of T. The ratio of the volume of T' to that of T can be expressed as a common fraction m/n. What is the value of $m + n$?

Problem 10. In a regular tetrahedron with the edge length of 18, the centers of three lateral faces are connected to form a triangle. The area of the triangle is expressed as $m\sqrt{n}$ in simplest radical form, where m and n are positive integers. Find $m + n$.

☆**Problem 11.** A tetrahedron has the edge lengths shown. Find the square of the distance between the midpoints of the two sides with the lengths of 41 and 13.

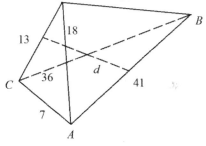

Problem 12. Let $A-BCD$ be a regular tetrahedron with the edge length of 8. E and F, R are two points on the edges AB and CD, respectively such that $AE = 1$, $CF = 2$. The length of EF can be written as $m\sqrt{n}$, where m and n are relatively prime. Find m^n.

☆**Problem 13.** $ABCD$ is a rectangle with $AB = 12\sqrt{3}$, $AD = 13\sqrt{3}$. The center of the rectangle is P. Triangle ABP is cut and removed. The figure is then folded along PA and PD to form a tetrahedron. The four faces of the tetrahedron are all isosceles triangles. Find the volume of this tetrahedron.

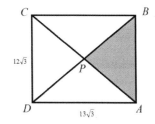

Problem 14. If the volume of a tetrahedron is doubled without changing its shape, the factor by which the surface area is increased is written as $\sqrt[m]{n}$. Find n^m.

Problem 15. The distance between the centroids of any two faces of a regular tetrahedron of edge length 1 can be expressed as a common fraction m/n. Find $m + n$.

Problem 16. (USAMO) If the sum of the lengths of the six edges of a perpendicular tetrahedron $PABC$ (i.e., $\angle APB = \angle BPC = \angle CPA = 90°$) is S, determine its maximum volume.

SOLUTIONS:

Problem 1. Solution:
Draw $PO \perp$ to the plane ABC at O. O is the centroid of $\triangle ABC$. Connect AO and extend AO to meet BC at D.
We know that $AD \perp BC$. Connect PD. $PD \perp BC$. PO is the height of the tetrahedron and PD is the slant height.

We know that $AO = \dfrac{2}{3}AD = \dfrac{2}{3} \times \dfrac{\sqrt{3}}{2}a = \dfrac{\sqrt{3}}{3}a$.

Applying Pythagorean Theorem to right triangle POA:
$$PO = \sqrt{PA^2 - OA^2} = \sqrt{b^2 - (\dfrac{\sqrt{3}}{3}a)^2} = \dfrac{\sqrt{3}}{3}\sqrt{3b^2 - a^2}.$$

The area of $\triangle ABC$ is $S = \dfrac{\sqrt{3}}{4}a^2$.

The volume of the tetrahedron be $P-ABC$ is
$$V = \dfrac{1}{3}S \times PO = \dfrac{1}{3} \times \dfrac{\sqrt{3}}{4}a^2 \times \dfrac{\sqrt{3}}{3}\sqrt{3b^2 - a^2} = \dfrac{a^2}{12}\sqrt{3b^2 - a^2}.$$

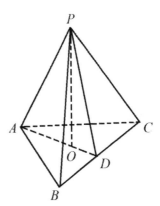

Problem 2. Solution: 069.
Let E be the midpoint of BC. Connect DE, and AE.
Since $AB = AC$, and $DB = DC$, $AE \perp BC$, and $DE \perp BC$.

Thus we know that BC is $\perp$ to the plane AED.
Applying Pythagorean Theorem to right triangle ABE:
$AE = \sqrt{AB^2 - BE^2} = \sqrt{17^2 - 8^2} = 15$.
Applying Pythagorean Theorem to right triangle DEC:
$DE = \sqrt{CD^2 - CE^2} = \sqrt{10^2 - 8^2} = 6$.
In triangle ADE, $AD^2 + DE^2 = (3\sqrt{21})^2 + 6^2 = 225$ and $AE^2 = 15^2 = 225$.
So $AD^2 + DE^2 = AE^2$.

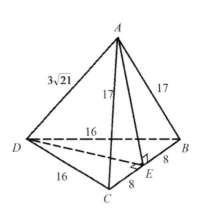

Thus we see that triangle ADE is a right triangle with $\angle ADE = 90°$.
So the area of the triangle ADE is $S = \dfrac{1}{2}AD \times DE = \dfrac{1}{2} \times 3\sqrt{21} \times 6 = 9\sqrt{21}$.

The volume of the tetrahedron $A-BCD$ is $2 \times V_{A-MCD}$

$$= V_{A-BCD} = V_{B-ADE} + V_{C-ADE} = \frac{1}{3} S_{\triangle ADE} \times BE + \frac{1}{3} \times S_{\triangle ADE} \times EC$$

$$= \frac{1}{3} S_{\triangle ADE} \times BC = \frac{1}{3} \times 9\sqrt{21} \times 16 = 48\sqrt{21}.$$ The answer is $48 + 21 = 69$.

Problem 3. Solution: 005.
Let E be the midpoint of BC. Connect CE, and AE.
Since $AB = AD$ and $CB = CD$, $AE \perp BD$, and $CE \perp BD$.
Thus we know that BD is $\perp$ to the plane AEC.

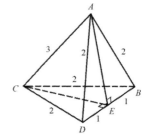

Thus $V_{A-BCD} = V_{D-ACE} + V_{BC-ACE} = \frac{1}{3} S_{\triangle AEC} \times BE + \frac{1}{3} \times S_{\triangle AEC} \times DE$

$$= \frac{1}{3} S_{\triangle AEC} \times BD.$$

Since $AB = BC = CD = DA = BD = 2$, $AE = CE = \frac{AB}{2} \sqrt{3} = \sqrt{3}$.

Let $\angle AEC = \alpha$.

Applying the law of cosine to triangle AEC:

$$\cos \alpha = \frac{AE^2 + CE^2 - AC^2}{2 \times AE \times CE} = \frac{(\sqrt{3})^2 + (\sqrt{3})^2 - 3^2}{2 \times \sqrt{3} \times \sqrt{3}} = -\frac{1}{2}.$$

So $\alpha = 120°$.

Thus $S_{\triangle AEC} = \frac{1}{2} AE \times CE \sin \alpha = \frac{1}{2} \times \sqrt{3} \times \sqrt{3} \sin 120° = \frac{3}{4} \sqrt{3}$.

Therefore $V_{A-BCD} = \frac{1}{3} S_{\triangle AEC} \times BD = \frac{1}{3} \times \frac{3}{4} \sqrt{3} \times 2 = \frac{\sqrt{3}}{2}$. The answer is $3 + 2 = 5$.

Problem 4. Solution:
Since three lateral faces of the tetrahedron are mutually perpendicular, PA, PB, and PC are mutually perpendicular.

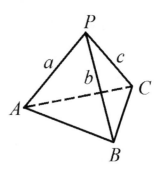

Let $PA = a$, $PB = b$, and $PC = c$.

$$\frac{1}{2} ab = x^2 \qquad (1)$$

$$\frac{1}{2} bc = y^2 \qquad (2)$$

$$\frac{1}{2}ca = z^2 \qquad (3)$$

$(1) \times (2) \times (3): (abc)^2 = 8(xyz)^2 \Rightarrow abc = 2\sqrt{2}xyz \qquad (4)$

$V_{A-PBC} = \frac{1}{3}S_{\triangle PBC} \times PA = \frac{1}{3} \times \frac{1}{2} \times a \times b \times c = \frac{1}{6} \times abc = \frac{1}{6} \times 2\sqrt{2}xyz = \frac{\sqrt{2}}{3}xyz$.

Problem 5. Solution: 015.

Draw $SM \perp BC$ at M. Connect AM.

We know that $SA \perp BS$ and $SA \perp CS$. So SA is $\perp$ to the plane SBC. Thus $AM \perp BC$.

Let $SA = a$, $SB = b$ and $SC = c$.

$\frac{1}{2}ab = \frac{3}{2}$ \qquad (1)

$\frac{1}{2}bc = 2$ \qquad (2)

$\frac{1}{2}ca = 6$ \qquad (3)

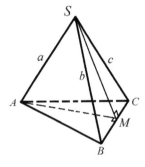

$(1) \times (2) \times (3): (abc)^2 = 12^2 \Rightarrow abc = 12 \qquad (4)$

$a = 3$, $b = 1$, and $c = 4$.

Applying Pythagorean Theorem to right $\triangle BSC$: $BC = \sqrt{b^2 + c^2} = \sqrt{17}$.

$S_{\triangle SBC} = \frac{1}{2}BC \times SM = \frac{1}{2} \times \sqrt{17} \times SM = 2 \Rightarrow SM = \frac{4}{\sqrt{17}}$.

Applying Pythagorean Theorem to right $\triangle SAM$: $AM = \sqrt{SA^2 + SM^2} = \sqrt{3^2 + \frac{16}{17}} = \frac{13}{\sqrt{17}}$.

$S_{\triangle ABC} = \frac{1}{2}BC \times AM = \frac{1}{2} \times \sqrt{17} \times \frac{13}{\sqrt{17}} = \frac{13}{2}$. The answer is $13 + 2 = 15$.

Problem 6. Solution: 009.

Let the centroid of $\triangle ABC$ be O.

Connect AO and extend AO to meet BC at D.

Connect SO and SD.

We know that $AB = BC = CA = 6$.

AD is the median on BC and $AD = \dfrac{\sqrt{3}}{2} AB = 3\sqrt{3}$.

$AO = \dfrac{2}{3} AD = 2\sqrt{3}$.

Applying Pythagorean Theorem to right ΔSOA:
$SO = \sqrt{SA^2 - AO^2} = \sqrt{(\sqrt{15})^2 - (2\sqrt{3})^2} = \sqrt{3}$.

$V_{S-ABC} = \dfrac{1}{3} S_{\Delta ABC} \times SO = \dfrac{1}{3} \times \dfrac{1}{2} \times (BC \times AD) = \dfrac{1}{3} \times (\dfrac{1}{2} \times 6 \times 3\sqrt{3}) = 9$.

☆**Problem 7.** Solution: 320.
Draw DP, the height of the tetrahedron $D-ABC$ to meet the plane ABC at P. Draw DH, the height of ΔBCD to meet BC at H. Connect PH. Since the angle between ABC and BCD is $30°$, $\angle DHP = 30°$.

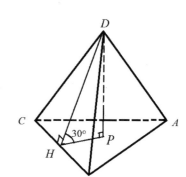

$S_{\Delta BCD} = \dfrac{1}{2} BC \times DH = \dfrac{1}{2} \times 10 \times DH = 80 \quad \Rightarrow$

$DH = 16$.

Note that ΔDHP is a $30°–60°–90°$ right triangle and

$DP = \dfrac{1}{2} DH = 8$.

The volume is then $V_{D-ABC} = \dfrac{1}{3} S_{\Delta ABC} \times DP = \dfrac{1}{3} \times 120 \times 8 = 320$.

Problem 8. Solution: 003.
Draw $BE \parallel CD$ such that $BE = CD$. Connect DE. Then $\angle ABE = 60°$. $DC \parallel$ the plane ABE. So the distance between the lines AB and CD is the same as the distance from point D to the plane ABE.

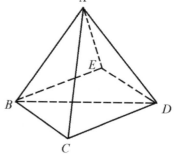

$V_{A-BCD} = V_{A-BDE} = V_{D-ABE} = \dfrac{1}{3} S_{\Delta ABE} \times DE$

$= \dfrac{1}{6} \times AB \times BE \times \sin \angle ABE \times DE = \dfrac{1}{2}$

$= \dfrac{1}{6} \times 1 \times \sqrt{3} \times \dfrac{\sqrt{3}}{2} \times 2 = \dfrac{1}{2}$.

The answer is $1 + 2 = 3$.

☆**Problem 9.** Solution: 028.

Let the length of each edge be a.
Let the centers be O, P, Q, and R. Connecting them we get T'.

Draw DOE, the heights of equilateral triangle ABD.
Draw CPE, the heights of equilateral triangle ABC.
By (2.2), the volume of the original tetrahedron is
$V_O = \dfrac{\sqrt{2}}{12} a^3$.

We see that the length of each edge of the smaller tetrahedron is OP. Since

$\triangle DCE \sim \triangle OPE$, $OP = \dfrac{1}{3} DC = \dfrac{a}{3}$.

Since the original tetrahedron and the new tetrahedron (V_n) are similar, we have

$\dfrac{V_N}{V_O} = \left(\dfrac{OP}{DC}\right)^3 = \dfrac{1}{27}$.

The answer is $1 + 27 = 28$.

Problem 10. Solution: 012.
Method 1:
Let a be the side length of the tetrahedron.
Let D, E, and F be the centers of the lateral faces.
Connect SD and extend to meet AB at G.
Connect SE and extend to meet BC at H.
G and H are the midpoints of AB and BC, respectively.

So $GH = \dfrac{1}{2} a$.

Connect DE.
$\triangle DEF$ is an equilateral triangle. The plane $DEF \parallel$ to the plane ABC.

$\triangle SDE \sim \triangle SGH$. $\dfrac{SD}{SG} = \dfrac{DE}{GH}$ $\Rightarrow$ $\dfrac{2}{3} = \dfrac{DE}{\tfrac{1}{2}a}$ $DE = \dfrac{a}{3}$.

The area of the triangle $\triangle DEF$ is $\dfrac{\sqrt{3}}{4}\left(\dfrac{a}{3}\right)^2 = \dfrac{\sqrt{3}}{4}\left(\dfrac{18}{3}\right)^2 = 9\sqrt{3}$. The answer is $9 + 3 = 12$.

Method 2:

Let a be the side length of the tetrahedron.
Let D, E, and F be the centers of the lateral faces.
Connect SD and extend to meet AB at G.
Connect SE and extend to meet BC at H.
Connect SF and extend to meet AC at I.
G and H are the midpoints of AB and BC, respectively.
Connect DE, DF, FE. Connect GH, HI, IG.
Both $\triangle DEF$ and $\triangle GHI$ is an equilateral triangle.

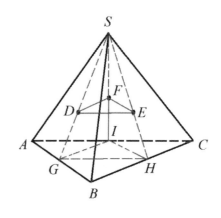

$GH = \dfrac{1}{2}a$.

The area of $\triangle GHI$ is $\dfrac{1}{4} \times \dfrac{\sqrt{3}}{4}(18)^2 = \dfrac{81\sqrt{3}}{4}$.

$DE = \dfrac{a}{3}$.

The ratio of the area of $\triangle DEF$ to the area of $\triangle GHI$ is

$$\dfrac{S_{\triangle DEF}}{S_{\triangle GHI}} = \left(\dfrac{DE}{GH}\right)^2 = \left(\dfrac{\frac{a}{3}}{\frac{a}{2}}\right)^2 = \dfrac{4}{9} \Rightarrow S_{\triangle DEF} = \dfrac{4}{9} S_{\triangle GHI} = \dfrac{4}{9} \times \dfrac{81\sqrt{3}}{4} = 9\sqrt{3}.$$

The answer is $9 + 3 = 12$.

☆**Problem 11.** Solution: 137.
Let the midpoints of AB and CD be M and N, respectively. Connect MC and MD.

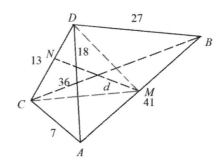

We see that DM is the median of $\triangle ABD$, CM is the median of $\triangle CAB$, and NM is the median of $\triangle CMD$.

Applying the median length formula in $\triangle ABD$, $\triangle CAB$, and $\triangle CMD$:

$DM^2 + DM^2 = AD^2 - AM^2 + BD^2 - BM^2$ (1)
$CM^2 + CM^2 = CA^2 - AM^2 + CB^2 - BM^2$ (2)
$NM^2 + NM^2 = DM^2 - DN^2 + CM^2 - CN^2$ (3)

(1), (2), and (3) can be written as:

$$2DM^2 = AD^2 - (\frac{AB}{2})^2 + BD^2 - (\frac{AB}{2})^2 \qquad (4)$$

$$2CM^2 = CA^2 - (\frac{AB}{2})^2 + CB^2 - (\frac{AB}{2})^2 \qquad (6)$$

$$2NM^2 = DM^2 - (\frac{CD}{2})^2 + CM^2 - (\frac{CD}{2})^2 \qquad (6)$$

Substituting (4) and (5) into (6):
$$4NM^2 = AD^2 + BD^2 + CA^2 + CB^2 - AB^2 - CD^2 = 18^2 + 27^2 + 7^2 + 36^2 - 41^2 - 13^2 = 548$$
$$NM^2 = d^2 = \frac{548}{4} = 137.$$

Problem 12. Solution: 015.
Draw $EG \parallel AC$ to meet BC at G.
Draw $FH \parallel AC$ to meet AD at H.
Connect EH and GF.
Since $AC = 8$ and $AE = 1$, $EG = 7$.
Since $CF = 2$, $AH = 2$, $FH = 6$.
Applying the law of cosine to triangle AEH:
$$EH = \sqrt{1^2 + 2^2 - 2 \times 2 \cos 60°} = \sqrt{3}.$$

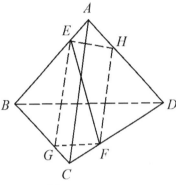

Similarly, we get $FG = \sqrt{3}$. $EGFH$ is an isosceles trapezoid.
The diagonal of the isosceles trapezoid is $EF^2 + GH^2 = EH^2 + FG^2 + 2FH \times EG$
$$2EF^2 = (\sqrt{3})^2 + (\sqrt{3})^2 + 2 \times 6 \times 7 \quad \Rightarrow \quad EF = \sqrt{45} = 3\sqrt{5}.$$
The answer is $3^5 = 243$.

☆**Problem 13.** Solution: 594.
Method 1:
Let M be the midpoint of DC.
Connect PM, AM.
Since $PD = PC$ and $AD = AC$, $PM \perp DC$, and $AM \perp DC$.
Thus DC is $\perp$ to the plane PMA.
Let V be the volume of the tetrahedron $P–ADC$.
$$V = \frac{1}{3} \times S_{\triangle PMA} \times MD + \frac{1}{3} \times S_{\triangle PMA} \times MC == \frac{1}{3} \times S_{\triangle PMA} \times CD = 4\sqrt{3} S_{\triangle PMA}$$
Now we calculate $S_{\triangle PMA}$.

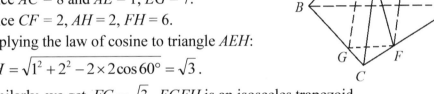

Note that $PA = \frac{1}{2}\sqrt{(13\sqrt{3})^2 + (12\sqrt{3})^2} = \frac{1}{2}\sqrt{313 \times 3}$

$PM = \frac{1}{2}AD = \frac{13}{2}\sqrt{3}$

$AM = \sqrt{(13\sqrt{3})^2 - (6\sqrt{3})^2} = \sqrt{133 \times 3}$

We also have $\cos \angle PAM = \dfrac{\frac{1}{4} \times 313 \times 3 + 133 \times 3 - \frac{1}{4} \times 169 \times 3}{2 \times \frac{1}{2}\sqrt{313 \times 3} \times \sqrt{133 \times 3}} = \dfrac{169}{\sqrt{313 \times 133}}$

$\sin \angle PAM = \sqrt{1 - \dfrac{169^2}{313 \times 133}} = \dfrac{66\sqrt{3}}{\sqrt{313 \times 133}}$.

$S_{\triangle PMA} = \frac{1}{2} PA \times AM \times \sin \angle PAM = \frac{1}{2} \times \frac{1}{2}\sqrt{313 \times 3} \times \sqrt{133 \times 3} \times \dfrac{66\sqrt{3}}{\sqrt{313 \times 133}} = \dfrac{99}{2}\sqrt{3}$.

Therefore $V = 4\sqrt{3} S_{\triangle PMA} = 4 \times \sqrt{3} \times \dfrac{99}{2}\sqrt{3} = 594$.

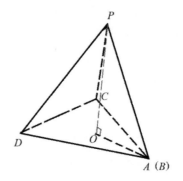

Method 2:

$PA = \frac{1}{2}\sqrt{(13\sqrt{3})^2 + (12\sqrt{3})^2} = \frac{1}{2}\sqrt{313 \times 3}$

The height on CD is $\sqrt{133 \times 3}$.

$S_{\triangle ACD} = \frac{1}{2} \times CD \times AM = \frac{1}{2} \times 12\sqrt{3} \times \sqrt{133 \times 3} = 18\sqrt{133}$

Draw $PO \perp$ to the plane ACD at O. O is the circumcenter $\triangle ACD$.

$R = \dfrac{AD \times AC \times CD}{4 S_{\triangle ACD}} = \dfrac{13^2 \times 3 \times 12\sqrt{3}}{4 \times 18\sqrt{133}} = \dfrac{169\sqrt{3}}{2\sqrt{133}} = AO$.

Applying Pythagorean Theorem to right $\triangle POA$:

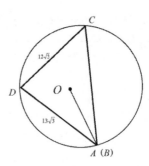

$$PO = \sqrt{PA^2 - AO^2} = \sqrt{(\frac{1}{2}\sqrt{313 \times 3})^2 - (\frac{169\sqrt{3}}{2\sqrt{133}})^2} = \frac{99\sqrt{133}}{133}.$$

$$V = \frac{1}{3} \times S_{\triangle ACD} \times PO = \frac{1}{3} \times 18 \times \sqrt{133} \times \frac{99\sqrt{133}}{133} = 6 \times 99 = 594.$$

Problem 14. Solution: 064.

Let V_1 be the volume of the new tetrahedron and V_2 be the volume of the original tetrahedron.

$$V_2 = \frac{1}{12}\sqrt{2}a_2^3 \tag{1}$$

$$S_2 = \sqrt{3}a_2^2 \tag{2}$$

$$V_1 = \frac{1}{12}\sqrt{2}a_1^3 \tag{3}$$

$$S_1 = \sqrt{3}a_1^2 \tag{4}$$

(1) ÷ (3): $\dfrac{V_1}{V_2} = \dfrac{\frac{1}{12}\sqrt{2}a_1^3}{\frac{1}{12}\sqrt{2}a_2^3} = (\dfrac{a_1}{a_2})^3 = 2 \Rightarrow \dfrac{a_1}{a_2} = 2^{\frac{1}{3}} \Rightarrow (\dfrac{a_1}{a_2})^2 = 2^{\frac{2}{3}}$ (5)

(2) ÷ (4): $\dfrac{S_1}{S_2} = \dfrac{\sqrt{3}a_1^2}{\sqrt{3}a_2^2} = (\dfrac{a_1}{a_2})^2$ (6)

Substituting (5) into (6): $\dfrac{S_1}{S_2} = (\dfrac{a_1}{a_2})^2 = \sqrt[3]{4}$. The answer is $4^3 = 64$.

Problem 15. Solution: 004.

In $\triangle ABC$, AM one of the medians with length $\dfrac{\sqrt{3}}{2}$. Similarly, the median DM in $\triangle BCD$ has length $\dfrac{\sqrt{3}}{2}$. The centroids for each of these triangles is located 2/3rds the way from the vertex to the opposite side, so $PM = QM = \dfrac{1}{3}(\dfrac{\sqrt{3}}{2}) = \dfrac{\sqrt{3}}{6}$.

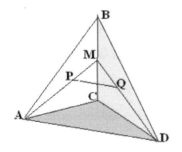

Since $\triangle PMC \sim \triangle AMD$, $\dfrac{PM}{PQ} = \dfrac{AM}{AD}$ $\Rightarrow \dfrac{\frac{\sqrt{3}}{6}}{PQ} = \dfrac{\frac{\sqrt{3}}{2}}{1}$ $\Rightarrow PQ = \dfrac{1}{3}$.

The answer is $1 + 3 = 4$.

Problem 16. Solution:

Let the three edges perpendicular to each other be $PA = a$, $PB = b$, $PC = c$.

$$S = a + b + c + \sqrt{a^2 + b^2} + \sqrt{b^2 + c^2} + \sqrt{c^2 + a^2}$$

$$\geq a + b + c + \sqrt{2ab} + \sqrt{2bc} + \sqrt{2ca} \geq 3\sqrt[3]{abc} + 3\sqrt[3]{\sqrt{2ab}\cdot\sqrt{2bc}\cdot\sqrt{2ca}}$$

$$= 3\sqrt[3]{abc} + 3\sqrt{2}\sqrt[3]{abc} = 3(1+\sqrt{2})\sqrt[3]{abc}$$

Equality holds if and only if $a = b = c$.

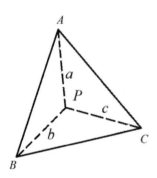

Since $V = \dfrac{1}{3} \times \dfrac{1}{2} abc = \dfrac{1}{6} abc$, $S \geq 3(1+\sqrt{2})\sqrt[3]{6V}$

$\Rightarrow \quad S^3 \geq 27(1+\sqrt{2})^3 \times 6V$

$\Rightarrow \quad V \leq \dfrac{S^3}{162(1+\sqrt{2})^3} \leq \dfrac{(5\sqrt{2}-7)S^3}{162}$.

Equality holds if and only if $a = b = c$.

The maximum volume is $\dfrac{(5\sqrt{2}-7)S^3}{162}$.

BASIC KNOWLEDGE

The maximum number of planes that can be formed by n points is $\binom{n}{3}$ (3.1)

Theorem. Through three non-collinear points one and only one plane can be passed, in other words, three non-collinear points determine a plane.

There are m planes in which no two planes are parallel, no three are collinear, and no four are concurrent. The number of parts of the planes divided among themselves is

$$N = 1 + 1 + 2 + 3 + 4 + \ldots + (m-1) = 1 + \frac{(m(m-1))}{2} = \frac{1}{2}(m^2 - m + 2) \quad (3.2)$$

The maximum number of regions into which a plane can be divided by n lines

$$\binom{n}{0} + \binom{n}{1} + \binom{n}{2} \quad (3.3)$$

The maximum number of regions into which space can be divided by n planes.

$$\binom{n}{0} + \binom{n}{1} + \binom{n}{2} + \binom{n}{3} \quad (3.4)$$

Or in the explicit form: $\frac{1}{6}(n+1)(n^2 - n + 6) = \frac{1}{6}(n^3 + 5n + 6)$

Euler's formula:
$F + V = E + 2$ (3.5)
F: number of faces, V: number of vertices, and E: number of edges of a polyhedron.

Proof:
The sum of angles in a n-gon is $(n-2)\pi$. Each edge contributes to two faces, so the total sum is $(2E - 2F)\pi$.

Now let's count the same angles the other way. Each interior vertex is surrounded by triangles and contributes a total angle of 2π to the sum. The vertices on the outside face contribute $2(\pi - 3\theta V)$, where θ denotes the exterior angle of the polygon. The total exterior angle of any polygon is 2π, so the total angle is $2\pi V - 4\pi$.

Combining these two formulas and dividing through by 2π, we see that $V - 2 = E - F$, or equivalently $V - E + F = 2$.

Polyhedron	Faces	Vertices	Edges
Tetrahedron	4	4	6
Cube	6	8	12
Octahedron	8	6	12
Icosahedron	20	12	30
Dodecahedron	12	20	30

Edges and faces formula

$$E = \frac{F \times S}{2} \tag{3.6}$$

E is the number of edges of the solid, F is the number of faces of the solid or net, and S is the number of sides of the faces.

The following convex polyhedron has 4 square faces and 8 triangular faces. The number of edges of the polyhedron is

$$E = \frac{F \times S}{2} = \frac{4 \times 4 + 8 \times 3}{2} = 20.$$

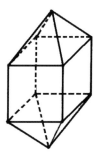

EXAMPLES

1. Dividing Regions

Example 1. There are ten planes in which no two planes are parallel, no three are collinear, and no four are concurrent. The number of intersecting lines is l. The number of intersecting points is p. The number of line segments of these intersecting lines divided among themselves is s. What is the value of $l + p + s$?

Solution: 570.
Since no two planes are parallel, any two planes must have one intersecting line. The number of intersecting lines formed by 10 planes is $l = \binom{10}{2} = 45$

Since no three planes are collinear and no two planes are parallel, any three planes must have one intersecting point. The number of intersecting points formed by 10 planes is $p = \binom{10}{3} = 120$.

Since an intersecting line formed by two planes is cut by the rest of 8 planes and is then divided into $(10 - 1) = 9$ segments, the number of line segments of these intersecting lines divided among themselves is $s = (10-1) \times \binom{10}{2} = 405$.

The answer is $45 + 120 + 405 = 570$.

Notes:

For m planes, the number of intersecting lines is $l = \binom{m}{2}$. The number of intersecting points is $p = \binom{m}{3}$. The number of line segments of these intersecting lines divided among themselves is $s = (m-1) \times \binom{m}{2}$.

Example 2. Find the maximum number of regions into which space can be divided by n planes.

Solution:
We prove this lemma first: the maximum number of regions into which plane can be divided by n lines is $\binom{n}{0} + \binom{n}{1} + \binom{n}{2}$.

Apparently, we get the maximum number of regions when (1) no three lines are concurrent and (2) n lines are mutually intersecting.

Let a_k be the maximum number of regions formed by k lines. Then we add the $k + 1^{\text{th}}$ line. The $k + 1^{\text{th}}$ line intersects every one of the k lines and produces k points of intersection. These k points divide the $k +$ 1th line into $k + 1$ sections. Each section will divide the region it goes through into two regions. So the number of regions increased by adding the $k+1^{\text{th}}$ line is the same as the number of sections the $k + 1^{\text{th}}$ line is divided, which is $k + 1$.

45

So we get the recursion formula: $a_{k+1} = a_k + k + 1$.

Solve the problem recursively:

$a_k = a_{k-1} + n = n + n - 1 + a_{k-2} = \cdots$
$= n + n - 1 + \cdots + 2 + a_1 = n + n - 1 \cdots + 2 + 1 + 1$
$= \binom{n}{0} + \binom{n}{1} + \binom{n}{2}.$

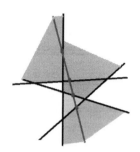

Let b_k be the maximum number of regions k planes divide the space. Then we add the $k + 1^{th}$ plane. The $k + 1^{th}$ plane intersects every one of the k planes and produces k lines of intersection. These k lines divide the $k + 1$th plane into at most $\binom{n}{0} + \binom{n}{1} + \binom{n}{2}$ parts.

Each part will divide the region it goes through into two regions. So the number of regions increased by adding the $k + 1^{th}$ plane is the same as the number of parts the $k + 1^{th}$ plane is divided, which is $\binom{n}{0} + \binom{n}{1} + \binom{n}{2}$.

So we get the recursion formula: $b_{k+1} = b_k + a_k$.

Solve the problem recursively:

$b_n = a_{n-1} + a_{n-2} + \cdots + a_1 + b_1 = \binom{n}{2} + \binom{n-1}{2} + \cdots + \binom{2}{2} + (n-1) + 2$

$= \binom{n}{0} + \binom{n}{1} + \binom{n}{2} + \binom{n}{3}.$

Or in the explicit form: $\frac{1}{6}(n+1)(n^2 - n + 6) = \frac{1}{6}(n^3 + 5n + 6)$.

Example 3. What is the minimum number of planes required to divide a cube into at least 300 pieces?

Solution: 013.

We know that the maximum number of regions divided by n planes is $\frac{1}{6}(n^3 + 5n + 6) \le 300$.

We see $\frac{1}{6}(12^3 + 5 \times 12 + 6) = 299$, $\frac{1}{6}(13^3 + 5 \times 13 + 6) = 378$.

So 12 planes can divide the space into 299 parts. We use a cube big enough to contain these 299 parts. Then we use the 13th plane to cut this cube such that it only divides one part into two so we get exactly 300 parts.
So the answer is 13.

2. Euler's Formula:

Example 4. The diagram shown is the net of a regular dodecahedron. In a regular dodecahedron, three edges come together at each vertex.
When the net of this dodecahedron is put together, the solid has x vertices and y edges. What is the value of $x + y$?

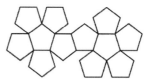

Solution: 050.
We know that $F + V = E + 2$, which can be rearranged to: $V + E = 2E + 2 - F$
We also know that $E = \dfrac{F \times S}{2}$ (two sides of the net will become one edge when folded),
so $E = 12 \times 5 \div 2 = 30$.
$F = 12$
$x + y = V + E = 2E + 2 - F = 2 \times 30 + 2 - 12 = 50$.

☆**Example 5.** The truncated cuboctahedron is a convex polyhedron with 26 faces: 12 squares, 8 regular hexagons and 6 regular octagons. There are three faces at each vertex: one square, one hexagon, and one octagon. How many segments joining vertices of the polyhedron are inside the polyhedron rather than on a face or edge?

Solution: 840.
By the Edges and Faces formula, the number of edges of the polyhedron is
$$E = \dfrac{F \times S}{2} = \dfrac{12 \times 4 + 8 \times 6 + 6 \times 8}{2} = 72.$$

By Euler's formula, $F + V = E + 2$, the number of vertices of the polyhedron is $V = E + 2 - F = 72 + 2 - 26 = 48$.

Each square has two face diagonals so we get $2 \times 12 = 24$ diagonals for 12 squares.

Each hexagon has $\binom{6}{2} - 6 = 9$ face diagonals so we get $9 \times 8 = 72$ diagonals for 8 hexagons.

Each octagon has $\binom{8}{2} - 8 = 20$ face diagonals so we get $6 \times 20 = 120$ diagonals for 6 octagons.

So total number of segments on the faces is $24 + 72 + 120 = 216$.

The number of segments of the convex polyhedron is $\binom{48}{2} = 1128$.

The answer is $1128 - 72 - 216 = 840$.

Example 6. A regular polyhedron has all faces of equilateral triangles. There are five edges joining each vertex of the polyhedron. F is the number of faces, V is the number of vertices, and E is the number of edges of the polyhedron. Find the value of $\frac{1}{9} F \times V \times E$.

Solution: 800.

We know that $F + V = E + 2$ \hfill (1)

By the Edges and Faces formula, we have:

$$E = \frac{F \times S}{2} = \frac{3F}{2} \quad \Rightarrow \quad F = \frac{2E}{3} \quad (2)$$

We know that five edges join each vertex, so we have $5V$ edges possible. However, each edge is connecting two vertices, we double counted the number of edges ($5V$). The number of edges is actually $E = \frac{5V}{2} \quad \Rightarrow \quad V = \frac{2E}{5}$ \hfill (3)

Substituting (2) and (3) into (1): $\frac{2E}{3} + \frac{2E}{5} = E + 2 \quad \Rightarrow \quad E = 30$.

$V = \frac{2E}{5} = 12$, $F = \frac{2E}{3} = 20$.

$\frac{1}{9} F \times V \times E = \frac{1}{9} \times F \times V \times E = \frac{1}{9} \times 20 \times 12 \times 30 = 800$.

This is a regular icosahedron.

Example 7. The number of vertices of a convex polyhedron is V. Find the sum of the interior angles of all polygon faces in terms of V.

Solution: $(V - 2) \times 360°$.
Let F be the number of faces, and E be the number of edges of the polyhedron.
Let $n_1, n_2, \ldots n_F$ be the number of sides of each face, respectively. where $n_1, n_2, \ldots n_F$ are positive integers ≥ 3.
The sum of the interior angles of each face is $(n_1 - 2) \times 180°$, $(n_2 - 2) \times 180°$, …, $(n_F - 2) \times 180°$.
Let M be the sum of all the angles and $M = [(n_1 + n_2 + \ldots n_F) - 2F] \, 180°$ (1)
Since every two sides forms an edge, $2E = (n_1 + n_2 + \ldots + n_F)$ (2)
Substituting (2) into (1): $M = [(2E - 2F)] \, 180° = (E - F) \times 360°$ (3)
We know that $F + V = E + 2$. Thus $E - F = V - 2$ (4)
Substituting (4) into (3): $M = (V - 2) \times 360°$.

3. Counting points, lines, shapes, planes, and solids

Example 8. (1991 China High School Math Contest) How many equilateral triangles can be formed using three vertices of a cube?

Solution: 008.
Method 1:
There are 8 vertices of a cube. ABC is the base (equilateral triangle) of the tetrahedron $D - ABC$. Each vertex corresponds to exactly one such tetrahedron, which in turn, has an equilateral triangle base. So the answer is 8.

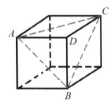

Method 2:
Only the face diagonals can form equilateral triangles.
There are $6 \times 2 = 12$ face diagonals of a cube.

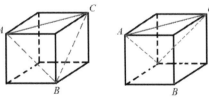

If we take one face diagonal, say AC, we can form two equilateral triangles with other face diagonals. With 12 face diagonals, the number of face diagonals appear $2 \times \binom{12}{1} = 24$ times. Since every such equilateral triangle has 3 sides, the number of equilateral triangles is $24 \div 3 = 8$.

☆**Example 9.** The sum of the areas of all triangles whose vertices are also vertices of a unit cube is $\sqrt{x} + \sqrt{y} + \sqrt{z}$, where x, y, and z are positive integers. Find $x + y + z$.

Solution: 480.

We know that there are $\binom{8}{3} = 56$ triangles whose vertices are the vertices of the unit cube.

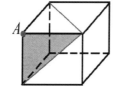

The first type of triangle is right with area $\frac{1 \times 1}{2} = \frac{1}{2}$, and there are 24 of them, 4 on each face.

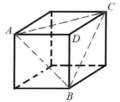

The second type of triangle is equilateral with area $\frac{\sqrt{3}}{4} \times (\sqrt{2})^2 = \frac{\sqrt{3}}{2}$. There are 8 of these because each of these triangles is uniquely determined by the three vertices adjacent to one of the 8 vertices of the cube.

The third type of triangle is right with area $\frac{1 \times \sqrt{2}}{2} = \frac{\sqrt{2}}{2}$. There are 24 of these because there are four space-diagonals and each determines six triangles, one with each cube vertex that is not an endpoint of the diagonal.

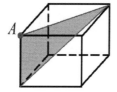

The total area is $24 \times \frac{1}{2} + 8(\frac{\sqrt{3}}{2}) + 24(\frac{\sqrt{2}}{2}) = 12 + 4\sqrt{3} + 12\sqrt{2} = \sqrt{144} + \sqrt{48} + \sqrt{288}$.

The answer is $144 + 48 + 288 = 480$.

Example 10. The number of planes that go through exactly four midpoints of the edges of a cube is m and the number of planes that go through exactly six midpoints of the edges of the cube is n. Find $m + n$.

Solution: 025.
Case 1: four points are in the same plane (figure *a*, 3 planes; figure *b*, 6 planes, and figure *c*, 12 planes).
Case 2: 6 points are in the same plane (figure *d*, 4 places).
So the answer is $3 + 6 + 12 + 4 = 25$.

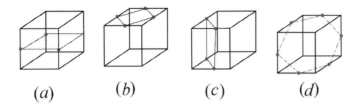

(a)　　　(b)　　　(c)　　　(d)

Example 11. (2002 China High School Math Contest) As shown in the figure, $P_1, P_2, \cdots, P_{10}$ are vertices or midpoints of the edges of a tetrahedron. How many quadruples (P_1, P_i, P_j, P_k) ($1 \leq i \leq k \leq 10$) are there such that these four points are in the same plane?

Solution: 033.

There are $3 \times \binom{1}{1}\binom{5}{3} = 30$ quadruples with points on three lateral faces of the tetrahedron (figure a).

There are $3 \times \binom{1}{1}\binom{3}{3} = 3$ quadruples points with one point the midpoint of any edge and three points in the opposite edge (figures b, c, and d).

The answer is $30 + 3 = 33$.

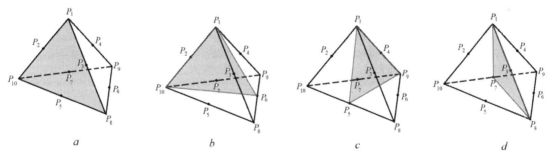

a　　　b　　　c　　　d

Example 12. Four points are selected from 10 points as shown in the figure such that these fours points are not in the same plane. These points are either vertices or midpoints of the edges of the tetrahedron. The probability that these four points are not coplanar is $\dfrac{m}{n}$, where m and n are positive integers relatively prime. Find $m + n$.

Solution: 117.

The number of ways of selecting 4 points from 10 points is $\binom{10}{4} = 210$.

There are $4 \times \binom{6}{4} = 60$ quadruples with points on four faces (3 lateral faces and one base face) of the tetrahedron (figure *a*).

There are $6 \times \binom{1}{1}\binom{3}{3} = 6$ quadruples points with one point the midpoint of any edge and three points in the opposite edge (figures *b*).

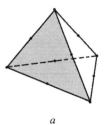
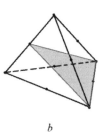
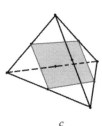

a   *b*   *c*

There are $3 \times \binom{4}{4} = 3$ quadruples points from six midpoints of the edges (figures *c*).

The numerator is $210 - (60 + 6 + 3) = 141$.
The probability is $141/210 = 47/70$. $m + n = 117$.

4. Coloring

Example 13. In how many ways can a cube be painted by six different colors such that each face has a different color? (If you can reorient a cube to look like another cube, then the two cubes are not distinct.)

Solution: 030.
Method 1:
We have $6! = 720$ ways to color the cube with 6 different colors. But some can be reoriented to get others.
For a painted cube, we can select any one face as the bottom face. We have 6 ways to do so. Then we select one lateral face as the front face. We have 4 ways to do so. We see that this cube have $6 \times 4 = 24$ different positions. That is every way is counted 24 times. The answer is $6!/24 = 720/24 = 30$.

Method 2:
We can use any color for the face facing down. We then choose one color from the rest of 5 colors to paint the top face. We have 5 ways to do so.

Then we use any one of the 4 colors left to paint the front face, and we can choose one color from the rest 3 colors left to paint the back face. We have 3 ways to do so. We have now two colors left and we have 2 ways to paint the left and right faces.
The answer is $1 \times 5 \times 1 \times 3 \times 2 = 30$.

Example 14. (1995 China High School Math Contest) You are given five different colors. In how many ways can the vertices of a pyramid be painted by one or more colors such that each vertex is painted one color and two vertices sharing the same edge have the different color? (If you can reorient a pyramid to look like another pyramid, then the two pyramids are not distinct.)

Solution: 420.
P must have the different color from $A, B, C,$ and D.
Case 1: We use 3 colors.
B and D can be the same color and A and C can be the same color. We have $\binom{5}{3} \times \binom{3}{1} \times 2 = 60$ ways to color.

Case 2: We use 4 colors.
B and D can be the same color and A and C can be the same color. We have
$\binom{5}{4} \times \binom{4}{1} \times 3 \times 2 \times 2 \times 1 = 240$ ways to color.

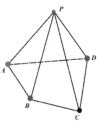 

Case 3: We use 5 colors.
All the vertices have the different color. We have $5! = 120$ ways to color.
The answer is $60 + 240 + 120 = 420$.

Note: There exists a formula for similar types of problems which can be derived using a recursion method. $(m(m-2)[(m-2)^{n-1} + (-1)^n]$
n is the number of lateral edges of the pyramid and m is the number of colors available.

PROBLEMS

Problem 1. There are ten planes in which no two planes are parallel, no three are collinear, and no four are concurrent. Find N, the number of parts of the planes divided among themselves.

Problem 2. Find maximum number of regions into which space can be divided by 10 planes.

Problem 3. What is the minimum number of planes required to divide a cube into 64 pieces?

Problem 4. A convex polyhedron has twelve faces and 8 vertices. There are two vertices with six edges coming together at each vertex. The rest of vertices with n edges come together at each vertex. Find n.

☆**Problem 5.** A convex polyhedron has 36 faces, 24 of which are triangular, and 12 of which are quadrilaterals. Find the number of space diagonals the polyhedron has. (A *space diagonal* is a line segment connecting two vertices which do not belong to the same face).

☆ **Problem 6.** P is a convex polyhedron with 15 faces, 10 of the faces are equilateral triangles and 5 are squares. A *space diagonal* is a line segment connecting two vertices which do not belong to the same face. How many space diagonals does P have?

Problem 7. A regular polyhedron has all faces of regular pentagons. There are three edges joining each vertex of the polyhedron. F is the number of faces, V is the number of vertices, and E is the number of edges of the polyhedron. Find the value of $\frac{1}{9} F \times V \times E$.

Problem 8. A convex polyhedron has all polygon faces with an odd number of sides. Show that the number of faces is even.

Problem 9. The number of vertices of a convex polyhedron is 6. Find the last three digits of the sum of the interior angles of all polygon faces.

☆ **Problem 10.** A convex polyhedron has 32 faces, each of which has 3 or 5 sides. At each of it's V vertices, T triangles and P pentagons meet. Find the value of $100P + 10T + V$. You may assume Euler's formula ($V + F = E + 2$, where F is the number of faces and E the number of edges).

Problem 11. (1989 China High School Math Contest) How many acute triangles can be formed using three vertices of a rectangular prism?

Problem 12. (1998 China High School Math Contest) Taking three points from the following 26 points at a time: 8 vertices of a cube, the midpoints of 12 edges of the cube, the centers of 6 faces, and the center of the cube, how many of these triples are collinear?

Problem 13. (1991 Japan Olympiad) How many planes are there that go through at least three midpoints of the edges of a cube?

Problem 14. Four points are selected from 10 points as shown in the figure such that these four points are not in the same plane. These points are either vertices or midpoints of the edges of the tetrahedron. How many ways are there?

Problem 15. Four points are selected from 8 vertices of a cube. How many tetrahedrons can be formed from the four points selected?

Problem 16. (1996 China High School Math Contest) You are given six different colors. In how many ways can a cube be painted by one or more colors such that each face is painted one color and two faces sharing the same edge will have two different colors? (If you can reorient a cube to look like another cube, then the two cubes are not distinct.)

Problem 17. You are given four different colors. In how many ways can the vertices of the pyramid as shown in the figure be painted by one or more colors such that each vertex is painted one color and two vertices sharing the same edge have the different color? (If you can reorient a pyramid to look like another pyramid, then the two pyramids are not distinct.)

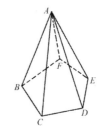

SOLUTIONS

Problem 1. Solution: 460.
Let us consider plane a first. Nine other planes intersect with the plane a and to form 9 intersecting lines in plane a. No two of these 9 lines are parallel and no three are collinear.

We know that one line (formed on the second plane when intersecting with the plane a) divides the plane a into $1 + 1 = 2$ parts.

The second line (formed the third plane intersecting with the plane a) meets the first line and the intersecting point divides the second line into two sections, and each section divides the plane a into two parts. So two lines divide the plane a into $1 + 1 + 2$ parts.

Similarly, the third line (formed the fourth plane intersecting with the plane a) joins in and it is divided by the first and the second lines into three section with each section dividing the plane a into three parts. So we get $1 + 1 + 2 + 3 = 7$ parts.

Repeat the procedure until the 8th line (formed the 9th plane intersecting with the plane a) is cut into 9 sections by the former 8 lines. Then we get

$$1+1+2+3+4+\ldots+9 = 1+\frac{(1+9)\times 9}{2} = 46 \text{ parts.}$$

Since we have 10 planes in our problem, the answer is then $N = 10 \times 46 = 460$.

Problem 2. Solution: 176.
$$N = \binom{n}{0} + \binom{n}{1} + \binom{n}{2} + \binom{n}{3} = \binom{10}{0} + \binom{10}{1} + \binom{10}{2} + \binom{10}{3} = 1 + 10 + 45 + 120 = 176.$$

Problem 3. Solution: 007.
We have $\frac{1}{6}(n+1)(n^2 - n + 6) = 64$.
Solving for n: $n = 7$.

Problem 4. Solution: 004.
We know that $F + V = E + 2 \implies V + F - E = 2 \implies 8 + 12 - E = 2$.

$E = 18$.

By the Edges and Faces formula, we have:

$$E = \frac{F \times S}{2} = \frac{2 \times 6 + 6 \times N}{2} = 18 \quad \Rightarrow \quad n = 4.$$

☆**Problem 5.** Solution: 241.

$F = 24 + 12 = 36$.

By the Edges and Faces formula, the number of edges of the polyhedron is

$$E = \frac{F \times S}{2} = \frac{24 \times 3 + 12 \times 4}{2} = 60.$$

We know that $F + V = E + 2$. The number of vertices is $V = E + 2 - F = 60 + 2 - 36 = 26$.

Each quadrilateral has two face diagonals so we get $2 \times 12 = 24$ diagonals for 12 quadrilaterals.

The number of segments of the convex polyhedron is $\binom{26}{2} = 325$.

The answer is $325 - 60 - 24 = 241$.

☆ **Problem 6.** Solution: 031.

$F = 15$.

By the Edges and Faces formula, the number of edges of the polyhedron is

$$E = \frac{F \times S}{2} = \frac{5 \times 4 + 10 \times 3}{2} = 25.$$

We know that $F + V = E + 2$. The number of vertices is $V = E + 2 - F = 25 + 2 - 15 = 12$.

Each square has two face diagonals so we get $2 \times 5 = 10$ face diagonals for 5 squares.

The number of segments of the convex polyhedron is $\binom{12}{2} = 66$.

The answer is $66 - 25 - 10 = 31$.

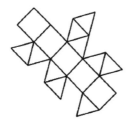

Problem 7. Solution: 800.

We know that $F + V = E + 2$ \hfill (1)

By the Edges and Faces formula, we have:

$$E = \frac{F \times S}{2} = \frac{5F}{2} \quad \Rightarrow \quad F = \frac{2E}{5} \quad (2)$$

We know that three edges join each vertex, so we have $3V$ edges possible. However, each edge is connecting two vertices. So we double counted the number of edges ($3V$). The number of edges is actually $E = \frac{3V}{2} \Rightarrow V = \frac{2E}{3}$ \hfill (3)

Substituting (2) and (3) into (1): $\frac{2E}{5} + \frac{2E}{3} = E + 2 \Rightarrow E = 30$.

$V = \frac{2E}{3} = 20$, $F = \frac{2E}{5} = 12$.

$\frac{1}{9} F \times V \times E = \frac{1}{9} \times F \times V \times E = \frac{1}{9} \times 20 \times 12 \times 30 = 800$.

This is a regular dodecahedron.

Problem 8. Solution:

Let F be the number of faces, V be the number of vertices, and E be the number of edges of the polyhedron.

The number of sides of each polygon is $2n_1 + 1$, $2n_2 + 1$, $2n_3 + 1$,..., $2n_F + 1$, where n_1, n_2,...n_F are positive integers.

By the Edges and Faces formula, we have:

$$E = \frac{F \times S}{2} \Rightarrow E = \frac{F \times [(2n_1 + 1) + (2n_2 + 1) + \cdots + (2n_F + 1)]}{2} = (n_1 + n_2 + \cdots + n_F) + \frac{F}{2}$$

We know that $F + V = E + 2$. Thus $V + F - (n_1 + n_2 + \cdots + n_F) - \frac{F}{2} = 2 \quad \Rightarrow$

$$\frac{F}{2} = 2 + (n_1 + n_2 + \cdots + n_F) - V \qquad \Rightarrow F = 2[2 + (n_1 + n_2 + \cdots + n_F) - V].$$

Therefore the number of faces is even.

Problem 9. Solution: 440.

Let F be the number of faces, and E be the number of edges of the polyhedron.

Let $n_1, n_2, \ldots n_6$ be the number of sides of each face, respectively, where $n_1, n_2, \ldots n_6$ are positive integers ≥ 3.

The sum of the interior angles of each face is $(n_1 - 2) \times 180°$, $(n_2 - 2) \times 180°$, …, $(n_6 - 2) \times 180°$.

Let M be the sum of all the angles and $M = [(n_1 + n_2 + \ldots n_6) - 2F]\, 180°$ \hfill (1)

Since every two sides forms an edge, $2E = (n_1 + n_2 + \ldots + n_6)$ \hfill (2)

Substituting (2) into (1): $M = [(2E - 2F)]\, 180° = (E - F) \times 360°$ \hfill (3)

We know that $F + V = E + 2$. Thus $E - F = V - 2$ \hfill (4)

Substituting (4) into (3): $M = (6 - 2) \times 360° = 1440$.

The solid is an octahedron.

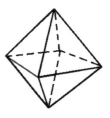

☆ **Problem 10.** Solution: 250.

We know that $F = 32$

The total number of triangles is $\dfrac{VT}{3}$ and the total number of pentagons is $\dfrac{VP}{5}$. So $\dfrac{VT}{3} + \dfrac{VP}{5} = 32 \qquad \Rightarrow \qquad V(5T + 3P) = 32 \times 15$ \hfill (1)

By the Edges and Faces formula, we have:

$$E = \frac{F \times S}{2} = \frac{3 \times \dfrac{VT}{3} + 5 \dfrac{VP}{5}}{2} \qquad \Rightarrow \qquad 2E = VT + VP \qquad (2)$$

We know that $F + V = E + 2$ \hfill (3)

Substituting (2) into (3): $32 + V = \dfrac{VT + VP}{2} + 2 \qquad \Rightarrow 60 = V(T + P - 2)$ \hfill (4)

(1) ÷ (4): $\dfrac{5T + 3P}{T + P - 2} = \dfrac{32 \times 15}{60} = 8 \qquad \Rightarrow 5T + 3P = 8T + 8P - 16 \Rightarrow 3T + 5P = 16$

We see that $P < 4$.

$2P \equiv 4 \mod 3 \implies P = 2$ and $T = 2$.
Substituting the values of T and P into (4) we get $V = 30$.
$100P + 10T + V = 250$.

Problem 11. Solution: 008.
We have 8 vertices. The number of possible triangles formed by any three of the 8 vertices is $\binom{8}{3} = 56$. These triangles are either right triangles or acute triangles.

We examine the cases where the vertex as the intersection point of two legs of a right triangle. We get 6 right triangles with each vertex of the cube. So we get $6 \times 8 = 48$ right triangles.
The answer is $56 - 48 = 8$.

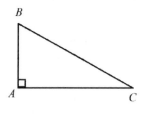

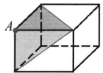 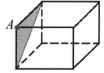 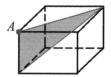 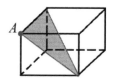 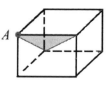

Method 2:
If one of the three sides of a triangle is the edge of the cube, the triangle will be right triangle. Any triangle with no edge of the cube will be an acute triangle.

There are 8 vertices of a cube. ABC is the base (acute triangle) of the tetrahedron $D - ABC$. Each vertex corresponds to exactly one such tetrahedron, which in turn, has an equilateral triangle base. So the answer is 8.

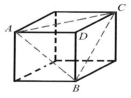

Method 3:
We have 8 vertices. The number of possible triangles formed by any three of the 8 vertices is $\binom{8}{3} = 56$.

The rectangular prism has 6 rectangular faces and 2 + 2 + 2 = 6 diagonal faces as shown in the figure below. Any three vertices of each rectangular face will form $\binom{4}{3} = 4$ right triangles. So we have 12 × 4 = 48 right triangles.

The answer is 56 − 48 = 8.

     6   2   2   2

Problem 12. Solution: 049.

Case 1: the line segment with two vertices as the end points (figure a). Any two vertices will be able to form a collinear triple with one other point either on the face or the edge. So we have $\binom{8}{2} = \frac{8 \times 7}{2} = 28$ such triples.

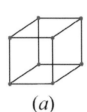 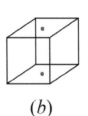 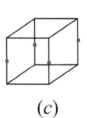

                (a)   (b)   (c)

Case 2: the line segment with center points of the faces as the end points (figure b). Any two center points will be able to form a collinear triple with the center of the cube. So we have $\frac{6 \times 1}{2} = 3$ such triples.

Case 3: the line segment with midpoints of the faces as the end points (figure c). Any two midpoints will be able to form a collinear triple with one other point (either on the face or the center of the cube). So we have $\frac{12 \times 3}{2} = 18$ such triples.

The answer is 28 + 3 + 18 = 49.

Problem 13. Solution: 081.

A plane is determined by three points that are not collinear.

We know that none of the three edges of a cube are collinear. So we have at most $\binom{12}{3} = 220$ planes.

Case 1: four points are in the same plane (figure a, 3 planes; figure b, 6 planes, and figure c, 12 planes).

Case 2: 6 points are in the same plane (figure d, 4 planes).

So the answer is $220 - 3[\binom{4}{3}-1] + 6[\binom{4}{3}-1] + 12[\binom{4}{3}-1] + 4[\binom{6}{3}-1] = 220 - 139 = 81$.

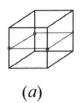 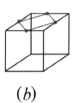 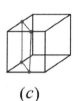

(a)   (b)   (c)   (d)

Problem 14. Solution: 141.

The number of ways of selecting 4 points from 10 points is $\binom{10}{4} = 210$.

There are $4 \times \binom{6}{4} = 60$ quadruples with points on four faces (3 lateral faces and one base face) of the tetrahedron (figure a).

There are $6 \times \binom{1}{1}\binom{3}{3} = 6$ quadruples points with one point the midpoint of any edge and three points in the opposite edge (figures b).

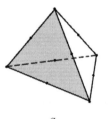 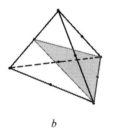 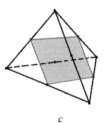

a   b   c

There are $3 \times \binom{4}{4} = 3$ quadruples points from six midpoints of the edges (figures c).

The answer is $210 - (60 + 6 + 3) = 141$.

Problem 15. Solution: 058.

The number of ways to select 4 points is $\binom{8}{4} = 70$.

Any four points that are coplanar could not form a tetrahedron.

We have 6 faces of the cube (figure *a*) and 2 + 2 + 2 diagonal faces (figures *b*, *c*, and *d*).

The answer is 70 – 12 = 58.

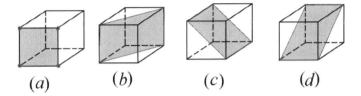

(*a*) (*b*) (*c*) (*d*)

Problem 16. Solution: 320.

At most we can use 6 colors and at least we need to use 3 colors.

Case 1: 6 colors. We have 6!/24 = 30 ways to paint the cube with 6 different colors.

Case 2: 5 colors. We choose one color from 6 colors. Then we choose one from 5 colors to paint the top and the bottom faces. We have 4 colors to paint 4 lateral faces. Any one color will go the front face. So we have 3 ways to paint the back face. Now we have two colors left to paint the left and right faces. They will only generate one new way. So we have $\binom{6}{5} \times \binom{5}{1} \times 3 = 90$ to paint the cube with 5 different colors.

Case 3: 4 colors. Let the top and the bottom faces have the same color and front and back faces have the same color.

We have $\binom{6}{4} \times \binom{4}{2} \times \frac{2 \times 1}{2} = 90$ to paint the cube with 4 different colors.

Case 4: 3 colors. Let the opposite faces have the same color.

We have $\binom{6}{3} = 20$ to paint the cube with 3 different colors.

The answer is 30 + 90 + 90 + 20 = 230.

Note: the original official solution was 30 + 180 + 90 + 20 = 320 ways which was wrong.

Problem 17. Solution: 120.

By the formula, the number of ways is $(m(m-2)[(m-2)^{n-1} + (-1)^n] =$
$(4(4-2)[(4-2)^{5-1} + (-1)^5] = 8 \times 15 = 120$

n is the number of lateral edges of the pyramid and *m* is the number of colors available.

Chapter 4 Similar Triangles

BASIC KNOWLEDGE

Similar triangles are triangles whose corresponding angles are congruent and whose corresponding sides are in proportion to each other. Similar triangles have the same shape but are not necessarily the same size.

The symbol for "similar" is ~. The notation $\triangle ABC \sim \triangle A'B'C'$ is read as "triangle ABC is similar to triangle A-prime B-prime C-prime."

Principles of Similar Triangles

Principle 1. *(AA)* If two angles of one triangle are congruent respectively to two angles of the other triangle, the two triangles are similar by *AA* (angle, angle).

Corollary of Principle 2: Two right triangles are similar if they have one congruent acute angle.

Principle 2. (*SAS*) If two sides of one triangle are proportional to the corresponding parts of another triangle, and the ***included*** angles are congruent, the two triangles are similar by *SAS* (side, angle, side).

If $\dfrac{a}{c} = \dfrac{b}{d}$ and $\alpha = \beta$, then two triangles are similar.

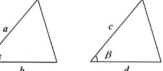

Principle 3. (*SSS*) If three corresponding sides (segments) of two triangles are in proportion, the two triangles are similar by *SSS* (side, side, side).

If $\dfrac{a}{a_1} = \dfrac{b}{b_1} = \dfrac{c}{c_1}$, then $\triangle ABC \sim \triangle A_1B_1C_1$.

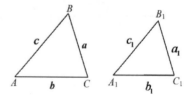

Principle 4. (HL) If the corresponding hypotenuse and one leg of two right triangles are in proportion, the two triangles are similar by *HL* (hypotenuse, leg).

Theorem 1. Corresponding sides (segments) of similar triangles are in proportion to each other.

50 AIME Lectures — Chapter 4 Similar Triangles

If $\triangle ABC \sim \triangle A_1B_1C_1$, then $\dfrac{a}{a_1} = \dfrac{b}{b_1} = \dfrac{c}{c_1}$

and the ratio of the areas is as follows:

$\dfrac{S_{\triangle ABC}}{S_{\triangle A_1B_1C_1}} = \left(\dfrac{a}{a_1}\right)^2 = \left(\dfrac{b}{b_1}\right)^2 = \left(\dfrac{c}{c_1}\right)^2$

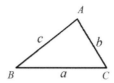
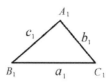

Theorem 2. A line parallel to a side of a triangle cuts off a triangle similar to the given triangle.

If $DE // BC$, then $\triangle ABC \sim \triangle ADE$

$\dfrac{AD}{AB} = \dfrac{AE}{AC} = \dfrac{DE}{BC}$

$\dfrac{AD}{DB} = \dfrac{AE}{EC} \quad \Rightarrow \quad \dfrac{AD}{AE} = \dfrac{DB}{EC}$

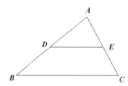

Theorem 3. If $\angle ACB = \angle ADC = 90°$, then

$AC^2 = AB \times AD$ (1)

$BC^2 = AB \times BD$ (2)

$CD^2 = AD \times BD$ (3)

$CD \times AB = AC \times BC$ (4)

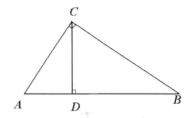

PROBLEMS INVOLVED IN ONE OR TWO PAIRS OF SIMILAR TRIANGLES

☆ **Example 1.** In rectangle $ABCD$, $AB = 50\sqrt{6}$. Let E be the midpoint of AD. What is the largest integer less than AD if lines AC and BE are perpendicular?

Solution: 173.
As shown in the figures, we see that $\alpha + \beta = 90°$ and $\alpha + \gamma = 90°$.
Thus $\beta = \gamma$.
$\triangle BAE \sim \triangle CBA$.

$\dfrac{AB}{BC} = \dfrac{AE}{AB} \quad \Rightarrow \quad \dfrac{50\sqrt{6}}{2AE} = \dfrac{AE}{50\sqrt{6}}$

$\Rightarrow \quad \sqrt{2}AE = 50\sqrt{6}$

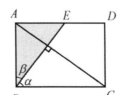
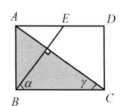

65

$\Rightarrow \quad \sqrt{2} \times \sqrt{2} AE = 50\sqrt{6} \times \sqrt{2} \quad \Rightarrow \quad 2AE = AD = 100\sqrt{3}$.

Since $173 < 100\sqrt{3} < 174$, the answer is 173.

☆**Example 2.** As shown in the figure, ABCD is a square with AB = 1. Four points E, F, G, H lie on sides AB, CD, DA, respectively, with AE = BF = CG = DH. The area of the shaded small square is area of the ABCD can be expressed as $\frac{1}{2113}$. What is the value of $\frac{1}{BE}$?

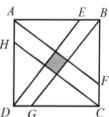

Solution: 033.

Draw $EK \perp BG$ at K. Let J be the point of intersection of AF and BG. $x = 1/BE$.

Right triangle $BKE \sim BAF$ ($\angle BEK = \angle BAJ$, $\angle BJA = \angle BKE = 90°$).

$$\frac{AB}{EK} = \frac{BF}{BK} \Rightarrow \frac{1}{\frac{1}{\sqrt{2113}}} = \frac{1 - \frac{1}{x}}{\sqrt{\frac{1}{x^2} - (\frac{1}{\sqrt{2113}})^2}}$$

$$\Rightarrow \sqrt{2113} = \frac{\frac{x-1}{x}}{\sqrt{\frac{1}{x^2} - \frac{1}{2113}}} \Rightarrow \sqrt{2113} = \frac{\frac{x-1}{x}}{\frac{\sqrt{2113-x^2}}{x\sqrt{2113}}}$$

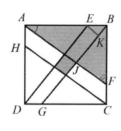
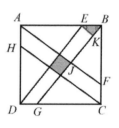

$\Rightarrow \sqrt{2113 - x^2} = x - 1 \Rightarrow 2113 - x^2 = (x-1)^2$

$x = 33$ or $x = -32$ (ignored).

☆**Example 3:** (1984 AIME) A point P is chosen in the interior of $\triangle ABC$ so that when lines are drawn through P parallel to the sides of $\triangle ABC$, the resulting smaller triangles, t_1, t_2 and t_3 in the figure, have areas 4, 9 and 49, respectively. Find the area of $\triangle ABC$.

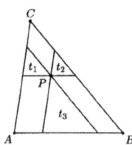

Solution: 144.

Method 1:

Let R and T be the two points that the lines drawn parallel through P intersect with AB, with R being the point closer to A.

The ratio of the corresponding sides of areas t_1, t_2 and t_3 is:

$PM : PN : RT = \sqrt{4} : \sqrt{9} : \sqrt{49} = 2 : 3 : 7$.

Or $AR : RT : BT = 2 : 3 : 7$.
$AB : RT = 12 : 7$.
$S_{\triangle ABC} : S_{\triangle PRT} = (AB : RT)^2 = 12^2 : 7^2$.
Therefore $S_{\triangle ABC} = \dfrac{144}{49} \times 49 = 144$.

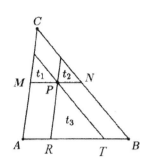

Method 2 (our solution):
Let the area of $\triangle ABC$ be S. We know that t_1, t_2, t_3 are all similar to $\triangle ABC$ and we label each side of the triangles as shown in the figure.

We use the triangle t_2 ($\triangle PNQ$) in our calculation (t_1 or t_3 can also be used):

$$\dfrac{9}{S} = \left(\dfrac{3x}{12x}\right)^2 \quad \Rightarrow \quad \dfrac{9}{S} = \left(\dfrac{1}{4}\right)^2 = \dfrac{1}{16} \Rightarrow \quad S = 9 \times 16 = 144.$$

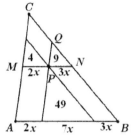

☆ **Example 4:** In $\triangle ABC$ shown below, $AB = 34$, $BC = 51$ and $CA = 68$. Moreover, P is an interior point chosen so that the segments DE, FG and HI are each of length d, contain P, and are parallel to the sides AB, BC and CA, respectively. Given that $d = p/q$, where p and q are relatively prime positive integers, find $p + q$.

Solution: 419.
$EH = BC - (BE + HC) = BC - (FP + PG) = 51 - d$.

Similarly $GD = 68 - d$.
We know that $\triangle DPG \sim \triangle ABC$, so $\dfrac{DP}{AB} = \dfrac{GD}{CA}$

$\Rightarrow DP = \dfrac{GD}{CA} \cdot AB = \dfrac{68-D}{68} \cdot 34 = 34 - \dfrac{1}{2}d.$

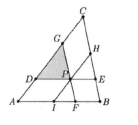
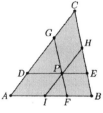

We also know that $\triangle PEH \sim \triangle ABC$.
Therefore $\dfrac{PE}{AB} = \dfrac{EH}{BC}$

$$\Rightarrow PE = \frac{EH}{BC} \cdot AB = \frac{51-d}{51} \cdot 34 = 34 - \frac{2}{3}d.$$

Hence $d = DP + PE = 68 - \frac{5}{6}d \Rightarrow d = 408/11.$

The answer is $408 + 11 = 419.$

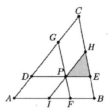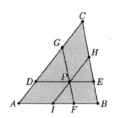

Example 5. As shown in the figure, a point P is chosen in the interior of $\triangle ABC$ and lines are drawn through P parallel to the sides of $\triangle ABC$. Show that $\dfrac{DE}{BC} + \dfrac{FG}{CA} + \dfrac{LH}{AB} = 2.$

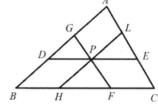

Proof:

We know that $\triangle BFG \sim \triangle BCA$, so $\dfrac{FG}{CA} = \dfrac{BF}{BC}$ \quad (1)

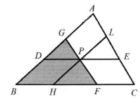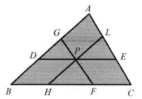

We know that $\triangle CHL \sim \triangle CBA$, so $\dfrac{LH}{AB} = \dfrac{CH}{BC}$ \quad (2)

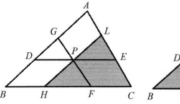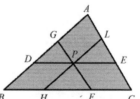

Then we can have: $\dfrac{DE}{BC} + \dfrac{FG}{CA} + \dfrac{LH}{AB} = \dfrac{DE}{BC} + \dfrac{BF}{BC} + \dfrac{CH}{BC} = \dfrac{DE + BF + CH}{BC}$

We see that $DE = DP + PE = BH + FC$. So $\dfrac{DE}{BC} + \dfrac{FG}{CA} + \dfrac{LH}{AB} = \dfrac{BH + FC + BF + CH}{BC} = \dfrac{(BH+CH)+(FC+BF)}{BC} = \dfrac{2BC}{BC} = 2$

Example 6: (1997 China Shandong Province Middle School Math Contest) As shown in the figure below, *ABCD* is a parallelogram. *A, E, F*, and *G* are on the same line. *BD* is the diagonal. Which one of the following is true?

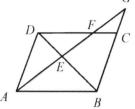

(A) $AE^2 = EF \times FG$

(B) $AE^2 = EF \times EG$

(C) $AE^2 = EG \times FG$

(D) $AE^2 = EF \times AG$

Solution: A.

$\triangle AEB \sim \triangle DEF \quad \Rightarrow \quad \dfrac{EA}{EF} = \dfrac{EB}{ED} \quad (1)$

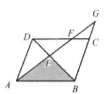 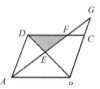

$\triangle DAE \sim \triangle BGE \quad \Rightarrow \quad \dfrac{EG}{EA} = \dfrac{EB}{ED} \quad (2)$

$\dfrac{EA}{EF} = \dfrac{EG}{EA} \quad \Rightarrow \quad AE^2 = EF \times EG.$

 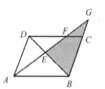

☆**Example 7. (1998 AIME)** Let *ABCD* be a parallelogram. Extend *DA* through *A* to a point *P*, and let *PC* meet *AB* at *Q* and *DB* at *R*. Given that *PQ* = 735 and *QR* = 112, find *RC*.

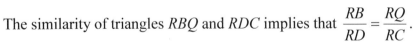

Solution: 308.

Method 1 (official solution):

The similarity of triangles *RBC* and *RDP* implies that

$\dfrac{RC}{RP} = \dfrac{RB}{RD}.$

The similarity of triangles *RBQ* and *RDC* implies that $\dfrac{RB}{RD} = \dfrac{RQ}{RC}$.

Thus $\dfrac{RC}{RP} = \dfrac{RQ}{RC}$, or

$RC^2 = RQ \times RP = 112 \times 847 = 16 \times 7 \times 7 \times 121.$

Hence $RC = 4 \times 7 \times 11 = 308$.

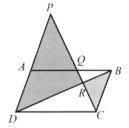 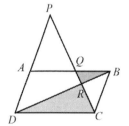

Method 2: (our solution).

$\triangle DRC \sim \triangle BRQ \quad \Rightarrow \quad \dfrac{QR}{RC} = \dfrac{QB}{DC} \quad \Rightarrow \quad \dfrac{112}{RC} = \dfrac{DC - AQ}{DC} = 1 - \dfrac{AQ}{DC}$ (1)

$\triangle APQ \sim \triangle DPC \quad \Rightarrow \quad \dfrac{AQ}{DC} = \dfrac{PQ}{PC} \quad \Rightarrow \quad \dfrac{AQ}{DC} = \dfrac{735}{735 + 112 + RC}$ (2)

Substituting (2) into (1): $\dfrac{112}{RC} = 1 - \dfrac{735}{735 + 112 + RC} \quad \Rightarrow \quad RC = 308$.

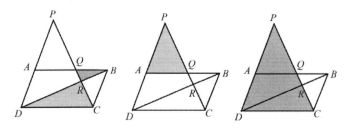

Method 3 (our solution):
$RC^2 = RQ \times RP = 112 \times (735 + 112)$
$RC = \sqrt{112 \times (735 + 112)} = 308$.

Example 8. In parallelogram $ABCD$, point E is the midpoint of AB, and point F is on AD so that $\dfrac{AF}{AD} = \dfrac{1}{3}$. Let G be the point of intersection of AC and FE. Find $\dfrac{AC}{AG}$.

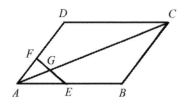

Solution: 006.
Extend FE through E to H and to meet the extension of CB at H.

We know that $AD \parallel CH$. So $\triangle AEF \sim \triangle BEH$ (Figure 1).
$\dfrac{AF}{BH} = \dfrac{AE}{EB} \Rightarrow BH = AF$. So we know that $CH = CB + BH = AD + AF = 4AF$.

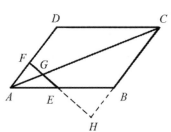

We know that $AF \parallel CH$. So $\triangle AGF \sim \triangle CGH$ (Figure 2).
$\dfrac{AF}{CH} = \dfrac{AG}{GC} \quad \Rightarrow \quad \dfrac{AF}{5AF} = \dfrac{AG}{GC} = \dfrac{1}{5} \quad \Rightarrow \quad \dfrac{GC}{AG} = 5$

$$\Rightarrow \quad \frac{AC-AG}{AG}=5 \Rightarrow \quad \frac{AC}{AG}-1=5 \quad \Rightarrow \quad \frac{AC}{AG}=6.$$

Figure 1   Figure 2

☆ **Example 9.** (2009 AIME) In parallelogram $ABCD$, point M is on AB so that $\frac{AM}{AB}=\frac{17}{1000}$, and point N is on AD so that $\frac{AN}{AD}=\frac{17}{2009}$. Let P be the point of intersection of AC and MN. Find $\frac{AC}{AP}$.

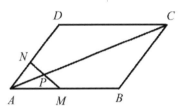

Solution: 177.

Method 1 (official solution):

Let point S be on AC such that NS is parallel to AB. Because $\triangle ASN$ is similar to $\triangle ACD$, $AS/AC = (AP + PS)/AC = AN/AD = 17/2009$.

Because $\triangle PSN$ is similar to $\triangle PAM$, $PS/AP = SN/AM =$

$$\frac{\frac{17}{2009}CD}{\frac{17}{1000}AB}=\frac{1000}{2009}, \text{ and so } \frac{PS}{AP}+1=\frac{3009}{2009}. \text{ Hence}$$

$$\frac{\frac{17}{2009}AC}{AP}=\frac{3009}{2009}, \text{ and } \frac{AC}{AP}=177.$$

Method 2 (our solution):

Extend NM through M to E and to meet the extension of CB at E. We label the line segments as shown in the figure 1.
We know that $AD // CE$. So $\triangle AMN \sim \triangle BME$ (Figure 1).

$$\frac{AN}{BE}=\frac{AM}{MB} \quad \Rightarrow \quad \frac{17y}{BE}=\frac{17x}{983x} \quad \Rightarrow \quad BE=983y.$$

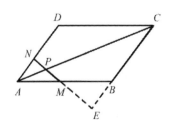

71

We know that $AN // CE$. So $\triangle APN \sim \triangle CPE$ (Figure 2). $\dfrac{AN}{CE} = \dfrac{AP}{PC}$ $\Rightarrow$

$\dfrac{17y}{(2009+983)y} = \dfrac{AP}{AC-AP}$ $\Rightarrow$ $\dfrac{AC}{AP} - 1 = \dfrac{2992}{17}$ $\Rightarrow$ $\dfrac{AC}{AP} = \dfrac{2992}{17} + 1 = 177$.

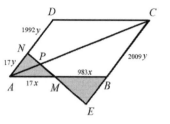

Figure 1   Figure 2

Example 10. In triangle ABC, BM is the median on AC. AE and AF trisect BC and meet BM at G and H, respectively. $BG : GH : HM = x : y : z$. Find the value of $x + y + z$, where x, y, and z are positive integers relatively prime.

Solution: 010.
Method 1:
Connect FM. We see that $FM // AE$ since M is the midpoint of AC and F is the midpoint of EC.
$MF = \dfrac{1}{2} AE = \dfrac{1}{2}(GE + AG) = 2GE$. So $AG = 3GE$ and
$MF = \dfrac{2}{3} AG$.

We know that $AG // MF$. So $\triangle AGH \sim \triangle FMH$. $\dfrac{AG}{MF} = \dfrac{GH}{HM} = \dfrac{3}{2}$.

We also know that $BG = GM$. So $BG : GH : HM = 5 : 3 : 2$. The answer is $5 + 3 + 2 = 10$.

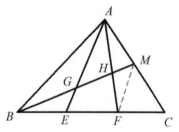 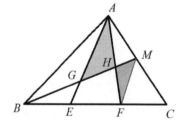

Method 2:
Draw *CP* // *AF* and *CQ* // *AE* through point *C* and to meet the extension of *BM* at *P* and *Q*, respectively. We see that $\triangle AGM \equiv \triangle CQM$ ($\angle GAM = \angle QCM$, $AM = MC$, $\angle AMG = \angle CMQ$). So $GM = MQ$. Similarly we get $HM = MP$.

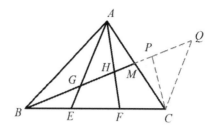

Let $BG = x$, $GH = y$, $HM = z$.

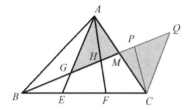 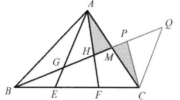 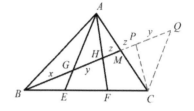

We know that *GE* // *CQ*. So $\triangle BEG \sim \triangle BCQ$. $\dfrac{BG}{BQ} = \dfrac{BE}{BC} = \dfrac{1}{3}$.

Therefore $x = y + z$ (1)

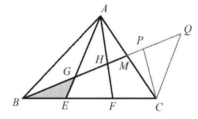 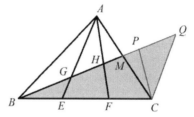

We know that *HF* // *PC*. So $\triangle BFH \sim \triangle BCP$. $\dfrac{BH}{BP} = \dfrac{BF}{BC} = \dfrac{2}{3}$ $\Rightarrow \dfrac{x+y}{2x+z} = \dfrac{2}{3}$.

Therefore $3y = 2z + x$ (2)

Substituting (1) into (2): $\dfrac{y}{z} = \dfrac{2}{3}$. So $x : y : z = 5 : 3 : 2$. The answer is $5 + 3 + 2 = 10$.

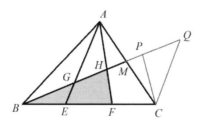 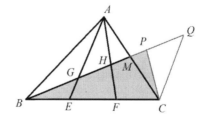

Method 3:
Extend *BM* to *N* such that *MN = BM*. Connect *AN, CN*. *ABCN* is a parallelogram because the diagonals bisect each other. Thus *AF // BC*. *AN = BC = 3BE*.

We know that *AN //BC*. So $\triangle BEG \sim \triangle NAG$.
$\dfrac{NG}{BG} = \dfrac{AN}{BE} = 3$. So *NG = 3BG*.

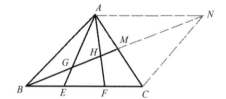

BN = BG + GN = 4BG.
BG = BN/4.

We know that *AN //BC*. So $\triangle ANH \sim \triangle FBH$. $\dfrac{NH}{BH} = \dfrac{AN}{BF} = \dfrac{3}{2}$. So *NH = 3BH/2*.

BN = BH + HN = 5BH/2.
So *BH = 2BN/5*.

Thus $GH = BH - BG = \dfrac{2}{5}BN - \dfrac{1}{4}BN = \dfrac{3}{20}BN$.

$HM = BM - BH = \dfrac{1}{2}BN - \dfrac{2}{5}BN = \dfrac{1}{10}BN$.

$BG : GH : HM = \dfrac{1}{4} : \dfrac{3}{20} : \dfrac{1}{10} = 5 : 3 : 2$

The answer is 5 + 3 + 2 = 10.

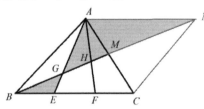 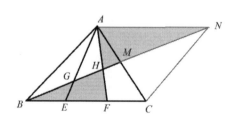

PROBLEMS INVOLVED IN MORE SIMILAR TRIANGLES

Example 11. In triangle *ABC*, *DE // BC*, *BE* and *CD* meet at *O*. *AO* meets *DE* at *N*, and *BC* at *M*, respectively. Show *AN : AM = ON : OM*.

Solution:
We know that *DE // BC*. So we have

$\triangle ADN \sim \triangle ABM \quad \Rightarrow \quad \dfrac{AN}{AM} = \dfrac{AD}{AB}$ (1)

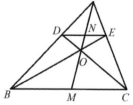

74

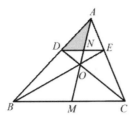 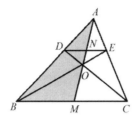

$\triangle ADE \sim \triangle ABC \quad \Rightarrow \quad \dfrac{AD}{AB} = \dfrac{DE}{BC} \quad (2)$

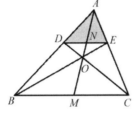 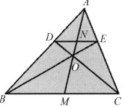

$\triangle ODE \sim \triangle OCB \quad \Rightarrow \quad \dfrac{DE}{BC} = \dfrac{OD}{OC} \quad (3)$

$\triangle ODN \sim \triangle OCM \quad \Rightarrow \quad \dfrac{OD}{OC} = \dfrac{ON}{OM} \quad (4)$

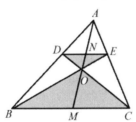 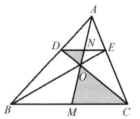

Substituting (2), (3), and (4) into (1): $AN : AM = ON : OM$.

Method 2 (by Kevin Wang)

$\triangle DOE \sim \triangle COB \quad \Rightarrow \quad \dfrac{DE}{BC} = \dfrac{NO}{OM} \quad (1)$

$\triangle ADE \sim \triangle ABC \quad \Rightarrow \quad \dfrac{DE}{BC} = \dfrac{AN}{AM} \quad (2)$

Thus $\dfrac{DE}{BC} = \dfrac{AN}{AM} = \dfrac{NO}{OM}$.

☆**Example 12.** (2005 AIME II Problem 14) In $\triangle ABC$, $AB = 13$, $BC = 15$, and $CA = 14$. Point D is on BC with $CD = 6$. Point E is on BC such that $\angle BAE = \angle CAD$. Given that $BE = p/q$, where p and q are relatively prime positive integers, find q.

Solution: 463.
Method 1 (official solution):
Let $m\angle BAE = \alpha = m\angle CAD$, and let $\beta = m\angle EAD$. Then

$$\frac{BD}{DC} = \frac{[ABD]}{[ADC]} = \frac{(1/2)AB \cdot AD \sin BAD}{(1/2)AD \cdot AC \sin CAD} = \frac{AB}{AC} \cdot \frac{\sin(\alpha+\beta)}{\sin \alpha}.$$

Similarly,
$$\frac{BE}{EC} = \frac{AB}{AC} \cdot \frac{\sin BAE}{\sin CAE} = \frac{AB}{AC} \cdot \frac{\sin \alpha}{\sin(\alpha+\beta)},$$

and so
$$\frac{BE}{EC} = \frac{AB^2 \cdot DC}{AC^2 \cdot BD}.$$

Substituting the given values yields $BE/EC = (13^2 \cdot 6)/(14^2 \cdot 9) = 169/294$. Therefore $BE = (15 \cdot 169)/(169 + 294) = (3 \cdot 5 \cdot 13^2)/463$. Because none of 3, 5, and 13 divides 463, $q = 463$.

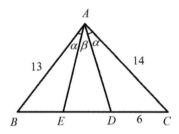

Method 2 (our solution):
Draw $BF // AC$ to meet the extension of AE at G and AD at F.

We know that $AC // BF$. So $\triangle ADC \sim \triangle FDB$ (figure 1). $\dfrac{AC}{BF} = \dfrac{DC}{BD} \Rightarrow \dfrac{14}{BF} = \dfrac{6}{9}$

$\Rightarrow \quad BF = \dfrac{14 \times 9}{6} = 21$

We know that $\angle BAG = \angle BFA = \alpha$ and $\angle ABG = \angle ABF$ (figures 2 and 3). So $\triangle ABG \sim \triangle ABF$. $\dfrac{AB}{BF} = \dfrac{BG}{AB} \Rightarrow \dfrac{13}{21} = \dfrac{BG}{13} \Rightarrow BG = \dfrac{169}{21}$

We know that $AC \parallel BF$. So $\triangle BGE \sim \triangle CAE$ (figure 4). $\dfrac{BG}{AC} = \dfrac{BE}{CE}$ $\Rightarrow$

$\dfrac{\frac{169}{21}}{14} = \dfrac{x}{15-x}$ $\Rightarrow$ $x = \dfrac{2535}{463}$.

The answer is 463.

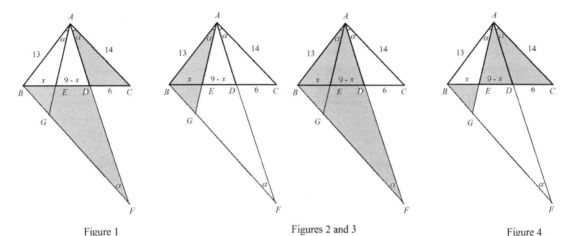

Figure 1   Figures 2 and 3   Figure 4

☆**Example 13.** (2002 AIME II) In triangle ABC, point D is on BC with $CD = 2$ and $DB = 5$, point E is on AC with $CE = 1$ and $EA = 3$, $AB = 8$, and AD and BE intersect at P. Points Q and R lie on AB so that PQ is parallel to CA and PR is parallel to CB. It is given that the ratio of the area of triangle PQR to the area of triangle ABC is m/n, where m and n are relatively prime positive integers. Find $m + n$.

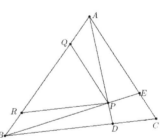

Solution: 901.

Method 1 (official solution):

Draw the line through E parallel to AD, and let K be its intersection with BC.

Because $CD = 2$ and $KC : KD = EC : EA = 1 : 3$, it follows that $KD = 3/2$.

Therefore, $\dfrac{QP}{AE} = \dfrac{BP}{BE} = \dfrac{BD}{BK} = \dfrac{5}{5 + \frac{3}{2}} = \dfrac{10}{13}$. Thus

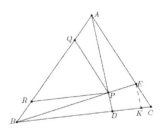

$$\frac{QP}{AC} = \frac{3}{4} \cdot \frac{10}{13} = \frac{15}{26}.$$

Since triangles *PQR* and *CAB* are similar, the ratio of their areas is $(15/26)^2 = 225/676$. Thus $m + n = 901$.

Method 2 (our solution):
Draw the line through *D* parallel to *BE*, and let *F* be its intersection with *AC*.

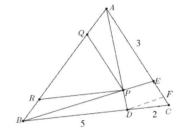

Observe that triangles *BEC* and *DFC* are similar.
$$\frac{BC}{DC} = \frac{EC}{FC} \quad \Rightarrow \quad \frac{7}{2} = \frac{1}{FC} \quad \Rightarrow \quad FC = \frac{2}{7}$$
So $EF = \frac{5}{7}$.

Triangles *RPA* and *BDA* are similar.

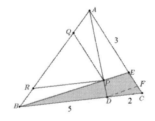 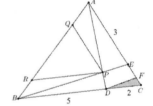

It follows that $\frac{RP}{BD} = \frac{AP}{AD}$.

Since triangles *ADF* and *APE* are similar, so $\frac{AE}{AF} = \frac{AP}{AD}$.

Thus, $\frac{RP}{BD} = \frac{AP}{AD} = \frac{AE}{AF} = \frac{3}{3 + \frac{5}{7}} = \frac{21}{26}$,

and so $\frac{S_{\triangle ARP}}{S_{\triangle ABD}} = (\frac{RP}{BD})^2 = (\frac{21}{26})^2$.

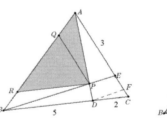 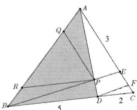

We also know that
$\frac{S_{\triangle ABD}}{S_{\triangle ABC}} = (\frac{5}{7})^2 = \frac{25}{49} \Rightarrow S_{\triangle ABD} = \frac{25}{49} S_{\triangle ABC}$.

After substitution, we have
$\frac{S_{\triangle ARP}}{S_{\triangle ABD}} = \frac{S_{\triangle ARP}}{\frac{25}{49} S_{\triangle ABC}} = (\frac{21}{26})^2$.

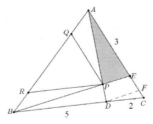 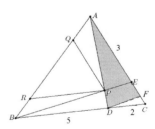

Finally, $\dfrac{S_{\triangle ARP}}{S_{\triangle ABC}} = (\dfrac{21}{26})^2 \times \dfrac{25}{49} = \dfrac{225}{676}$. Thus $m + n = 901$.

This is the problem 13 in 2002 AIME II, and here we have provided a different solution from the official one.

PROBLEMS

Problem 1. In rectangle *ABCD*, *BD* is the diagonal. $AE \perp BD$. $CF \perp BD$. $BE = 1$ and $EF = 2$. The area of the *ABCD* can be expressed as $m\sqrt{n}$. What is $100(m + n)$?

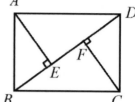

Problem 2. In quadrilateral *ABCD*, $AD = DC = 1$. $\angle DCB = 90°$. The extensions of *BC* and *AD* meet at *P*. Find the smallest value of $AB \times S_{\triangle PAB}$.

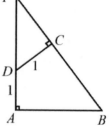

☆**Problem 3.** A point *P* is chosen in the interior of $\triangle ABC$ so that when lines are drawn through *P* parallel to the sides of $\triangle ABC$, the resulting smaller triangles, $S_1 = 9$ cm², $S_2 = 16$ cm², and $S_3 = x$ cm² in the figure, respectively. Find the value of *x* if the area of $\triangle ABC$ is 225 cm².

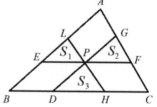

☆**Problem 4:** As shown in the figure, $\triangle ABC$ has the sides $AB = 9$, $BC = 10$, and $CA = 15$. $DE = FG = HI$. DE //BC, FG // AB, and HI // AC. DE, FG, and HI meet at *P*. Find the product of *a* and *b* if $DE = a/b$, where *a* and *b* are positive integers relatively prime.

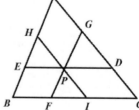

Problem 5: A point *P* is chosen in the interior of $\triangle ABC$ so that when lines are drawn through *P* parallel to the sides of $\triangle ABC$. Show that
$$\frac{HF}{BC} + \frac{EL}{CA} + \frac{GD}{AB} = 1.$$

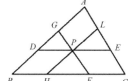

Problem 6. A point *P* is chosen in the interior of $\triangle ABC$ so that when lines are drawn through *P* parallel to the sides of $\triangle ABC$ such that $HI = FG = ED$. $AB = 12$, $BC = 8$, and $CA = 6$. The ratios of $AI : IF : FB$ can be expressed in the simplest form of $a : b : c$. a, b, c are positive integers relatively prime. Find the value of $a + b + c$.

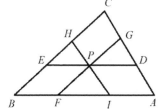

Problem 7. (1998 China Middle School Math Contest) As shown in the figure below, *ABCD* is a square. *A, E, F,* and *G* are in the same line. $AE = 5$ cm and $EF = 3$ cm. Find the sum of *a* and *b* if $FG = a/b$, where *a* and *b* are positive integers relatively prime.

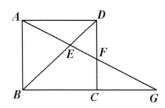

☆**Problem 8.** Let *ABCD* be a parallelogram. Extend *DC* through *C* to a point *G*, and let *AG* meet *DB* at *E* and *BC* at *F*. Show that $AF \times EG = AE \times AG$.

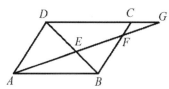

Problem 9. Let *ABCD* be a parallelogram. Extend *BC* through *C* to a point *E*, and let *AE* meet *BD* at *G* and *DC* at *F*. Show that $\dfrac{GD^2}{GB^2} = \dfrac{GF}{GE}$.

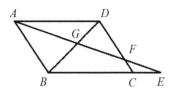

☆**Problem 10.** In parallelogram $ABCD$, point M is on AB so that $\dfrac{AM}{MB} = \dfrac{17}{1000}$, and point N is on AD so that $\dfrac{AN}{ND} = \dfrac{17}{2009}$. Let P be the point of intersection of AC and MN. Find $\dfrac{PC}{PA}$.

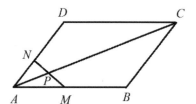

Problem 11. In triangle ABC, AD is the median on BC. BG and BH divide AD into three parts such that $AE : EF : FD = 4:3:1$. $AG : GH : HC = x : y : z$. Find the value of $x + y + z$, where x and y are positive integers relatively prime.

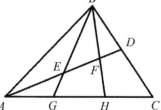

Problem 12. In triangle AMS, $BD \parallel MS$, BR and DN meet at C. AP goes through C and meets BD at O, and MS at P, respectively. Show $PM : PN = PS : PR$.

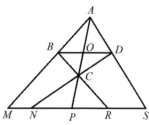

Problem 13. In parallelogram $ABCD$, M is the midpoint of AB. The diagonals AC and BD meet DM and CM at G and H, respectively. GH meets AD at E and BC at F.
Show that $EG = GH = HF$.

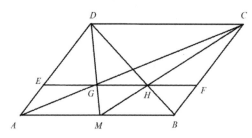

Problem 14. In trapezoid $ABCD$, $AB \parallel CD$, $AB < CD$. EJ meets AD at F, DB at G, AC at H, BC at I, respectively, as shown in the figure. Find DC/AB if $EF = FG = GH = HI = IJ$.

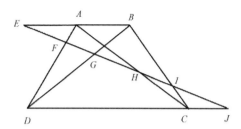

Problem 15. In isosceles triangle ABC, AD is the height on BC. Draw the height CE on AB. Draw $DF \perp CE$ and meets CE at F. Draw $FG \perp AD$ and meets AD at G. Show that $\dfrac{FG}{AG} = \left(\dfrac{BD}{AD}\right)^3$.

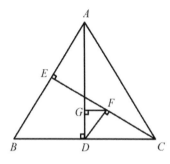

Problem 16. (USAMO) A convex hexagon $ABCDEF$ is inscribed in a circle such that $AB = CD = EF$ and diagonals AD, BE, and CF are concurrent. Let P be the intersection of AD and CE. Prove that $\dfrac{CP}{PE} = \dfrac{AC^2}{CE^2}$.

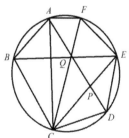

SOLUTIONS

Problem 1. Solution: 700.

We see that $\triangle BAE \cong \triangle CBA$ ($\angle BAE = \angle DCF$, $AB = CD$, $\angle ABE = \angle CDF$).
Thus $BE = FD$. $BD = 1 + 2 + 1 = 4$. $ED = 1 + 2 = 3$.
$\triangle BAE \sim \triangle ADE$ (The height AE divides right triangle ABD into two similar triangles).

$$\frac{AE}{ED} = \frac{BE}{AE} \quad \Rightarrow \quad AE = \sqrt{ED \times BE} = \sqrt{3 \times 1} = \sqrt{3}.$$

The area of the $ABCD$ is $BD \times AE = 4\sqrt{3}$. The answer is $10(4 + 3) = 700$.

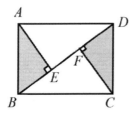 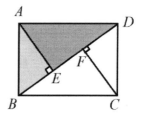

Problem 2. Solution: 004.

Let $PD = x$. $PC = \sqrt{x^2 - 1}$.

We see that $\triangle PCD \sim \triangle PAB$ ($\angle P = \angle P$, $\angle PCD = \angle PAB = 90°$).

Thus $\dfrac{CD}{AB} = \dfrac{PC}{PA} \quad \Rightarrow \quad AB = \dfrac{CD \times PA}{PC} = \dfrac{x+1}{\sqrt{x^2-1}}$

$$AB \times S_{\triangle PAB} = \frac{1}{2} AB^2 \times PA = \frac{(x+1)^3}{2(x^2-1)} = \frac{(x+1)^2}{2(x-1)}.$$

Let $y = \dfrac{(x+1)^2}{2(x-1)}$.

Then we have $2(x-1)y = (x+1)^2 \Rightarrow$
$x^2 + 2(1-y)x + (1 + 2y) = 0$.

We know that x is real number. So $\Delta = 4(1-y)^2 - 4(1+2y) = 4y(y-4) \geq 0$.
Since $y > 0$, $y \geq 4$. The smallest value of y is 4 (when $x = 3$).

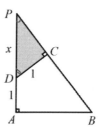 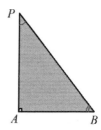

☆**Problem 3.** Solution: 064.
We label the figure as shown.
We know that $EF \parallel BC$ and $LH \parallel AC$. So $\angle LEP = \angle B$.

$\angle ELP = \angle A$. Thus $\triangle LEP \sim \triangle ABC \Rightarrow \dfrac{S_1}{S_{\triangle ABC}} = \dfrac{EP^2}{BC^2}$ \qquad (1)

We know that $EBDP$ is a parallelogram, $EP = BD$.

(1) can be written as $\dfrac{\sqrt{S_1}}{\sqrt{S_{\triangle ABC}}} = \dfrac{BD}{BC}$ \qquad (2)

Similarly we get: $\dfrac{\sqrt{S_2}}{\sqrt{S_{\triangle ABC}}} = \dfrac{CH}{BC}$ \qquad (3)

$\dfrac{\sqrt{S_3}}{\sqrt{S_{\triangle ABC}}} = \dfrac{DH}{BC}$ \qquad (4)

(2) + (3) + (4): $\dfrac{\sqrt{S_1}}{\sqrt{S_{\triangle ABC}}} + \dfrac{\sqrt{S_2}}{\sqrt{S_{\triangle ABC}}} + \dfrac{\sqrt{S_3}}{\sqrt{S_{\triangle ABC}}} = \dfrac{BD + CH + DH}{BC} = 1$

$\Rightarrow \sqrt{S_{\triangle ABC}} = \sqrt{S_1} + \sqrt{S_2} + \sqrt{S_3} \Rightarrow S_{\triangle ABC} = (\sqrt{S_1} + \sqrt{S_2} + \sqrt{S_3})^2$

$\Rightarrow 225 = (\sqrt{9} + \sqrt{16} + \sqrt{x})^2 \Rightarrow x = 64$.

☆**Problem 4:** Solution: 180.
Method 1:
Let $DE = m$.
$EH = AB - (BE + AH) = AB - (FP + PG) = 9 - m$.

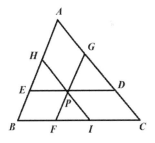

Similarly $GD = 15 - m$.

We know that $\triangle DPG \sim \triangle CBA$, so
$DP = \dfrac{BC}{AC} \cdot GD = \dfrac{10}{15}(15 - m) = 10 - \dfrac{2}{3}m$.

We also know that $\triangle PEH \sim \triangle CBA$.
Therefore $PE = \dfrac{BC}{AB} \cdot EH = \dfrac{10}{9}(9 - m) = 10 - \dfrac{10}{9}m$.

Hence $m = DP + PE = 20 - \dfrac{16}{9}m \Rightarrow m = a/b = 36/5$.

$ab = 36 \times 5 = 180$.

Method 2 (by Kevin Wang):
Let FI be x.
$FI : EH : GD = 10 : 9 : 15 = x : (x - 1) : (x + 5)$.

We know that $\triangle HEP \sim \triangle ABC$, so
$EP = \dfrac{BC}{AB} \cdot EH = \dfrac{10}{9}(x-1)$

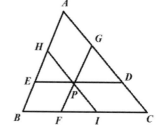

We also know that $\triangle GPD \sim \triangle ABC$.
Therefore $PD = \dfrac{BC}{AB} \cdot GD = \dfrac{10}{15}(x-5) = \dfrac{2}{3}(x-5)$

Hence $EP + PD + FI = 10 \Rightarrow \dfrac{10}{9}(x-1) + \dfrac{2}{3}(x-5) + x = 10$.

Solving for x: $x = 14/5$.
Thus $10 - x = 10 - 14/5 = 36/5$. The answer is $36 \times 5 = 180$.

Problem 5: Proof:
Since $DE \parallel BC$, $FG \parallel AC$, $LH \parallel AB$, $DP = BH$, $PE = FC$.
We know that $\triangle GDP \sim \triangle BCA$, so $\dfrac{GD}{AB} = \dfrac{DP}{BC}$ (1)

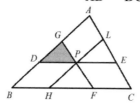 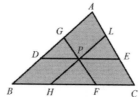

We know that $\triangle PEL \sim \triangle BCA$, so $\dfrac{LE}{AC} = \dfrac{PE}{BC}$ (2)

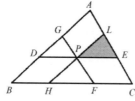 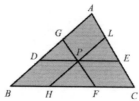

Then we can have: $\dfrac{HF}{BC} + \dfrac{EL}{CA} + \dfrac{GD}{AB} = \dfrac{HF}{BC} + \dfrac{PE}{BC} + \dfrac{DP}{BC} = \dfrac{HF + PE + DP}{BC}$

We see that $DP = BH$. $PE = FC$. So $\dfrac{HF}{BC} + \dfrac{EL}{CA} + \dfrac{GD}{AB} =$
$\dfrac{BH + FC + BF + CH}{BC} = \dfrac{(BH+CH)+(FC+BF)}{BC} = \dfrac{2BC}{BC} = 2\dfrac{BC}{BC} = 2$.

Problem 6. Solution: 009.
Let $AI = x$, $IF = y$, $FB = z$.
So $x + y + z = 12$ (1)
Since $DE \parallel AB$, $FG \parallel BC$, $IH \parallel AC$, both $AIPD$ and $FBEP$ are parallelograms. Thus $DP = IA = x$, $PE = FB = z$. $DE = FG = HI = x + z$.

We know that $\triangle AFG \sim \triangle ABC$, so
$$\frac{FG}{BC} = \frac{AF}{AB} \Rightarrow \frac{x+z}{8} = \frac{x+y}{12} \quad (2)$$

We know that $\triangle BIH \sim \triangle BAC$, so
$$\frac{HI}{AC} = \frac{BI}{AB} \Rightarrow \frac{x+z}{6} = \frac{y+z}{12} \quad (3)$$

Solving the system of equations (1), (2), and (3): $x = \frac{4}{3}$, $y = \frac{20}{3}$, $z = 4 = \frac{12}{3}$.
Thus $AI : IF : FB = 4 : 20 : 12 = 1 : 5 : 3$.
$a + b + c = 1 + 5 + 3 = 9$.

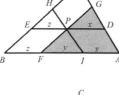
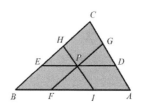
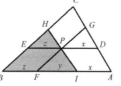
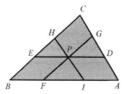

Problem 7. Solution: 019.

We know that $AB \parallel CD$. Thus, $\dfrac{AE}{EF} = \dfrac{BE}{ED}$ (1)

We also know that $CB \parallel AD$. Thus, $\dfrac{BE}{ED} = \dfrac{EG}{AE}$ (2)

From (1) and (2), we get $\dfrac{AE}{EF} = \dfrac{EG}{AE} \Rightarrow EG = \dfrac{AE^2}{EF} = \dfrac{25}{3}$.

So $FG = EG - EF = \dfrac{16}{3}$. The answer is $16 + 3 = 19$.

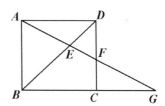

☆**Problem 8.** Proof:
We know that $AB \parallel DG$. So $\triangle ABE \sim \triangle GDE$
$$\frac{AE}{EG} = \frac{AB}{DG} \quad (1)$$
We know that $\angle ABC = \angle ADC$ and $\angle BAF = \angle G$. So $\triangle ABF \sim \triangle GDA$

$$\frac{AF}{AG} = \frac{AB}{DG} \qquad (2)$$

From (1) and (2), we get: $\frac{AE}{EG} = \frac{AF}{AG}$

$\Rightarrow \quad AF \times EG = AE \times AG$.

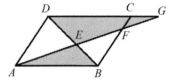
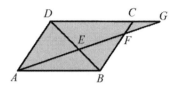

Problem 9. Proof:

We know that $AB // DC$. So $\triangle GDF \sim \triangle GBA$. $\Rightarrow \quad \dfrac{GD}{GB} = \dfrac{GF}{GA} \qquad (1)$

We know that $AB // AD$. So $\triangle GAD \sim \triangle GBE$. $\Rightarrow \quad \dfrac{GD}{GB} = \dfrac{GA}{GE} \qquad (2)$

$(1) \times (2)$: $\dfrac{GD^2}{GB^2} = \dfrac{GF}{GE}$.

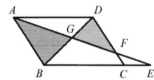
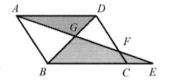

☆**Problem 10.** Solution: 178.

Extend NM through M to E and to meet the extension of CB at E. We label the line segments as shown in the figures.

We know that $AD // CE$. So $\triangle AMN \sim \triangle BME$ (Figure 1). $\dfrac{AN}{BE} = \dfrac{AM}{MB} \quad \Rightarrow$

$\dfrac{17y}{BE} = \dfrac{17x}{1000x} \quad \Rightarrow \quad BE = 1000y$.

We know that $AN // CE$. So $\triangle APN \sim \triangle CPE$ (Figure 2). $\dfrac{PC}{PA} = \dfrac{CE}{AN} = \dfrac{2026y + 1000y}{17y} = 178$

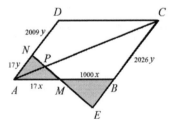
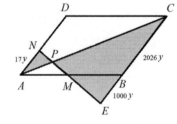

Figure 1   Figure 2

Problem 11. Solution: 009.
Extend AD to M and N and connect CM and CN such that $DM = DF$ and $DN = DE$. So $BFCM$ and $BECN$ are parallelograms since the diagonals bisect each other.
Thus $BE \parallel NC$, $BF \parallel MC$.

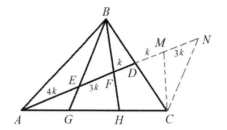

Let $AE = 4k$, $FE = 3k$, and $FD = k$. So $FMN = 3k$, and $DM = k$.

Since $BE \parallel NC$, $\triangle AGE \sim \triangle ACN$.
$$\frac{AE}{AN} = \frac{AG}{AC} = \frac{4k}{12k} = \frac{1}{3} \Rightarrow$$
$$AG = \frac{1}{3}AC = \frac{3}{9}AC$$

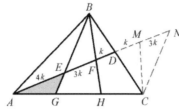 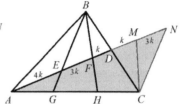

Since $BH \parallel MC$. $\triangle AHF \sim \triangle ACM$. $\dfrac{AF}{AM} = \dfrac{AH}{AC} = \dfrac{7k}{9k} = \dfrac{7}{9} \Rightarrow AH = \dfrac{7}{9}AC$.

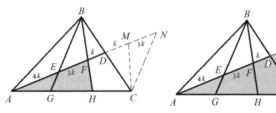

$GH = AH - AG = \dfrac{7}{9}AC - \dfrac{3}{9}AC = \dfrac{4}{9}AC$.

$HC = AC - AH = AC - \dfrac{7}{9}AC = \dfrac{2}{9}AC$.

$AG : GH : HC = 3 : 4 : 2$. The answer is $3 + 4 + 2 = 9$.

Problem 12. Proof:
We know that $BD \parallel MS$. So we have
$$\triangle ABO \sim \triangle AMP \quad \Rightarrow \quad \frac{PM}{BO} = \frac{AP}{AO} \qquad (1)$$

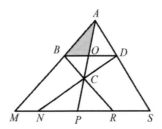 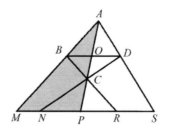

$\triangle AOD \sim \triangle APS \quad \Rightarrow \quad \dfrac{PS}{OD} = \dfrac{AP}{AO}$ \quad (2)

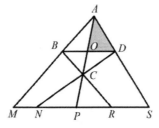 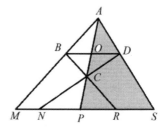

$\triangle ODC \sim \triangle PNC \quad \Rightarrow \quad \dfrac{PN}{OD} = \dfrac{PC}{OC}$ \quad (3)

$\triangle OBC \sim \triangle PRC \quad \Rightarrow \quad \dfrac{PR}{OB} = \dfrac{PC}{OC}$ \quad (4)

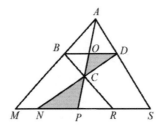 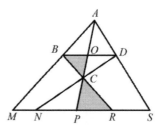

From (1) and (2), we get $\dfrac{PM}{BO} = \dfrac{PS}{OD}$ \quad (5)

From (3) and (4), we get $\dfrac{PN}{OD} = \dfrac{PR}{OB}$ \quad (6)

(5) ÷ (6): $PM : PN = PS : PR$.

Problem 13. Proof:
We know that $DC \parallel AB$. So we have
$\triangle AMG \sim \triangle CDG \quad \Rightarrow \quad \dfrac{MG}{DG} = \dfrac{AM}{CD} = \dfrac{1}{2}$ \quad (1)

$\triangle MBH \sim \triangle CDH \Rightarrow \dfrac{MH}{CH} = \dfrac{MB}{CD} = \dfrac{1}{2}$ (2)

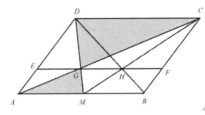
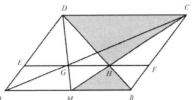

From (1) and (2), we get: $\dfrac{MH}{CH} = \dfrac{MG}{DG} = \dfrac{1}{2}$.

Thus we know that $GH \parallel DC$, and $EF \parallel DC \parallel AB$.

So we know that $\triangle DEG \sim \triangle DAM$.

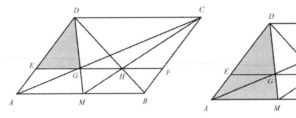

We have $\dfrac{EG}{AM} = \dfrac{DG}{DM} \Rightarrow EG = AM \times \dfrac{DG}{DM} = \dfrac{CD}{2} \times \dfrac{2GM}{2GM + GM} = \dfrac{CD}{3}$.

Similarly we get $HF = \dfrac{CD}{3}$.

$GH = EF - EG - HF = CD - \dfrac{CD}{3} - \dfrac{CD}{3} = \dfrac{CD}{3}$.

Therefore $EG = GH = HF$.

Problem 14. Proof:

We know that $DC \parallel AB$. So we have

$\triangle EAH \sim \triangle JCH \Rightarrow \dfrac{EA}{CJ} = \dfrac{EH}{HJ} = \dfrac{3}{2}$ (1)

$\triangle EBI \sim \triangle JCI \Rightarrow \dfrac{EB}{CJ} = \dfrac{EI}{IJ} = 4$ (2)

So we get $AB = EB - EA = 4CJ - \dfrac{3}{2}CJ = \dfrac{5}{2}CJ$

We also have $\triangle EBG \sim \triangle JDG \Rightarrow \dfrac{EB}{DJ} = \dfrac{EG}{GJ} = \dfrac{2}{3}$ (3)

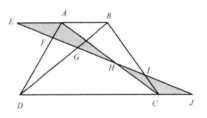
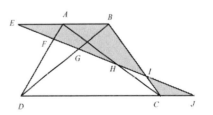

So we get $\frac{2}{3}DJ = 4CJ$ and $DJ = 6CJ$.
$CD = DJ - CJ = 5CJ$.
We see that $AB = \frac{1}{2}CD \Rightarrow \frac{DC}{AB} = 2$.

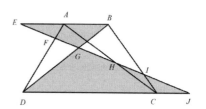

Problem 15. Proof:
Draw $FH \perp BC$. Extend GF to meet AC at K.
We know that $GF \parallel BD$. So we have

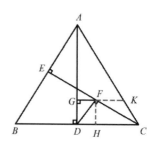

$\triangle ABD \sim \triangle DFG \Rightarrow \dfrac{FG}{GD} = \dfrac{BD}{AD}$ (1)

$\triangle CFI \sim \triangle ADB \Rightarrow \dfrac{FH}{CH} = \dfrac{BD}{AD}$ (2)

$\triangle AGK \sim \triangle ADB \Rightarrow \dfrac{KG}{AG} = \dfrac{BD}{AD}$ (3)

(1) × (2) × (3): $\dfrac{FG}{GD} \times \dfrac{FH}{CH} \times \dfrac{KG}{AG} = (\dfrac{BD}{AD})^3$ (4)

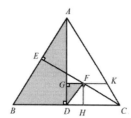 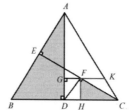 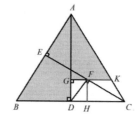

If we connect DK, we see that $\triangle KGD \sim \triangle CFH \Rightarrow \dfrac{KG}{CH} = \dfrac{GD}{FH}$ (5)

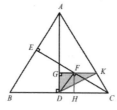 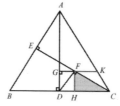

Substituting (5) into (4): $\dfrac{FG}{AG} = (\dfrac{BD}{AD})^3$.

Problem 16. Proof:
Since $CD = EF$, $CF \parallel DE$.
Thus $\triangle CPQ \sim \triangle EPD \Rightarrow \dfrac{CP}{PE} = \dfrac{CQ}{DE}$ (1)

We also know that $\angle QDE = \angle ACE$, $\angle QED = \angle AEC$.

Thus $\triangle QDE \sim \triangle ACE \Rightarrow \dfrac{QD}{DE} = \dfrac{AC}{CE}$ \hfill (2)

Similarly, $\triangle CQD \sim \triangle ACE \Rightarrow \dfrac{CQ}{QD} = \dfrac{AC}{CE}$ \hfill (3)

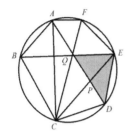 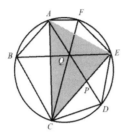 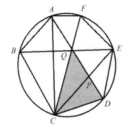 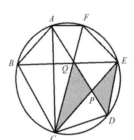

$$\dfrac{CP}{PE} = \dfrac{CQ}{DE} = \dfrac{CQ}{DQ} \times \dfrac{DQ}{DE} = \dfrac{AC^2}{CE^2}.$$

BASIC KNOWLEDGE

1. FORMULAS

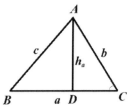

1. $S_\triangle = \dfrac{1}{2} a h_a = \dfrac{1}{2} b h_b = \dfrac{1}{2} c h_c$ \hfill (1)

2. Let $h_a = b \sin C$, $h_b = c \sin A$, and $h_c = a \sin B$. Equation (1) becomes:

$$S_\triangle = \dfrac{1}{2} bc \sin A = \dfrac{1}{2} ac \sin B = \dfrac{1}{2} ab \sin C \quad (2)$$

3. $S_\triangle = \sqrt{s(s-a)(s-b)(s-c)}$ \hfill (3)

$s = \dfrac{1}{2}(a+b+c)$

4. $S_\triangle = s \cdot r$ \hfill (4)

where $s = \dfrac{1}{2}(a+b+c)$. The figure to the right shows triangle ABC and its inscribed circle O of radius r.

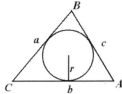

5. $S_\triangle = \dfrac{abc}{4R}$ \hfill (5)

Figure to the right shows the triangle ABC and its circumcircle O of radius R.

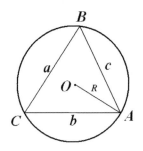

2. THEOREMS

Theorem 1: The ratio of the areas of any two triangles is:

$$\frac{S_{\triangle ABC}}{S_{\triangle A_1B_1C_1}} = \frac{\frac{1}{2} \times AB \times H}{\frac{1}{2} \times A_1B_1 \times H_1} = \frac{AB \times H}{A_1B_1 \times H_1}$$

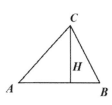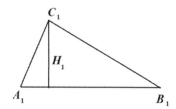

Theorem 2: If two triangles have the same base, the ratio of the areas is the ratio of the heights.

$$\frac{S_{\triangle ABD}}{S_{\triangle ABC}} = \frac{H}{h}$$

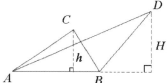

Theorem 3: If two triangles have the same height, the ratio of the areas is the ratio of the bases.

$$\frac{S_{\triangle ABC}}{S_{\triangle ADC}} = \frac{AB}{AD}; \quad \frac{S_{\triangle ABC}}{S_{\triangle DBC}} = \frac{AB}{DB}; \quad \frac{S_{\triangle ADC}}{S_{\triangle BDC}} = \frac{AD}{DB}.$$

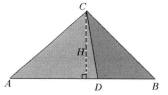

Theorem 4(a): If $AB//CD$, then $S_{\triangle ABC} = S_{\triangle ABD}$ and $S_{\triangle AED} = S_{\triangle BEC}$ (Same base and same height).

4(b): If $S_{\triangle AED} = S_{\triangle BEC}$, then $AB//CD$.

4(c): If $S_{\triangle ABC} = S_{\triangle ABD}$, then $AB//CD$.

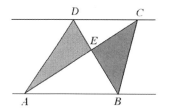

Theorem 5: $\dfrac{S_{\triangle AEC}}{S_{\triangle BEC}} = \dfrac{AD}{DB}$

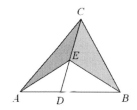

Theorem 6: $\dfrac{S_{\triangle AEC}}{S_{\triangle BEC}} = \dfrac{S_{\triangle AED}}{S_{\triangle BED}} = \dfrac{AD}{DB}$.

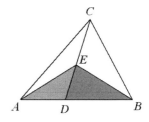

Theorem 7: If $AE = n$ and $EC = m$, then $\dfrac{S_{\triangle AED}}{S_{\triangle EDC}} = \dfrac{n}{m}$ and $\dfrac{S_{\triangle AEB}}{S_{\triangle EBC}} = \dfrac{n}{m}$.

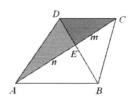

Theorem 8: If $AE = n$ and $EC = m$, then $\dfrac{S_{\triangle ABD}}{S_{\triangle BDC}} = \dfrac{n}{m}$

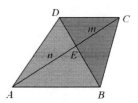

Theorem 9: If $DE = n$ and $DC = m$, then $\dfrac{S_{\triangle AEB}}{S_{\triangle ABC}} = \dfrac{n}{m}$

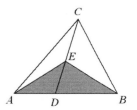

Theorem 10: The ratio of the areas of two similar triangles is the same as the ratio of the squares of their corresponding sides.

Theorem 11: In convex quadrilateral $ABCD$, two diagonals AC and BD divide the four areas with the relationship $S_1 \times S_3 = S_2 \times S_4$.

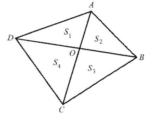

Proof:

$S_1 \times S_3 = \dfrac{1}{2} AO \times DO \sin \angle AOD \times \dfrac{1}{2} BO \times CO \sin \angle BOC$

$$S_2 \times S_4 = \frac{1}{2} AO \times BO \sin(180° - \angle AOB) \times \frac{1}{2} DO \times CO \sin(180° - \angle DOC)$$

$$= \frac{1}{2} AO \times DO \sin \angle AOD \times \frac{1}{2} BO \times CO \sin \angle BOC$$

Thus $S_1 \times S_3 = S_2 \times S_4$.

Theorem 12: In convex quadrilateral $ABCD$, O is any point on the diagonal AC. Connect DO and BO. $S_1 \times S_3 = S_2 \times S_4$.

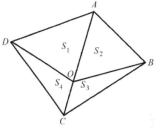

Theorem 13: In triangle ABC, O is any point on CD. Connect AO and BO. $S_1 \times S_3 = S_2 \times S_4$.

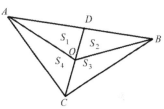

Theorem 14: In parallelogram $ABCD$, E is any point on CD. Connect AE and BE. $S_3 = S_1 + S_2 = \frac{1}{2} S_{ABCD}$.

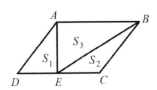

Theorem 15: In parallelogram $ABCD$, O is any point inside Connect AO, BO, CO, and DO. $S_1 + S_3 = S_2 + S_4$.

Theorem 16: In trapezoid ABCD, with AB//CD, let $S_{\triangle ABO} = m^2$, $S_{\triangle DOC} = n^2$. the following relationship of areas is true: $S_{ABCD} = (m+n)^2$

Proof:

Since $\triangle ABO \sim \triangle CDO$, $\dfrac{AO^2}{OC^2} = \dfrac{S_{\triangle AOB}}{S_{\triangle COD}} = \dfrac{m^2}{n^2}$

Simplifying yields $\dfrac{AO}{OC} = \dfrac{m}{n}$.

We also know that $\dfrac{AO}{OC} = \dfrac{S_{\triangle AOB}}{S_{\triangle COB}}$, so $S_{\triangle COB} = mn$.

Since $S_{\triangle AOD} = S_{\triangle COB}$, $S_{\triangle AOD} = mn$.

Therefore $S_{ABCD} = m^2 + mn + mn + n^2 = m^2 + 2mn + n^2 = (m+n)^2$.

Theorem 17: For any trapezoid ABCD, the following relationship of areas is true: $S_{\triangle AOD} = s = \sqrt{ab}$

Proof:

We know that: $S_{ABCD} = (\sqrt{a} + \sqrt{b})^2$

Or $2s + a + b = (\sqrt{a} + \sqrt{b})^2$

$\Rightarrow \quad 2s = (\sqrt{a} + \sqrt{b})^2 - a - b = a + b + 2\sqrt{ab} - a - b \quad \Rightarrow \quad s = 2\sqrt{ab}$.

Theorem 18: In triangle ABC, AD, BE, and CF meet at O. Let the areas of six small triangles be p, q, r, m, n, and k, respectively, as shown in the figure. Then

$pqr = mnk$ (1)

$\dfrac{1}{p} + \dfrac{1}{q} + \dfrac{1}{r} = \dfrac{1}{m} + \dfrac{1}{n} + \dfrac{1}{k}$ (2)

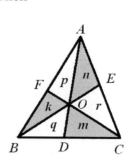

Proof:
We begin by proving (1) first.
By Ceva's Theorem:

$$\frac{AF}{FB} \times \frac{BD}{DC} \times \frac{CE}{EA} = 1 \qquad (3)$$

By Theorem 6, we have

$$\frac{AF}{FB} = \frac{p}{k} \qquad (4)$$

$$\frac{BD}{DC} = \frac{q}{m} \qquad (5)$$

$$\frac{CE}{EA} = \frac{r}{n} \qquad (6)$$

Substituting (4), (5), and (6) into (3) yields

$$\frac{p}{k} \times \frac{q}{m} \times \frac{r}{n} = 1 \quad \Rightarrow \quad pqr = mnk$$

Now we will prove (2):

By Theorem (5), we have:

$$\frac{q}{m} = \frac{BD}{CD} = \frac{p+k}{n+r} \quad \Rightarrow \quad qn + qr = mp + mk \qquad (7)$$

Similarly we get
$$rp + rk = nq + nm \qquad (8)$$
$$pq + pm = kn + kr \qquad (9)$$

(7) + (8) + (9):

$$qr + rp + pq = kn + mk + nm \qquad (10)$$

Dividing left hand side by *pqr* and right hand side by *mnk*:

$$\frac{1}{p} + \frac{1}{q} + \frac{1}{r} = \frac{1}{m} + \frac{1}{n} + \frac{1}{k}.$$

Example 1. (1995 China Hope Cup Math Contest) As shown in the figure, the area of triangle ABC is 18. Points D, E, and F are on sides AB, BC and AC respectively, and $AD = 4$, $DB = 5$. Find the area of triangle ABE if triangles ABE and quadrilateral $DBEF$ have the same areas.

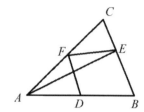

Solution: 010.
Method 1 (our solution):
Connect DE.

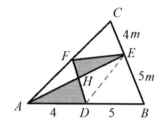

We know that $S_{\triangle ADH} = S_{\triangle EFH}$.

By **Theorem 4 (c)**, $DE \parallel AF$.
So $\triangle ABC \approx \triangle DBE$. $\dfrac{AD}{DB} = \dfrac{CE}{EB} = \dfrac{4m}{5m}$.

By **Theorem 3**, $\dfrac{S_{\triangle ABE}}{S_{\triangle ABC}} = \dfrac{5}{9}$ $\Rightarrow S_{\triangle ABE} = \dfrac{5m}{9m} \times S_{\triangle ABC} = 10$.

Method 2:
Connect DE, DC.

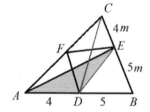 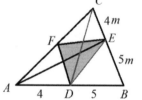

We know that $S_{DBEF} = S_{\triangle ABE}$. So
$S_{\triangle ADE} = S_{\triangle EDF}$.

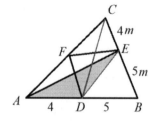 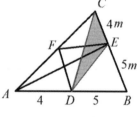

By **Theorem 4 (c)**, $DE \parallel AF$.

By **Theorem 4 (a)**, $S_{\triangle ADE} = S_{\triangle CDE}$.
Thus $S_{\triangle ABE} = S_{\triangle BDC}$. Since $AD = 4$, and $DB = 5$, $S_{\triangle BDC} = \dfrac{5}{9} S_{ABC} = \dfrac{5}{9} \times 18 = 10$.

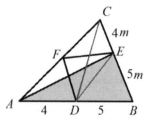 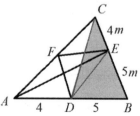

Example 2. $ABCD$ is a 64×64 square, E is the midpoint of AD, P is the midpoint of CE, F is the midpoint of BP. Find the area of triangle DFB.

Solution: 256.
Connect BE. Connect DP and extend it to meet BC at Q. It is easy to see that $EDQB$ is a parallelogram. Then we have $DP \parallel EB$.
By **Theorem 4 (a)**, $S_{\Delta DPE} = S_{\Delta DPB}$

$S_{\Delta DPE} = \frac{1}{2} S_{\Delta DCE} = \frac{1}{2} \times \frac{1}{4} S_{ABCD}$. Thus

$S_{\Delta DFB} = \frac{1}{2} S_{\Delta DPB} = \frac{1}{16} S_{ABCD} = \frac{1}{16} \times 64^2 = 256$.

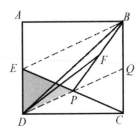 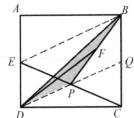 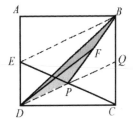

Example 3. (ARML) In triangle ABC, P and Q are the midpoints of AB and AC respectively; R and S are trisection points of BC (with R closer to B). PS and QR intersect in T. If the area of the triangle ABC is 60, compute the area of triangle PQT.

Solution: 009.
Method 1 (official solution):
If $RS = 2x$, $BC = 6x$ and $PQ = 3x$, $\Delta PQT \sim \Delta RST$ and the ratio of their sides is 3:2. If altitude $AH = 10k$, then $w = 5k$, $y = 3k$, and $z = 2k$. Area of $\Delta ABC = \frac{1}{2} \times 10k \times 6x = 30kx = 60$, so $kx = 2$. Area of $\Delta PQT = \frac{1}{2} \times 3k \times 3x = 9kx/2 = 9$.

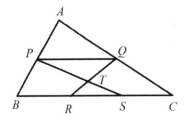

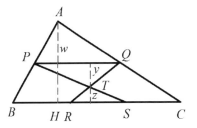

Method 2 (our solution):
$\Delta PQT \sim \Delta RST$ and the ratio of their areas is 9: 4 or 18: 8. Since $PT : ST = 3:2$, the ratio of the areas of ΔPRT and ΔRST is 12:8.

We also know that the area of $\triangle PRS$ is
$= \frac{1}{2} \times (\frac{1}{3}BC) \times (\frac{1}{2}h) = \frac{1}{6}S_{\triangle ABC} = 10$, or $12x + 8x = 10$ $\Rightarrow$ $x = 1/2$.
The area of triangle PQT is 9.

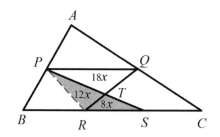

Example 4. (1985 AIME) As shown in the figure on the right, $\triangle ABC$ is divided into six smaller triangles by lines drawn from the vertices through a common interior point. The areas of four of these triangles are as indicated. Find the area of $\triangle ABC$.

Solution: 315.
Method 1 (official Solution):
Let the areas of two unknown triangles be x and y.

$\dfrac{40}{30} = \dfrac{40 + y + 84}{30 + 35 + x}$ (1)

$\dfrac{35}{x} = \dfrac{35 + 30 + 40}{x + 84 + y}$ (2)

$\dfrac{84}{y} = \dfrac{84 + x + 35}{y + 40 + 30}$ (3)

Solving we get: $x = 70$, $y = 56$.

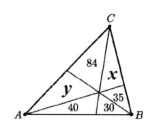

The area is then $30 + 35 + 70 + 84 + 56 + 40 = 315$.

Method 2 (our solution):
We label the points D and E as shown in the figure.
Looking at triangles ADC and BDC, by the Theorem 5, we have
$\dfrac{84 + m}{n + 35} = \dfrac{40}{30}$ (1)

Looking at triangles ADB and DEB, by the Theorem 3, we have
$\dfrac{AD}{DE} = \dfrac{40 + 30}{35} = 2$.
Looking at triangles ADC and DEC, by the Theorem 3, we have
$\dfrac{m + 84}{n} = \dfrac{AD}{DE} = 2$ $\Rightarrow$ $84 + m = 2n$ (2)

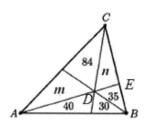

Substituting (2) into (1), we get: $\dfrac{2n}{n+35} = \dfrac{4}{3}$ $\Rightarrow$ $6n = 4n + 140$ $\Rightarrow$ $n = 70$.
Substituting $n = 70$ into (2), we get $m = 56$.

Therefore the area of $\triangle ABC$ is $84 + 40 + 30 + 35 + 126 = 315$.

Method 3 (our solution):
For any triangle, we know that following relationship is true:

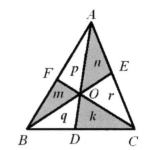

$$pqr = mnk \qquad (1)$$
$$\dfrac{1}{p} + \dfrac{1}{q} + \dfrac{1}{r} = \dfrac{1}{m} + \dfrac{1}{n} + \dfrac{1}{k} \qquad (2)$$

For our case, let the areas of two unknown triangles be m and n.
We have
$$84 \times 40 \times 35 = 30mn \qquad (3)$$
$$\dfrac{1}{84} + \dfrac{1}{40} + \dfrac{1}{35} = \dfrac{1}{m} + \dfrac{1}{n} + \dfrac{1}{30} \qquad (4)$$
or $mn = 3920$ \hfill (5)
$$\dfrac{1}{m} + \dfrac{1}{n} = \dfrac{1}{84} + \dfrac{1}{40} + \dfrac{1}{35} - \dfrac{1}{30} = \dfrac{9}{280} \qquad (6)$$

From (6), we have $\dfrac{1}{m} + \dfrac{1}{n} = \dfrac{m+n}{mn} = \dfrac{9}{280}$ \hfill (7)

Substituting (5) into (7), we get $m + n = \dfrac{9}{280} \times mn = \dfrac{9}{280} \times 3920 = 126$.
Therefore the area of $\triangle ABC$ is $84 + 40 + 30 + 35 + 126 = 315$.

Example 5. Triangle ABC is divided into four parts with the areas of three parts shown in the figure. $\dfrac{m}{n}$ is the area of the quadrilateral $ADOE$, where m and n are positive integers relatively prime. Find $m + n$.

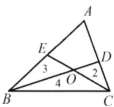

Solution: 044.
Method 1:

$$\frac{S_{\triangle BEO}}{S_{\triangle BAD}} = \frac{\frac{1}{2} BE \times BO \sin \angle EBO}{\frac{1}{2} BA \times BD \sin \angle ABD} = \frac{BE}{BA} \times \frac{S_{\triangle BOC}}{S_{\triangle BCD}}$$

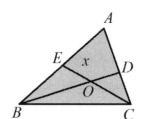

$$\frac{3}{3+x} = \frac{4}{6} \times \frac{BE}{BA} \quad (1)$$

$$\frac{BE}{BA} = \frac{S_{\triangle BCE}}{S_{\triangle BCA}} = \frac{7}{9+x} \quad (2)$$

So $\frac{3}{3+x} = \frac{4}{6} \times \frac{7}{9+x} \Rightarrow x = \frac{39}{5}$. $\quad m + n = 39 + 5 = 44$.

Method 2:

Connect AO. Let $S_{\triangle AEO} = a$ and $S_{\triangle ADO} = b$.

We have $\frac{3+a}{b} = \frac{4}{2}$ and $\frac{2+b}{a} = \frac{4}{3}$. Solving we get $a = \frac{21}{5}$ and $b = \frac{18}{5}$. $x = a + b = \frac{39}{5}$

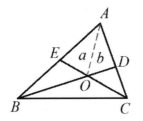 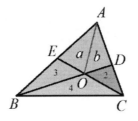 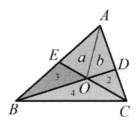

Method 3:

Connect DE. Let $S_{\triangle AED} = a$ and $S_{\triangle OED} = b$.

We have $\frac{a}{b+2} = \frac{a+b+3}{4}$ and $\frac{b}{2} = \frac{3}{4}$. Solving we get $b = \frac{3}{2}$ and $a = \frac{63}{10}$. $x = a + b = \frac{39}{5}$

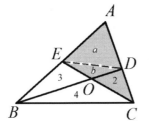 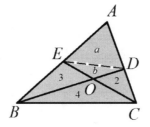 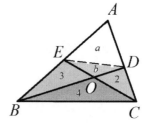

Example 6. As shown in the figure on the right, $\triangle ABC$ with the area of 40 square units is divided into three smaller triangles and one quadrilateral by lines drawn from two

vertices through a common interior point. Find the areas of quadrilateral $AEOD$ if $AE = BE$ and $\dfrac{AD}{DC} = \dfrac{2}{3}$.

Solution: 011.
Connect AO. Let $S_{\triangle AEO} = S_{\triangle BEO} = x$, $S_{\triangle AOD} = y$, $S_{\triangle COD} = z$, and $S_{\triangle COB} = w$.

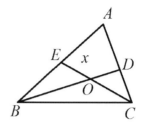

$S_{\triangle ACE} = \dfrac{1}{2} S_{\triangle ABC} = \dfrac{40}{2} = 20$ or $x + y + z = 20$ (1)

$x + w = 20 \Rightarrow x = 20 - w$ (2)

By **Theorem 5,** $\dfrac{2x}{w} = \dfrac{AD}{DC} = \dfrac{2}{3} \Rightarrow w = 3x$ (3)

Substituting (2) into (3): $w = 15$.

$w + z = \dfrac{3}{5} \times S_{\triangle ABC} = \dfrac{3}{5} \times 40 = 24 \Rightarrow z = 24 - w = 24 - 15 = 9$

Substituting $z = 9$ into (1): $x + y = 11$.

Example 7: (ARML) In triangle ABC, C is a right angle and M is on AC. A circle with radius r is centered at M, is tangent to AB, and is tangent to BC at C. If $AC = 5$ and $BC = 12$, compute r.

Solution: $\dfrac{12}{5}$.

Method 1 (official Solution):
Let N be the point of tangency of the circle with AB and draw MB, as shown to the right. Because $\triangle BMC$ and $\triangle BMN$ are right triangles sharing a hypotenuse, and MN and MC are radii, $\triangle BMC \cong \triangle BMN$. Thus $BN = 12$ and $AN = 1$. Also $\triangle ANM \sim \triangle ACB$ because the right triangles share $\angle A$, so $NM/AN = CB/AC$. Therefore $r/1 = 12/5$, so $r = 12/5$.

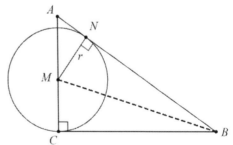

Method 2 (our solution):
$\triangle ABC$ is a $5 - 12 - 13$ right triangle with $AB = 13$. Drop a perpendicular to AB from M to meet AB at N, and connect BM.

$$S_{\triangle BMC} + S_{\triangle BAM} = S_{\triangle ABC} \quad \Rightarrow \quad \frac{BC \times MC}{2} + \frac{AB \times MN}{2} = \frac{BC \times AC}{2} \quad \Rightarrow$$

$$\frac{12 \times r}{2} + \frac{13 \times r}{2} = \frac{12 \times 5}{2} \quad \Rightarrow \quad 25r = 12 \times 5 \quad \Rightarrow \quad r = \frac{12}{5}.$$

Example 8. (1986 AIME) In $\triangle ABC$ shown below, $AB = 425$, $BC = 450$ and $CA = 510$. Moreover, P is an interior point chosen so that the segments DE, FG and HI are each of length d, contain P, and are parallel to the sides AB, BC and CA, respectively. Find d.

Solution: 306.
(our solution)

$$\frac{S_{\triangle CDE}}{S_{\triangle ABC}} = \frac{d^2}{AB^2} \qquad (1)$$

$$\frac{S_{\triangle BHI}}{S_{\triangle ABC}} = \frac{d^2}{AC^2} \qquad (2)$$

$$\frac{S_{\triangle AGF}}{S_{\triangle ABC}} = \frac{d^2}{BC^2} \qquad (3)$$

$$\frac{S_{\triangle PIF}}{S_{\triangle ABC}} = \frac{(AB-d)^2}{AB^2} \qquad (4)$$

$$\frac{S_{\triangle PEH}}{S_{\triangle ABC}} = \frac{(BC-d)^2}{BC^2} \qquad (5)$$

$$\frac{S_{\triangle PGD}}{S_{\triangle ABC}} = \frac{(AC-d)^2}{AC^2} \qquad (6)$$

$(1) + (2) + (3) - [(4) + (5) + (6)]$:
$S_{\triangle ABC} = S_{\triangle CDE} + S_{\triangle BHI} + S_{\triangle AGF} - (S_{\triangle PIF} + S_{\triangle PHE} + S_{\triangle PGD})$

$$\Rightarrow \quad d\left(\frac{1}{AB} + \frac{1}{BC} + \frac{1}{AC}\right) = 2 \quad \Rightarrow \quad d = 306.$$

✰**Example 9.** (1997 China Hope Cup Math Contest) As shown in the figure, D, E, and F are points on BC, CA, and AB of an acute triangle ABC. AD, BE, and CF meet at P. $AP = BP = CP = 6$. If $PD = x$, $PE = y$, $PF = z$, and $xy + yz + zx = 28$. Find the value of xyz.

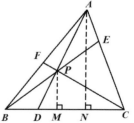

Solution: 024.
Draw $PM \perp BC$ at M, $AN \perp BC$ at N.

We know that $S_{\triangle PBC} = \frac{1}{2} PM \cdot BC$ and $S_{\triangle ABC} = \frac{1}{2} AN \cdot BC$.

Therefore $\dfrac{S_{\triangle PBC}}{S_{\triangle ABC}} = \dfrac{PM}{AN} = \dfrac{PD}{AD} = \dfrac{x}{x+6}$.

Similarly $\dfrac{S_{\triangle PAC}}{S_{\triangle ABC}} = \dfrac{y}{y+6}$ and $\dfrac{S_{\triangle PAB}}{S_{\triangle ABC}} = \dfrac{z}{z+6}$.

Adding them together we get:

$\dfrac{x}{x+6} + \dfrac{y}{y+6} + \dfrac{z}{z+6} = \dfrac{S_{\triangle PBC} + S_{\triangle PAC} + S_{\triangle PAB}}{S_{\triangle ABC}} = 1 \quad \Rightarrow$

$1 - \dfrac{6}{x+6} + 1 - \dfrac{6}{y+6} + 1 - \dfrac{6}{z+6} = 1 \quad \Rightarrow \quad \dfrac{3}{x+6} + \dfrac{3}{y+6} + \dfrac{3}{z+6} = 1$.

$3(yz + zx + xy) + 36(x + y + z) + 324 = xyz + 6(xy + yz + zx) + 36(x + y + z) + 216$.
We are given that $xy + yz + zx = 28$.
Hence $xyz = 108 - 3(xy + yz + zx) = 24$.

Example 10. (ARML) Given noncollinear points A, B, C, segment AB is trisected by points D and E, and F is the midpoint of segment AC. DF and BF intersect CE at G and H, respectively. If $[DEG] = 18$, compute $[FGH]$.

Solution: 9/5.
Method 1 (our solution):
We first connect DC and EF. Since E and F are the midpoints of DA and CA, respectively, $DC//EF$. Therefore, $[DEG] = [CFG]$.
Next, we connect GA. Triangle CFG and triangle AGF share the same height, and their bases are equal to each other since F is the midpoint of CA, so they have the same area. Similarly, $[DEG] = [AGF]$.
Thus, the areas of triangles DEG, CFG, AGF, and EAG equal 18.

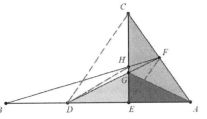

$[DFA] = [DEF] + [EFA] = 18 + 18 + 18 = 54$. Since E is the midpoint of DA, $[DEF] = [EFA] = \dfrac{\frac{1}{2}[DFA]}{2} = 27$. Triangles DEF and BDF share the same height and have equivalent bases, so $[BDF] = [DEF] = 27$.

As we determined already, $[AGF] = 18$ and $[DGA] = [DEG] + [EAG] = 18 + 18 = 36$. Triangles AGF and DGA share the same height, therefore the ratio of their bases:
$$\frac{FG}{GD} = \frac{1}{2}.$$

Let $[FGH] = x$. By the ratio above, we see that $[DGH] = 2x$.

Therefore $[BDF] = [BDH] + 2x + x$.

We have determined that the area of triangle $[BDF]$ is 27, and $[DEF] = [BDH]$. So the equation above becomes $27 = [DEH] + 2x + x$ \hfill (1)

We also know that $[DEH] = [DGH] + [DGE] = 18 + 2x$.

Substituting this into equation (1), we get $27 = 18 + 2x + 2x + x \Rightarrow x = 9/5$. The area of FGH is 9/5.

Method 2 (our solution):
We draw FK so that $FK//AB$ and FK meets CE at K.

Let $[FGH] = x$ and $[FKH] = y$.
Since $FK//AB$ and F is the midpoint of CA,
$$KF = \frac{1}{2}EA = \frac{1}{2}DE = \frac{1}{4}BE.$$
Because $FK//AB$, triangles FKG and DEG are similar to each other. Since the ratio of the area of two similar triangles is equal to the square of the ratio of their corresponding sides,

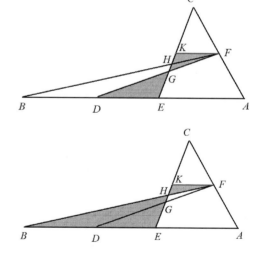

$$\frac{[FKG]}{[DEG]} = \left(\frac{FK}{DE}\right)^2 = \frac{1}{4} \Rightarrow [FKG] = \frac{18}{4} = \frac{9}{2}$$

$$\Rightarrow \quad x + y = \frac{9}{2} \hfill (1)$$

Because $FK//AB$, triangles FKH and BEH are similar to each other. Since the ratio of the area of two similar triangles is equal to the square of the ratio of their corresponding sides,

$$\frac{[FKH]}{[BEH]} = \left(\frac{FK}{BE}\right)^2 = \frac{1}{16} \qquad (2)$$

From method 1, $[BDF] = 27$, so $[BEH] = [BDF] - [HGF] + [DGE] = 27 - x + 18$.

Substituting this into equation (2), we get $[FKH] = \frac{1}{16}(27 - x + 18)$.

Or $y = \frac{1}{16}(27 - x + 18)$ \qquad (3)

Solving the system of equations (1) and (3) for x: $x = 9/5$.

Note: ARML has two official solutions (one used Menelaus's Theorem, and one used the method of mass points) for this problem.

Example 11. O is the circumcenter (the center of circumcircle O of radius R about triangle ABC, where the perpendicular bisectors of the sides intersect of triangle ABC. Show that $\frac{1}{AD} + \frac{1}{BE} + \frac{1}{CF} = \frac{2}{R}$.

Proof:

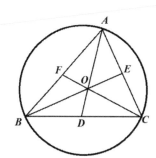

$$\frac{AO}{AD} = \frac{S_{\triangle ABO}}{S_{\triangle ABD}} = \frac{S_{\triangle ACO}}{S_{\triangle ACD}} = \frac{S_{\triangle ABO} + S_{\triangle ACO}}{S_{\triangle ABC}} \qquad (1)$$

$$\frac{BO}{BE} = \frac{S_{\triangle BCO} + S_{\triangle BAO}}{S_{\triangle ABC}} \qquad (2)$$

$$\frac{CO}{CD} = \frac{S_{\triangle CAO} + S_{\triangle CBO}}{S_{\triangle ABC}} \qquad (3)$$

(1) + (2) + (3):

$$\frac{AO}{AD} + \frac{BO}{BE} + \frac{CO}{CD} = \frac{2(S_{\triangle ABO} + S_{\triangle BCO} + S_{\triangle CAO})}{S_{\triangle ABC}} = \frac{2S_{\triangle ABC}}{S_{\triangle ABC}} = 2.$$

$OA = OB = OC = R$,

$$\therefore \frac{R}{AD} + \frac{R}{BE} + \frac{R}{CF} = 2, \quad \frac{1}{AD} + \frac{1}{BE} + \frac{1}{CF} = \frac{2}{R}.$$

✩Example 12. In triangle ABC, D, E, and F are on the sides CB, AC, and AB, respectively. Given that AD, BE, and CF are concurrent at the point P, and that $\frac{AP}{PD}+\frac{BP}{PE}+\frac{CP}{PF}=2015$, $\frac{AP}{PD}\times\frac{BP}{PE}\times\frac{CP}{PF}=m$. Find the last three digits of m.

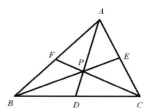

Solution: 017.

Let $S_{\triangle ABC}=S$, $S_{\triangle AFP}=S_1$, $S_{\triangle BCP}=S_2$. $S_{\triangle CAP}=S_3$.

$$\frac{AP}{PD}=\frac{S_1}{S_{\triangle BDP}}=\frac{S_3}{S_{\triangle CDP}}=\frac{S_1+S_3}{S_2}=\frac{S-S_2}{S_2} \tag{1}$$

Similarly, $\dfrac{BP}{PE}=\dfrac{S-S_3}{S_3}$ (2)

$\dfrac{CP}{PF}=\dfrac{S-S_1}{S_1}$ (3)

We are given that $\dfrac{AP}{PD}+\dfrac{BP}{PE}+\dfrac{CP}{PF}=2015$ (4)

Substituting (1), (2), (3) into (4): $\dfrac{S-S_1}{S_1}+\dfrac{S-S_2}{S_2}+\dfrac{S-S_3}{S_3}=2015$ (5)

(5) can be simplified into $\dfrac{S}{S_1}+\dfrac{S}{S_2}+\dfrac{S}{S_3}=2018 \Rightarrow$

$$2018 S_1 S_2 S_3 = S(S_1 S_2 + S_2 S_3 + S_3 S_1) \tag{6}$$

So $\dfrac{AP}{PD}\times\dfrac{BP}{PE}\times\dfrac{CP}{PF}=\dfrac{(S_2+S_3)(S_3+S_1)(S_1+S_2)}{S_1 S_2 S_3}$

$=\dfrac{(S_1+S_2+S_3)(S_1 S_2+S_2 S_2+S_3 S_1)-S_1 S_2 S_3}{S_1 S_2 S_3}$

$=\dfrac{S(S_1 S_2+S_2 S_2+S_3 S_1)}{S_1 S_2 S_3}-1=\dfrac{2018 S_1 S_2 S_3}{S_1 S_2 S_3}-1=2018-1=2017$. The answer is 017.

Example 13. (IMO) The diagonals AC and CE of the regular hexagon $ABCDEF$ are divided by the inner points M and N, respectively, so that $AM/AC = CN/CE = r$. Determine r if B, M, and N are collinear.

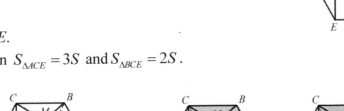

Solution: $\dfrac{\sqrt{3}}{3}$.

Connect BE and AE.

Let $S_{\triangle ABC} = S$. Then $S_{\triangle ACE} = 3S$ and $S_{\triangle BCE} = 2S$.

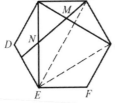 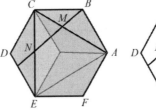 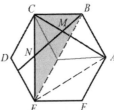

By **Theorem 3**,

$$\frac{S_{\triangle BCM}}{S_{\triangle ABC}} = \frac{CM}{AC} = \frac{AC - AM}{AC} = 1 - r \quad \Rightarrow \quad S_{\triangle BCM} = (1-r)S \tag{1}$$

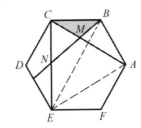 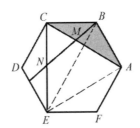

By **Formula (2)**, $\dfrac{S_{\triangle MCN}}{S_{\triangle ACE}} = \dfrac{\frac{1}{2} CN \times CM \times \sin \angle MCN}{\frac{1}{2} CE \times CA \times \sin \angle ACE} = \dfrac{CN \times CM}{CE \times CA} = r \times \dfrac{CM}{AC} = r(1-r)$

$$\Rightarrow \quad S_{\triangle MCN} = r(1-r) S_{\triangle ACE} = 3r(1-r)S \tag{2}$$

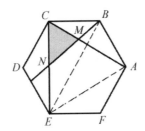 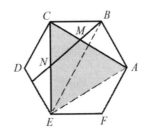

By **Theorem 3**, $\dfrac{S_{\triangle BCN}}{S_{\triangle BCE}} = \dfrac{CN}{CE}$ $\Rightarrow$ $S_{\triangle BCN} = rS_{\triangle BCE} = 2rS$ (3)

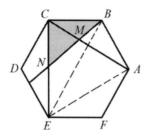 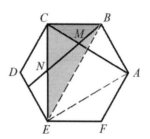

Since B, M, and N are collinear, we know that $S_{\triangle BCN} = S_{\triangle BCM} + S_{\triangle MCN}$ (4)

Substituting (1), (2), and (3) into (4): $3r^2 = 1$ $\Rightarrow$ $r = \dfrac{\sqrt{3}}{3}$.

Example 14. The area of $\triangle ABC$ is 1. As shown in the figure, D and E trisect BC. F and G trisect CA. The area of quadrilateral $PECF$ can be written as $\dfrac{m}{n}$, where m and n are positive integers relatively prime. Find $m + n$.

Solution: 007.

Since $EC = \dfrac{1}{3} BC$, $S_{\triangle AEC} = \dfrac{1}{3} S_{\triangle ABC} = \dfrac{1}{3}$.

Because $CF = \dfrac{1}{3} CA$, $S_{\triangle BCF} = \dfrac{1}{3} S_{\triangle ABC} = \dfrac{1}{3}$.

Connect PC and let $S_{\triangle PEC} = x$, $S_{\triangle PFC} = y$.

We have $S_{\triangle PBC} = 3x$, $S_{\triangle PCA} = 3y$.

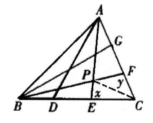

Therefore $x + 3y = \dfrac{1}{3}$ and $3x + y = \dfrac{1}{3}$.

Adding these two equations together, we get $4x + 4y = \dfrac{2}{3}$ $\Rightarrow$ $x + y = \dfrac{1}{6}$.

Hence $S_{PECF} = \dfrac{1}{6}$. $m + n = 1 + 6 = 7$.

PROBLEMS

Problem 1. As shown in the figure, the area of triangle *ABC* is 50. Points *D*, *E*, and *F* are on sides *AC*, *AB*, and *BC*, respectively, and *AD* = 6, *DB* = 9. Find the area of triangle *BCE* if triangles *CDG* and *EFG* have equal areas.

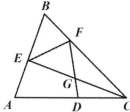

Problem 2. *ABCD* is a quadrilateral. *E* is the midpoint of the diagonal *BD*. *EF* // *AC*. If the area of triangle *ABF* is 1008, and the area of quadrilateral *ABCD* is *m*, find the last three digits of *m*.

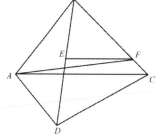

Problem 3. The area of the parallelogram *ABCD* is 800. *E* is a point on *DC*. *DE* : *EC* = 3:2. Find the area of triangle *AFB*.

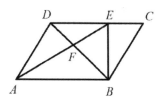

Problem 4. As shown in the figure, $\triangle ABC$ is divided into six smaller triangles by lines drawn from the vertices through a common interior point. The areas of four of these triangles are as indicated. Find the area $\triangle ABC$.

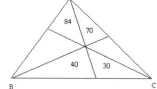

Problem 5. Triangle *ABC* is divided into four parts with the areas of three parts shown in the figure. Find the area of the quadrilateral *AEFD*.

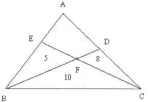

Problem 6. As shown in the figure on the right, $\triangle ABC$ with the area of 21 square units is divided into three smaller triangles and one quadrilateral by lines drawn from two vertices through a common interior point. Find the areas of quadrilateral *AEOD* if $\frac{AD}{DC} = \frac{1}{2}$, and $\frac{AE}{BE} = 2$.

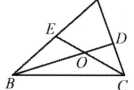

Problem 7. (AMC) Let *AB* be a diameter of a circle and *C* be a point on *AB* with $2 \cdot AC = BC$. Let *D* and *E* be points on the circle such that $DC \perp AB$ and *DE* is a second diameter. What is the ratio of the area of $\triangle DCE$ to the area of $\triangle ABD$?

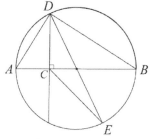

Problem 8. Let *P* be an interior point of $\triangle ABC$ and extend lines from the vertices through *P* to the opposite sides. Let *a*, *b*, *c*, and *d* denote the lengths of the segments indicated in the figure. Find the last three digits of the product *abc* if $a + b + c = 29$ and $d = 6$.

Problem 9. As shown in the figure, the area of parallelogram $ABCD$ is 1. E and F are the midpoints of AB and BC, respectively. AF meets CE at G and DE at H. The area of $\triangle EGH$ can be written as $\dfrac{m}{n}$, where m and n are positive integers relatively prime. Find $m + n$.

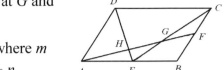

Problem 10. As shown in the figure, P is any point inside the triangle ABC. Line segment AP, BP, CP meet BC at D AC at E, and AB at F, respectively. Prove that $\dfrac{AF}{BF} \cdot \dfrac{BD}{CD} \cdot \dfrac{CE}{AE} = 1$.

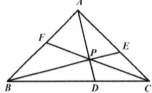

☆Problem 11. In triangle ABC, D, E, and F are on the sides CB, AC, and AB, respectively. AD, BE, and CF are concurrent at the point P. $\dfrac{AP}{PD} \times \dfrac{BP}{PE} \times \dfrac{CP}{PF} = 2017$, $\dfrac{AP}{PD} + \dfrac{BP}{PE} + \dfrac{CP}{PF} = m$. Find the last three digits of m.

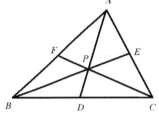

Problem 12. (USAMO) A given convex pentagon $ABCDE$ has the property that the area of each of the five triangles ABC, BCD, CDE, DEA, and EAB is unity. Find the area of the convex pentagon $ABCDE$

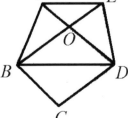

Problem 13. (1989 AIME 15) Point P is inside triangle ABC. Line segments APD, BPE, and CPF are drawn with D on BC, E on AC, and F on AB (see the figure below). Given that $AP = 6$, $BP = 9$, $PD = 6$, $PE = 3$, and $CF = 20$, find the area of triangle ABC.

Problem 14. (2007 IMO) In triangle ABC the bisector of angle BCA intersects the circumcircle again at R, the perpendicular bisector of BC at P, and the perpendicular bisector of AC at Q. The midpoint of BC is K and the midpoint of AC is L. Prove that the triangles RPK and RQL have the same area.

SOLUTIONS

Problem 1. Solution: 020.

Connect *DE*. Since triangle *DCG* has the same area as triangle *EFG*, *FC//ED* and $\triangle AED$ is similar to $\triangle ABC$.

$\dfrac{S_{\triangle AED}}{S_{\triangle ABC}} = \left(\dfrac{9}{15}\right)^2 = \dfrac{9}{25} \Rightarrow S_{\triangle AED} = \left(\dfrac{9}{15}\right)^2 = \dfrac{9}{25} \times S_{\triangle ABC} = 18$.

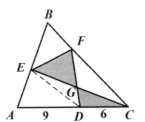

$\dfrac{S_{\triangle DCE}}{S_{\triangle AED}} = \dfrac{6}{9} = \dfrac{2}{3} \Rightarrow S_{\triangle DCE} = \dfrac{2}{3} \times S_{\triangle AED} = \dfrac{2}{3} \times 18 = 12$

$S_{\triangle ACE} = S_{\triangle AED} + S_{\triangle DCE} = 18 + 12 = 30$.

$S_{\triangle BCE} = S_{\triangle ABC} - S_{\triangle ACE} = 50 - 30 = 20$.

Problem 2. Solution: 016.

Connect *AE, CE*. Let *AF* and *CE* meet at *G*.
We know that *BE = DE*. So $S_{\triangle ADE} = S_{\triangle ABE}$ and $S_{\triangle DCE} = S_{\triangle BCE}$

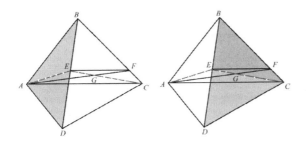

We also know that *EF // AC*. So $S_{\triangle AEF} = S_{\triangle CEF}$. $S_{\triangle AEG} = S_{\triangle CFG}$.

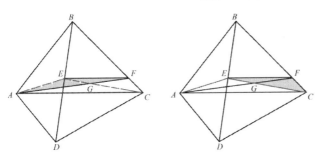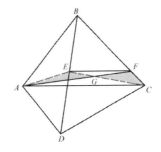

117

$S_{AFCD} = S_{\triangle ADE} + S_{\triangle DCE} - S_{\triangle AEG} + S_{CFG}$

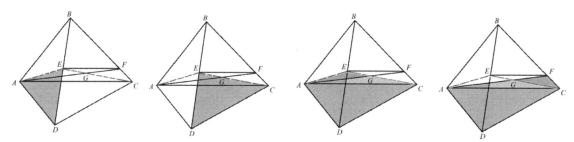

$S_{\triangle ABF} = S_{\triangle ABE} + S_{\triangle BCE} - S_{\triangle CFG} + S_{\triangle AEG}$.

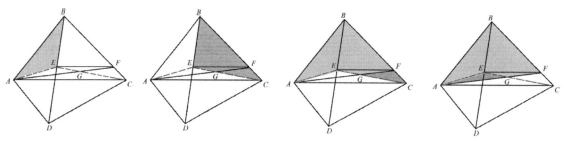

We see that $S_{AFCD} = S_{\triangle ABF} = 1008$.

The area of quadrilateral $ABCD$ is $1008 \times 2 = 2016$. The last three digits are 016.

Problem 3. Solution: 250.

Method 1:

We know that $DE : AB = 3:5$ and $S_{\triangle ABF} \approx S_{\triangle EDF}$.

Then $DF : FB = 3:5$ and $EF : FA = 3:5$.

So we can label the area of each region as shown in the figure.

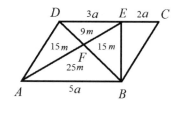

We see that $S_{\triangle ADB} = \frac{1}{2} S_{ABCD} = 400$, that is $15m + 25m = 400$ $\Rightarrow$ $m = 10$.

The area of triangle AFB is $25 \times 10 = 250$.

Method 2:

We label each region as shown in the figure.

We have $S_2^2 = S_1 \times S_3$ (1)

We also know that $S_2 + S_3 = \frac{1}{2} S_{ABCD} = 400$ (2)

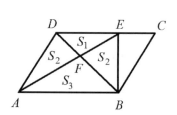

We see that $S_{\triangle BDE} : S_{\triangle BCE} = DE : EC = \frac{3}{2}$, and $S_{\triangle BDE} + S_{\triangle BCE} = S_{\triangle BCD} = \frac{800}{2} = 400$. We get $S_{\triangle BDE} = 240$ or $S_1 + S_2 = 240$ \qquad (3)

Solving the system of equations (1), (2), and (3), we get $S_1 = 90$, $S_2 = 150$, $S_3 = 250$.

Problem 4. Solution: 315.
Let x and y be the areas for the small triangles as shown in the figure.

$\dfrac{S_{\triangle ABO}}{S_{\triangle ACO}} = \dfrac{S_{\triangle BOD}}{S_{\triangle COD}} \Rightarrow \dfrac{84+x}{70+y} = \dfrac{40}{30}$

Similarly, we have $\dfrac{S_{\triangle ABO}}{S_{\triangle BCO}} = \dfrac{S_{\triangle AEO}}{S_{\triangle CEO}} \Rightarrow \dfrac{84+x}{40+30} = \dfrac{70}{y}$

Or $\dfrac{70+y}{70} = \dfrac{3}{4}\dfrac{70}{y}$.

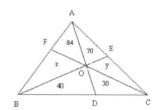

$x = 56$ and $y = 35$. The total area is $84 + 70 + 40 + 30 + 35 + 56 = 315$.

Problem 5. Solution: 022.
Connect AF.

$\dfrac{S_{\triangle ABF}}{S_{\triangle BFC}} = \dfrac{S_{\triangle AFD}}{S_{\triangle FDC}} \Rightarrow \dfrac{5+x}{10} = \dfrac{y}{8}$

Similarly, we have $\dfrac{S_{\triangle ACF}}{S_{\triangle BCF}} = \dfrac{S_{\triangle AEF}}{S_{\triangle EFB}} \Rightarrow \dfrac{8+y}{10} = \dfrac{x}{5}$

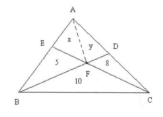

Solving the equations for x and y, we get $x = 10$, and $y = 12$. The area of $AEFD$ is 22.

Problem 6. Solution: 006.
Connect AO. Let $S_{\triangle AEO} = 2x$, $S_{\triangle BEO} = x$, $S_{\triangle AOD} = y$, $S_{\triangle COD} = 2y$, and $S_{\triangle COB} = w$.

$S_{\triangle ACE} = \dfrac{2}{3} S_{\triangle ABC} = \dfrac{2}{3} \times 21 = 14$ or $2x + 3y = 14$ \qquad (1)

$x + w = 7 \Rightarrow x = 7 - w$ \qquad (2)

By **Theorem 5,** $\dfrac{3x}{w} = \dfrac{AD}{DC} = \dfrac{1}{2} \Rightarrow w = 6x$ \qquad (3)

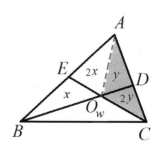

Substituting (2) into (3): $w = 6$.

$$w + 2y = \frac{2}{3} \times S_{\Delta ABC} = \frac{2}{3} \times 21 = 14 \quad \Rightarrow \quad y = \frac{14-w}{2} = \frac{14-6}{2} = 4.$$

$2x + y = 2 \times 1 + 4 = 6.$

Problem 7. Solution:
We have two solutions different from the official solution.
Method 1 (our solution):
Let the area of ΔDCE be $S_{\Delta DCE}$ and the area of ΔABD be $S_{\Delta ABD}$, and let the radius be r.
Let the area of ΔDCO be $S_{\Delta DCO}$ and $S_{\Delta DCE} = 2S_{\Delta DCO}$

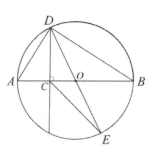

Since $2AC = BC$, and $AC + CB = 2r$, $AC = \frac{2}{3}r$, and $CO = \frac{1}{3}r$.

$$\frac{S_{\Delta DCE}}{S_{\Delta ABD}} = \frac{2S_{\Delta DCO}}{S_{\Delta ABD}} = \frac{2 \times \frac{1}{2} DC \times CO}{\frac{1}{2} AB \times CD} = \frac{2CO}{AB} = \frac{\frac{2}{3}r}{2r} = \frac{1}{3}.$$

Method 2 (our solution):
Let the area of ΔDCE be $S_{\Delta DCE}$ and the area of ΔABD be $S_{\Delta ABD}$, and let the radius be r.
Connect EF. ΔDEF is a right triangle, since DE is the diameter of the circle.
Since $2AC = BC$, and $AC + CB = 2r$, $AC = \frac{2}{3}r$, and $CO = \frac{1}{3}r$.

Therefore $EF = 2CO = \frac{2}{3}r$.

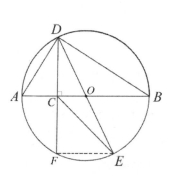

$$\frac{S_{\Delta DCE}}{S_{\Delta ABD}} = \frac{\frac{1}{2} DC \times EF}{\frac{1}{2} AB \times CD} = \frac{EF}{AB} = \frac{\frac{2}{3}r}{2r} = \frac{1}{3}.$$

Problem 8. Solution: 476.
Let $S_{\Delta ABC} = S$, $S_{\Delta APF} = S_1$, $S_{\Delta BPF} = S_2$.
$S_{\Delta BPD} = S_3$, $S_{\Delta CPD} = S_4$, $S_{\Delta CPE} = S_5$, $S_{\Delta APE} = S_6$.

Therefore

$$\frac{S_1+S_2}{S}=\frac{d}{c+d} \quad (1)$$

$$\frac{S_3+S_4}{S}=\frac{d}{a+d} \quad (2)$$

$$\frac{S_5+S_6}{S}=\frac{d}{b+d} \quad (3)$$

So $\dfrac{d}{a+d}+\dfrac{d}{b+d}+\dfrac{d}{c+d}=1$ (4)

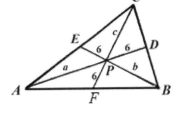

Solving (4) we have: $2d^3+(a+b+c)d^2-abc=0$

Therefore $abc = 36(a+b+c) + 432 = 1476$. The last three digits are 476.

Problem 9. Solution: 031.

Method 1:
Connect BG and DG.

Since $S_{\triangle ABF}=\dfrac{1}{2}S_{\triangle ABC}=S_{\triangle EBC}$, $S_{\triangle AEG}=S_{\triangle CFG}$.

Therefore $S_{\triangle BEG}=S_{\triangle AEG}=S_{\triangle CFG}=S_{\triangle BFG}=\dfrac{1}{3}S_{\triangle ABF}=\dfrac{1}{6}S_{\triangle ABC}=\dfrac{1}{12}S_{ABCD}=\dfrac{1}{12}$.

We also know that $S_{\triangle ADG}+S_{\triangle BCG}=\dfrac{1}{2}S_{ABCD}$. So $S_{\triangle ADG}=\dfrac{1}{3}$.

So $\dfrac{HE}{DH}=\dfrac{S_{\triangle AEH}}{S_{\triangle ADH}}=\dfrac{S_{\triangle GEH}}{S_{\triangle GDH}}=\dfrac{S_{\triangle AEH}+S_{\triangle GEH}}{S_{\triangle ADH}+S_{\triangle GDH}}=\dfrac{S_{\triangle AEG}}{S_{\triangle ADG}}=\dfrac{\frac{1}{12}}{\frac{1}{3}}=\dfrac{1}{4}$.

$S_{\triangle AEH}=\dfrac{1}{5}S_{\triangle DAE}=\dfrac{1}{5}\times(\dfrac{1}{4}S_{ABCD})=\dfrac{1}{20}$.

Therefore $S_{\triangle EGH}=S_{\triangle AEG}-S_{AEH}=\dfrac{1}{12}-\dfrac{1}{20}=\dfrac{1}{30}$.

The answer is $1 + 30 = 31$.

Method 2:
Draw $EP \parallel AD$ to meet HG at P.

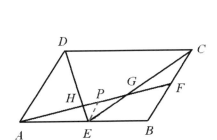

$$EG = EC \times \frac{EP}{FC+EP} = EC \times \frac{\frac{1}{2}BF}{BF+\frac{1}{2}BF} = \frac{EC}{3}$$

$$EH = ED \times \frac{EP}{AD+EP} = ED \times \frac{\frac{1}{2}BF}{BF+\frac{1}{2}BF} = \frac{ED}{5}.$$

So $\dfrac{S_{\triangle EGH}}{S_{\triangle ECD}} = \dfrac{EG \times EH}{EC \times ED} = \dfrac{1}{15}$.

We know that $S_{\triangle ECD} = \dfrac{1}{2} S_{ABCD} = \dfrac{1}{2}$. Thus $S_{\triangle EGH} = \dfrac{1}{30}$.

Method 3:
Connect AC to meet ED at P. Connect GP. We know that G is the centroid of triangle ABC.
Since $AE \parallel DC$,
$EP : PD = AE : CD = 1 : 2$.
$EG : GC = 1 : 2$.
Thus $EG : GC = EP : PD$.

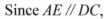

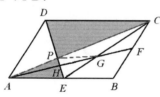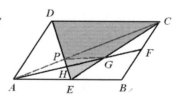

Then we know that $PG \parallel CD$, and $PG : CD = EG : EC = 1 : 3$.
$S_{\triangle EGP} : S_{\triangle ECD} = 1^2 : 3^2 = 1 : 9$.

So $S_{\triangle EGP} = \dfrac{1}{9} S_{\triangle ECD} = \dfrac{1}{18} S_{ABCD} = \dfrac{1}{18}$.

But $\triangle HGP \sim \triangle HAE$. $PH : HE = PG : AE = \dfrac{1}{3}CD : \dfrac{1}{2}CD = \dfrac{2}{3}$.

So $S_{\triangle EGH} = \dfrac{3}{5} S_{\triangle EGP} = \dfrac{3}{5} \times \dfrac{1}{18} = \dfrac{1}{30}$.

Problem 10. Solution:
Taking a closer look at $\triangle CAF$ and $\triangle CFB$, since they share the same vertex C, the ratio of their areas is the same as the ratio of their bases (AF and FB).

Therefore we have $\dfrac{AF}{BF} = \dfrac{\triangle APC}{\triangle BPC}$ (1)

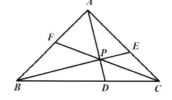

Similarly we have $\dfrac{BD}{CD} = \dfrac{\triangle APB}{\triangle APC}$ (2)

and $\dfrac{CE}{AE} = \dfrac{\triangle BPC}{\triangle APB}$ (3)

Multiplying (1), (2), and (3) together we get:

$$\dfrac{AF}{BF} \cdot \dfrac{BD}{CD} \cdot \dfrac{CE}{AE} = \dfrac{\triangle APC}{\triangle BPC} \cdot \dfrac{\triangle APB}{\triangle APC} \cdot \dfrac{\triangle BPC}{\triangle APB} = 1$$

Note that the conclusion is still valid if P is outside the triangle ABC. This is called "Ceva's Theorem".

☆Problem 11. Solution: 015.
Let $S_{\triangle ABC} = S$, $S_{\triangle AFP} = S_1$, $S_{\triangle BCP} = S_2$, $S_{\triangle CAP} = S_3$.

$\dfrac{AP}{PD} = \dfrac{S_1}{S_{\triangle BDP}} = \dfrac{S_3}{S_{\triangle CDP}} = \dfrac{S_1 + S_3}{S_2} = \dfrac{S - S_2}{S_2}$ (1)

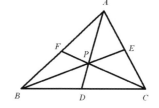

Similarly, $\dfrac{BP}{PE} = \dfrac{S - S_3}{S_3}$ (2)

$\dfrac{CP}{PF} = \dfrac{S - S_1}{S_1}$ (3)

(1) + (2) + (3): $\dfrac{AP}{PD} + \dfrac{BP}{PE} + \dfrac{CP}{PF} = \dfrac{S - S_1}{S_1} + \dfrac{S - S_2}{S_2} + \dfrac{S - S_3}{S_3} = \dfrac{S}{S_1} + \dfrac{S}{S_2} + \dfrac{S}{S_3} - 3$ (4)

(1) × (2) × (3): $\dfrac{AP}{PD} \times \dfrac{BP}{PE} \times \dfrac{CP}{PF} = \dfrac{(S_2 + S_3)(S_3 + S_1)(S_1 + S_2)}{S_1 S_2 S_3}$

$= \dfrac{(S_1 + S_2 + S_3)(S_1 S_2 + S_2 S_3 + S_3 S_1) - S_1 S_2 S_3}{S_1 S_2 S_3} = \dfrac{S(S_1 S_2 + S_2 S_3 + S_3 S_1)}{S_1 S_2 S_3} - 1$, or

$$\frac{S}{S_1} + \frac{S}{S_2} + \frac{S}{S_3} - 1 = 2017 \quad \Rightarrow \quad \frac{S}{S_1} + \frac{S}{S_2} + \frac{S}{S_3} = 2018 \tag{5}$$

Substituting (5) into (4): $\frac{AP}{PD} + \frac{BP}{PE} + \frac{CP}{PF} = \frac{S}{S_1} + \frac{S}{S_2} + \frac{S}{S_3} - 3 = 2018 - 3 = 2015$.

Problem 12. Solution: $\frac{5+\sqrt{5}}{2}$.

Let O be the intersection point of diagonals AD and BE.

Since $S_{\triangle AEB} = S_{\triangle AED} = 1$, by **Theorem 4(c):** $AE \parallel BD$; by **Theorem 4(a):** $S_{\triangle ABO} = S_{\triangle EDO}$.

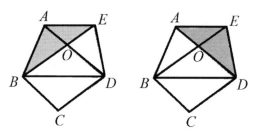

For the same reason we get $AD \parallel BC$, and $BE \parallel CD$.

Thus $BCDO$ is a parallelogram. $S_{\triangle BOD} = 1$.

Let $S_{\triangle AEO} = S$. By **Theorem 17,** we have $S_{\triangle ABO} \times S_{\triangle EDO} = S_{\triangle AEO} \times S_{\triangle BDO}$ or $(1-S)^2 = 1 \times S$

$\Rightarrow S^2 - 3S + 1 = 0$.

Solving we get: $S = \frac{-(-3) - \sqrt{(-3)^2 - 4 \times 1 \times 1}}{2} = \frac{3 - \sqrt{5}}{2}$.

We know that the area of the trapezoid $ABDE$ is $3 - S =$

$3 - \frac{3-\sqrt{5}}{2} = \frac{3+\sqrt{5}}{2}$.

The area of the convex pentagon $ABCDE$ is $1 + \frac{3+\sqrt{5}}{2} = \frac{5+\sqrt{5}}{2}$.

Problem 13. Solution: 108.
(We are giving a solution that is different from the official solution):

We see that $S_{\triangle PAB} = S_{\triangle PBD} = S_{\triangle PDC} = S_{\triangle PCA}$.

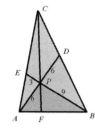
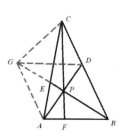

So $\dfrac{PC}{FC} = \dfrac{S_{\triangle PCA}}{S_{\triangle AFC}} \Rightarrow PC = \dfrac{S_{\triangle PCA}}{S_{\triangle AFC}} \times FC = \dfrac{3}{4} \times 20 = 15$.

Extend BP to G such that $PG = BP$. We know that $ABDG$ is a parallelogram. Since $BD = DC$, CG and DA are congruent and parallel and $CG = DA = 12$.
$CG^2 + PG^2 = 12^2 + 9^2 = 15^2 = PC^2$

Thus $CG \perp PG$, $AD \perp BG$. $S_{\triangle ABC} = S_{ABDG} = \dfrac{1}{2} AD \times BG = 108$.

Problem 14. Solution (our solution):
We want to prove:
$\dfrac{1}{2} CL \times CR \times \sin \angle 1 - \dfrac{1}{2} CL \times CQ \times \sin \angle 1 =$
$\dfrac{1}{2} CR \times CK \times \sin \angle 1 - \dfrac{1}{2} CP \times CK \times \sin \angle 1$

Or $\dfrac{1}{4} CA \times CR \times \sin \angle 1 - \dfrac{1}{4} CA \times CQ \times \sin c \angle 1 =$
$\dfrac{1}{4} CR \times CB \times \sin \angle 1 - \dfrac{1}{4} CP \times CB \times \sin \angle 1$

Or $CA \times CR - CA \times CQ = CR \times CB - CP \times CB$

Or $CA(CR - CQ) = CB(CR - CP)$ or $\dfrac{CA}{CB} = \dfrac{PR}{QR}$

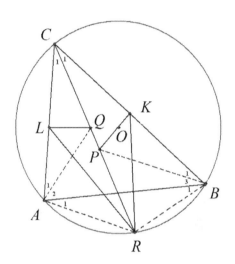

(1)
As shown in the figure, $\triangle ABC \sim \triangle AQR$ ($\angle BAC = \angle RAQ$, $\angle CBA = \angle ARC = \angle ARQ$).
So we have $\dfrac{CA}{CB} = \dfrac{AQ}{QR}$.

In other hand, $\triangle AQR$ is congruent to $\triangle RPB$ ($\angle QAR = \angle CAB = \angle PRB$, $\angle RBP = \angle CBA = \angle ARQ$, $AR = EB$).

Thus we have $AQ = PR$. Then we have $\dfrac{CA}{CB} = \dfrac{PR}{QR}$. We then know that equation (1) is true and we are done.

BASIC KNOWLEDGE

Menelaus' Theorem

A line intersects the sides or extension of the sides AB, BC and CA of $\triangle ABC$ at X, Y and Z, respectively. The following holds $\dfrac{AX}{BX} \cdot \dfrac{BY}{CY} \cdot \dfrac{CZ}{AZ} = 1$.

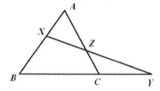

Proof:
Method 1:
Draw $CG // XY$ to meet AB at G.

Since $\triangle BYX \sim \triangle BCG$, we have $\dfrac{BY}{CY} = \dfrac{BX}{GX}$ (1)

Since $\triangle AGC \sim \triangle AXZ$, we have $\dfrac{CZ}{AZ} = \dfrac{GX}{AX}$ (2)

(1) × (2): $\dfrac{BY}{CY} \times \dfrac{CZ}{AZ} = \dfrac{BX}{GX} \times \dfrac{GX}{AX} = \dfrac{BX}{AX}$, or $\dfrac{AX}{BX} \cdot \dfrac{BY}{CY} \cdot \dfrac{CZ}{AZ} = 1$

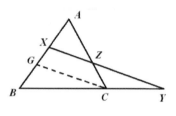

Method 2: Connect AY and CX.

$\dfrac{AX}{BX} = \dfrac{S_{\triangle AXY}}{S_{\triangle BXY}}$ (1)

$\dfrac{BY}{CY} = \dfrac{S_{\triangle BXY}}{S_{\triangle CXY}}$ (2)

$\dfrac{CZ}{AZ} = \dfrac{S_{\triangle CXY}}{S_{\triangle AXY}}$ (3)

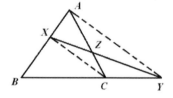

(1) × (2) × (3): $\dfrac{AX}{BX} \cdot \dfrac{BY}{CY} \cdot \dfrac{CZ}{AZ} = 1$.

We can use the following method to memorize this theorem.

$\triangle ABC$ is called the Menelaus' triangle and XYZ is called the transversal line. Point X is on AB, Y is on BC, and Z is on CA.

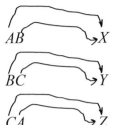 AX/BX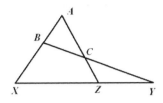

BY/CY

CZ/AZ

Multiplying them together we have: $\dfrac{AX}{BX}\cdot\dfrac{BY}{CY}\cdot\dfrac{CZ}{AZ}=1$.

(a). If the Menelaus' triangle is $\triangle AXZ$, points are B, Y, and C, we have

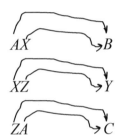 AB/XB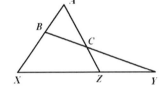

XY/ZY

ZY/AY

Multiplying them together we have: $\dfrac{AB}{XB}\cdot\dfrac{XY}{ZY}\cdot\dfrac{ZC}{AC}=1$.

(b). If the Menelaus' triangle is $\triangle CYZ$, points are B, X, and A, we have

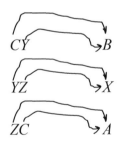 CY/YB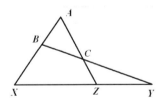

YX/ZX

ZA/CA

Multiplying them together we have: $\dfrac{CY}{YB}\cdot\dfrac{YX}{ZX}\cdot\dfrac{ZA}{CA}=1$.

(c). If the Menelaus' triangle is △BXY, points are A, Z, and C, we have

BX → A		BA/XA
XY → Z		XZ/YZ
YB → C		YC/BC

Multiplying them together we have: $\dfrac{BA}{XA} \cdot \dfrac{XZ}{YZ} \cdot \dfrac{YC}{BC} = 1$.

Note that there are two cases for three transversal points:

Case I: Two of them are on the sides of the Menelaus' triangle and one is on the extension of the third side.

Case II: All of the three points are on the extension of the sides of the Menelaus' triangle.

Converse of Menelaus' Theorem

If $\dfrac{AX}{BX} \cdot \dfrac{BY}{CY} \cdot \dfrac{CZ}{AZ} = 1$, then X, Y and Z are collinear. Three distinct points on a plane are said to be collinear if they lie on a straight line.

Ceva's Theorem

A Cevian line is specified by naming the vertex it passes through along with the point at which it intersects the opposite sideline.

Three distinct lines on a plane are said to be concurrent if they all go through the same point.

The cevians AX, BY and CZ of △ABC are concurrent if and

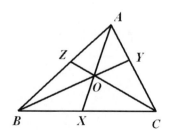

only if $\dfrac{AZ}{ZB} \cdot \dfrac{BX}{XC} \cdot \dfrac{CY}{YA} = 1$.

Proof:
Method 1:
Draw $GH // BC$ through A to meet the extensions of CZ and BY at G and H, respectively.
Then we have

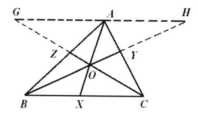

$\dfrac{CY}{AY} = \dfrac{BC}{AH}$; $\dfrac{AZ}{BZ} = \dfrac{GA}{BC}$; $\dfrac{BX}{AH} = \dfrac{OX}{AO}$; and $\dfrac{CX}{AG} = \dfrac{OX}{AO}$

$\therefore \dfrac{BX}{CX} = \dfrac{AH}{GA}$.

$\therefore \dfrac{CY}{AY} \cdot \dfrac{AZ}{BZ} \cdot \dfrac{BX}{CX} = \dfrac{BC}{AH} \cdot \dfrac{GA}{BC} \cdot \dfrac{AH}{GA} = 1$

Method 2:
We apply Menelaus' Theorem.
The Menelaus' triangle is $\triangle ABX$ and the transversal points are Z, C, and O.

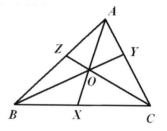

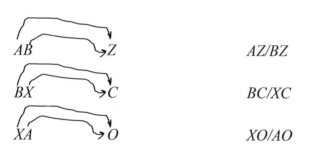

Multiplying them together, we have: $\dfrac{AZ}{BZ} \cdot \dfrac{BC}{XC} \cdot \dfrac{XO}{AO} = 1$ \hfill (1)

The Menelaus' triangle is $\triangle ACX$ and the transversal points are Y, B, and O.

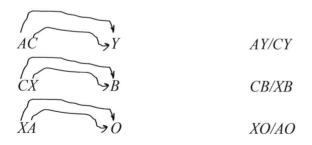

Multiplying them together we have: $\dfrac{AY}{CY} \cdot \dfrac{CB}{XB} \cdot \dfrac{XO}{AO} = 1$ (2)

(1) ÷ (2): $\dfrac{AZ}{BZ} \cdot \dfrac{BC}{CX} \cdot \dfrac{XO}{AO} = \dfrac{AY}{CY} \cdot \dfrac{CB}{XB} \cdot \dfrac{XO}{AO}$ or $\dfrac{AZ}{ZB} \cdot \dfrac{BX}{XC} \cdot \dfrac{CY}{YA} = 1$.

Method 3:
Let $S_{\triangle AOB} = S_1$, $S_{\triangle BOC} = S_2$, $S_{\triangle COA} = S_3$.
Then

$\dfrac{AZ}{ZB} = \dfrac{S_3}{S_2}$ (1)

$\dfrac{BX}{XC} = \dfrac{S_1}{S_3}$ (2)

$\dfrac{CY}{YA} = \dfrac{S_2}{S_1}$ (3)

(1) × (2) × (3): $\dfrac{AZ}{ZB} \cdot \dfrac{BX}{XC} \cdot \dfrac{CY}{YA} = 1$.

Note: Among the three points X, Y, and Z, there are an even number (0 or 2) of them on the extension of the sides the Menelaus' triangle.

Converse of Ceva' Theorem

If $\dfrac{AZ}{ZB} \cdot \dfrac{BX}{XC} \cdot \dfrac{CY}{YA} = 1$, then X, Y and Z are concurrent.

Ceva's theorem and its converse provide us with a criterion to determine whether three given cevians are concurrent.

A rule of thumb for these problems is to use Menelaus' Theorem for collinearity and Ceva's Theorem for concurrency.

Problem Proving Using Menelaus' Or Ceva

Example 1. As shown in the figure, $\triangle ABC$ is divided into three smaller triangles (with the areas of 5, 8, and 10 as indicated in the figure) and one quadrilateral of the area x. Find x.

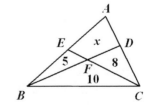

Solution: 022.

Applying Menelaus' Theorem to $\triangle CAE$ with the transversal line DBF: $\dfrac{CD}{AD} \cdot \dfrac{AB}{EB} \cdot \dfrac{EF}{CF} = 1$

$\Rightarrow \quad \dfrac{18}{x+5} \cdot \dfrac{23+x}{15} \cdot \dfrac{5}{10} = 1 \Rightarrow \quad x = 22$.

Example 2. As shown in the figure, in $\triangle ABC$, $AG = \dfrac{1}{3}AB$, $BE = \dfrac{1}{3}BC$, $CF = \dfrac{1}{3}CA$.
AN: NL: $LE = a$:b:c.
Find $a + b + c$.

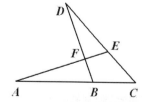

Solution: 010.
Let $AN = x$, $NL = y$, $LE = z$.
Applying Menelaus' Theorem to $\triangle AEB$ with the transversal points N, C, and G:
$\dfrac{AN}{EN} \cdot \dfrac{EC}{BC} \cdot \dfrac{BG}{AG} = 1$, or $\dfrac{x}{y+z} \cdot \dfrac{2}{3} \cdot \dfrac{2}{1} = 1 \Rightarrow \quad 4x = 3y + 3z$ (1)

Applying Menelaus' Theorem to $\triangle AEC$ with the transversal points L, B, and F:
$\dfrac{AL}{EL} \cdot \dfrac{EB}{CB} \cdot \dfrac{CF}{AF} = 1$, or $\dfrac{x+y}{z} \cdot \dfrac{1}{3} \cdot \dfrac{1}{2} = 1 \Rightarrow \quad x + y = 6z$ (2)

Solving (1) and (2): $x = y = 3z$.
AN: NL: $LE = 3 : 3 : 1$. $a + b + c = 10$.

Example 3. As shown in the figure, $\dfrac{AB}{BC} = \dfrac{DF}{FB} = 2$. $\dfrac{DE}{EC} + \dfrac{AF}{FE} = \dfrac{m}{n}$, where m and n are positive integers relatively prime. Find $m + n$.

Solution: 035.

Applying Menelaus' Theorem to $\triangle DBC$ with the transversal points F, A and E:
$\dfrac{DF}{BF} \cdot \dfrac{BA}{CA} \cdot \dfrac{CE}{DE} = 1 \quad \Rightarrow \quad \dfrac{DE}{CE} = \dfrac{DF}{BF} \cdot \dfrac{BA}{CA} = \dfrac{2}{1} \cdot \dfrac{2}{3} = \dfrac{4}{3}$

Applying Menelaus' Theorem to $\triangle ACE$ with the transversal points B, D and F: $\dfrac{AB}{CB} \cdot \dfrac{CD}{ED} \cdot \dfrac{EF}{AF} = 1 \Rightarrow \dfrac{AF}{EF} = \dfrac{DC}{ED} \cdot \dfrac{AB}{CB} = \dfrac{7}{4} \cdot \dfrac{2}{1} = \dfrac{7}{2}$.

$$\frac{DE}{EC} + \frac{AF}{FE} = \frac{4}{3} + \frac{7}{2} = \frac{29}{6}.$$
$m + n = 35$.

Example 4. As shown in the figure, ABC is a triangle, F, D, and E are points on AB, BC and CA respectively, and M is the point of intersection of AD, BE, and CF. Show that

$$\frac{AE}{CE} + \frac{AF}{BF} = \frac{AM}{MD}.$$

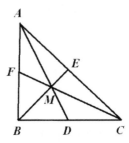

Proof:
Applying Menelaus' Theorem to $\triangle ABD$ with the transversal points F, C, M:

$$\frac{AF}{BF} \cdot \frac{BC}{DC} \cdot \frac{DM}{AM} = 1 \quad \Rightarrow \quad \frac{AF}{BF} = \frac{DC}{BC} \cdot \frac{AM}{DM} \qquad (1)$$

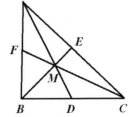

Applying Menelaus' Theorem to $\triangle ACD$ with the transversal points E, B, M:

$$\frac{AE}{CE} \cdot \frac{CB}{DB} \cdot \frac{DM}{AM} = 1 \quad \Rightarrow \quad \frac{AE}{CE} = \frac{DB}{CB} \cdot \frac{AM}{DM} \qquad (2)$$

(1) + (2): $\dfrac{AF}{BF} + \dfrac{AE}{CE} = \dfrac{AM}{MD}(\dfrac{DC}{BC} + \dfrac{DB}{CB}) = \dfrac{AM}{MD}.$

Example 5. (1988 AIME) Let P be an interior point $\triangle ABC$ and extend lines from the vertices through P to the opposite sides. Let a, b, c, and d denote the lengths of the segments indicated in the figure. Find the product abc if $a + b + c = 43$ and $d = 3$.

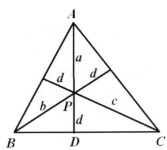

Solution: 441.
The official solution used the area method to solve this problem. We here use a different method.
We label E and F as shown in the figure.
Applying Menelaus' Theorem to $\triangle AFP$ and transversal line BCD:

$$\frac{AB}{FB} \cdot \frac{FC}{PC} \cdot \frac{PD}{AD} = 1$$

Applying Menelaus' Theorem to ΔBFP and transversal line ACE:

$\dfrac{BA}{FA} \cdot \dfrac{FC}{PC} \cdot \dfrac{PE}{BE} = 1$

$\therefore \dfrac{FB}{AB} = \dfrac{c+d}{c} \cdot \dfrac{d}{a+d}$, $\dfrac{AF}{AB} = \dfrac{c+d}{c} \cdot \dfrac{d}{b+d}$.

$\therefore \dfrac{c+d}{c}\left(\dfrac{d}{a+d} + \dfrac{d}{b+d}\right) = \dfrac{FB}{AB} + \dfrac{AF}{AB} = 1$.

$\dfrac{d}{a+d} + \dfrac{d}{b+d} = \dfrac{c}{c+d}$.

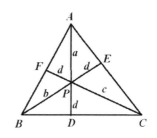

Since $d = 3$, $3(b + 3)(c + 3) + 3(a + 3)(c + 3) = c(a + 3)(b + 3)$.
$abc = 9(a + b + c) + 54 = 441$.

Example 6. (1983 China High School Math Contest) AC and BD are two diagonals of quadrilateral $ABCD$. Extensions of AB and DC meets at E and BC and AD meet at F. The extension of AC meets EF at G. Show that $EG = GF$.

Proof:

We know that DBD/EF. We have $\dfrac{AB}{BE} = \dfrac{AD}{DF}$ (1)

By Ceva's Theorem, $\dfrac{AB}{BE} \cdot \dfrac{EG}{GF} \cdot \dfrac{FD}{DA} = 1$ (2)

From (1) and (2), we get $\dfrac{EG}{GF} = 1$ that is $EG = GF$.

Example 7. In right ΔABC, P and Q are on BC and AC, respectively, such that $CP/CQ = 2$. Through the point of intersection, R, of AP and BQ, a line is drawn also passing through C and meeting AB at S. PQ extended meets AB at T. If the hypotenuse $AB = 10$ and $AC = 8$, find TS.

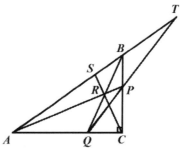

Solution: 024.
In right ΔABC, hypotenuse $AB = 10$, and $AC = 8$, so $BC = 6$.
In ΔABC, since AP, BQ, and CS are concurrent, $AQ/QC \times CP/PB \times BS/SA = 1$, by Ceva's Theorem.

Substituting, 6/2 × 2/4 × BS/(10 − BS) = 1, and BS = 4.
Now consider $\triangle ACB$ with transversal QPT.
AQ/QC × CP/BP × BT/AT = 1 (Menelaus' Theorem).
This may be restated as (AQ)(CP)(BT) = (QC)(PB)(AT).
Substituting, (6)(2)(BT) = (2)(4)(BT + 10).
Then BT = 20, and TS = 24.

Problem Solving Using Menelaus' Or Ceva With Similar Triangles

Example 8. ABCD is a parallelogram with bisects $\angle ADC = 128°$. M and N are two distinct points in AB and BC, respectively. AM = NC. AN and CM meet at Q. Find $\angle ADQ$.

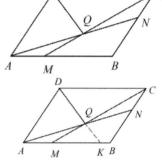

Solution: 064.
Extend DQ to meet AB at K.
Applying Menelaus' Theorem to $\triangle CBM$ with the transversal points N, A, and Q:

$$\frac{CN}{BN} \times \frac{BA}{MA} \times \frac{MQ}{CQ} = 1 \qquad (1)$$

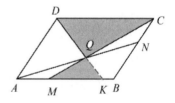

We see that $\triangle MKQ \sim \triangle CDQ$. So $\dfrac{MQ}{QC} = \dfrac{MK}{DC}$ (2)

Substituting (2) into (1): $\dfrac{CN}{BN} \times \dfrac{BA}{MA} \times \dfrac{MK}{DC} = 1$ (3)

Note that CN = AM and BA = DC, (3) becomes: MK = BN
    $\Rightarrow$ MK + AM = BN + CN.
Therefore AK = BC = AD $\Rightarrow$ $\angle ADK = \angle AKD$.
Since AB // DC, $\angle AKD = \angle KDC$.
$\angle ADQ = \angle ADK = 128° \div 2 = 64°$.

Example 9. (2009 AIME I) Triangle ABC has AC = 450 and BC = 300. Points K and L are located on AC and AB respectively so that AK = CK, and CL is the angle bisector of angle C. Let P be the point of intersection of BK and CL, and let M be the point on line BK for which K is the midpoint of PM. If AM = 180, find LP.

Solution: 072.

(our new solution):

Triangle $\triangle AKM \cong \triangle CKP$ (SAS). So $CP = AM = 180$.

Applying Menelaus' Theorem to $\triangle ACL$ with the transversal points $K, P,$ and B:

$$\frac{AK}{CK} \times \frac{CP}{LP} \times \frac{LB}{AB} = 1 \quad \Rightarrow \quad \frac{180}{LP} \times \frac{LB}{AB} = 1 \qquad (1)$$

By the angle bisector theorem,

$$\frac{CA}{AL} = \frac{CB}{LB} \quad \Rightarrow \quad \frac{450}{LB} = \frac{300}{AB-LB} \quad \Rightarrow \quad \frac{LB}{AB} = \frac{2}{5} \qquad (2)$$

Substituting (2) into (1): $\frac{2}{5} \times \frac{180}{LP} = 1 \Rightarrow \quad LP = 180 \times \frac{2}{5} = 72$.

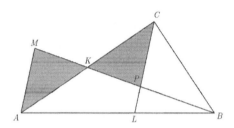 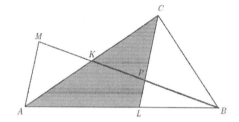

Example 10. (USAMO modified) Let ABC be a triangle with side lengths 6, 8, and 12 and let ω be its incircle with center I. Denote by $D_1, E_1,$ and F the points where ω is tangent to sides $BC, AC,$ and AB respectively. Denote by D_2 and E_2 the points on sides BC and AC, respectively, such that $CD_2 = BD_1$ and $CE_2 = AE_1$, and denote by P the point of intersection of segments AD_2 and BE_2. Circle ω intersects segment AD_2 at two points, the closer of which to the vertex A is denoted by Q. $Q, I,$ and D_1 are collinear. Prove that $AQ = D_2P$.

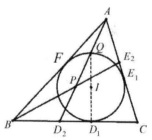

Solution:
Let $AB = 12, BC = 8,$ and $CA = 6$.
$BF + AF = 12$, $AE_1 + CE_1 = 6$, $BD_1 + CD_1 = 8$.
Noting that $CD_2 = BD_1$ or $BD_2 = CD_1$ and $CE_2 = AE_1$ or $AE_2 = CE_1$.
We have $CD_2 = BD_1 = 6$, and $CE_2 = AE_1 = 4$. So $CD_1 = 1$ and $BF = 7, AF = 5, BD_2 = 1$.

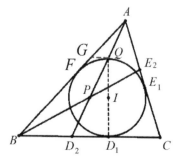

135

Draw $QG \parallel BC$ and meets AB at G. Since QD_1 is the diameter, GQ is the tangent to the circle. Let $GQ = GF = x$.

$$\frac{AQ}{AD_2} = \frac{x}{BD_2} = \frac{AG}{AB} = \frac{AF-x}{12} \Rightarrow \frac{x}{1} = \frac{5-x}{12} = \frac{5}{13} \Rightarrow x = \frac{5}{13}.$$

So $\dfrac{AQ}{AD_2} = \dfrac{\frac{5}{13}}{1} = \dfrac{5}{13}$ \hfill (1)

Applying Menelaus' Theorem to $\triangle AD_2C$ with the transversal points P, B, E_2:

$$\frac{AP}{D_2P} \times \frac{D_2B}{CB} \times \frac{CE_2}{AE_2} = 1 \Rightarrow \frac{AP}{D_2P} \times \frac{1}{8} \times \frac{5}{1} = 1 \Rightarrow \frac{AP}{D_2P} = \frac{8}{5}.$$

$$\frac{AP}{D_2P} = \frac{8}{5} = \frac{AD_2 - D_2P}{D_2P} = \frac{AD_2}{D_2P} - 1 \Rightarrow \frac{8}{5} = \frac{AD_2}{D_2P} - 1 \Rightarrow \frac{AD_2}{D_2P} = \frac{13}{5} \quad (2)$$

(1) × (2): $AQ = D_2P$.

Problem Solving Using Menelaus' Or Ceva With Area

Example 11. As shown in the figure on the right, $\triangle ABC$ with the area of 40 square units is divided into three smaller triangles and one quadrilateral by lines drawn from two vertices through a common interior point. Find the areas of quadrilateral $AEFD$ if $AE = BE$ and $\dfrac{AD}{DC} = \dfrac{2}{3}$.

Solution: 011.
Applying Menelaus' Theorem to $\triangle AEC$ with the transversal points B, F, and D:

$$\frac{AB}{EB} \times \frac{EF}{CF} \times \frac{CD}{AD} = 1 \Rightarrow \frac{2}{1} \times \frac{EF}{CF} \times \frac{3}{2} = 1 \Rightarrow \frac{EF}{CF} = \frac{1}{3}.$$

$EF = \dfrac{1}{3} CF = \dfrac{1}{4} EC$.

$S_{\triangle EBC} = \dfrac{1}{2} S_{\triangle ABC} = \dfrac{40}{2} = 20$. $S_{\triangle EBF} = \dfrac{1}{4} S_{\triangle EBC} = 5$, $S_{\triangle ADB} = \dfrac{2}{5} S_{\triangle ABC} = 16$.

$S_{AEFD} = S_{\triangle ADB} - S_{\triangle EBF} = 16 - 5 = 11.$

Example 12. In $\triangle ABC$, F, D, E are points on AB, BC, CA respectively such that $\frac{BD}{DC} = \frac{CE}{EA} = \frac{AF}{FB} = \frac{1}{2}$. A_1, B_1, and C_1 are the intersection points of the lines CF and BE, AD and CF, BE and CF, respectively. Suppose the area of $\triangle ABC$ is $S_{\triangle ABC}$ and the area of $\triangle A_1B_1C_1$ is $S_{\triangle A_1B_1C_1}$, $\frac{S_{\triangle A_1B_1C_1}}{S_{\triangle ABC}} = \frac{m}{n}$, where m and n are positive integers relatively prime. Find $m + n$.

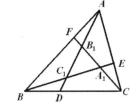

Solution: 008.

Applying Menelaus' Theorem to $\triangle ABD$ with the transversal points F, C, and B_1.

$$\frac{AF}{BF} \cdot \frac{BC}{CD} \cdot \frac{DB_1}{AB_1} = 1 \quad \Rightarrow \quad \frac{1}{2} \cdot \frac{3}{2} \cdot \frac{DB_1}{AB_1} = 1$$

Thus $\frac{AB_1}{B_1D} = \frac{3}{4}$ $\quad \Rightarrow \quad \frac{AB_1}{AD} = \frac{3}{7}$ $\quad \Rightarrow \quad \frac{S_{\triangle AB_1C}}{S_{\triangle ADC}} = \frac{3}{7}$

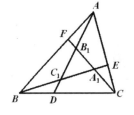

We know that $\frac{S_{\triangle ADC}}{S_{\triangle ABC}} = \frac{DC}{BC} = \frac{2}{3}$. So

$$\frac{S_{\triangle AB_1C}}{S_{\triangle ABC}} = \frac{S_{\triangle AB_1C}}{S_{\triangle ADC}} \cdot \frac{S_{\triangle ADC}}{S_{\triangle ABC}} = \frac{3}{7} \cdot \frac{2}{3} = \frac{6}{21} = \frac{2}{7}.$$

Similarly, $\frac{S_{\triangle BC_1A}}{S_{\triangle ABC}} = \frac{2}{7}$. $\quad \frac{S_{\triangle CA_1B}}{S_{\triangle ABC}} = \frac{2}{7}$.

Therefore $\frac{S_{\triangle A_1B_1C_1}}{S_{\triangle ABC}} = \frac{S_{\triangle ABC} - S_{\triangle AB_1C} - S_{\triangle BC_1A} - S_{\triangle CA_1B}}{S_{\triangle ABC}} = 1 - 3 \times \frac{2}{7} = \frac{1}{7}$. $m + n = 008$.

Example 13. In triangle ABC, M and N are trisection points of AC (with M closer to A), and X and Y are trisection points of BC (with Y closer to C). Connect BM, BN, and AY to form a quadrilateral $SRNM$ as shown in the figure. Find $m + n$ if $\frac{S_{SRNM}}{S_{\triangle ABC}} = \frac{m}{n}$, m and n are positive integers relatively prime.

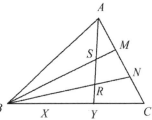

Solution: 047.

Applying Menelaus' Theorem to $\triangle BMC$ with the transversal points S, A, and Y:

$$\frac{BS}{MS} \times \frac{MA}{CA} \times \frac{CY}{BY} = 1 \quad \Rightarrow \quad \frac{BS}{MS} \times \frac{1}{3} \times \frac{1}{2} = 1 \quad \Rightarrow \quad \frac{BS}{MS} = 6.$$

Thus $\dfrac{BS}{BM} = \dfrac{6}{7}$.

Applying Menelaus' Theorem to $\triangle BNC$ with the transversal points R, A, and Y:

$$\frac{BR}{NR} \times \frac{NA}{CA} \times \frac{CY}{BY} = 1 \quad \Rightarrow \quad \frac{BR}{NR} \times \frac{2}{3} \times \frac{1}{2} = 1 \quad \Rightarrow \quad \frac{BR}{NR} = 3.$$

Thus $\dfrac{BR}{BN} = \dfrac{3}{4}$.

$$\frac{S_{\triangle BSR}}{S_{\triangle BMN}} = \frac{\frac{1}{2} BS \times BR \times \sin \angle SBR}{\frac{1}{2} BM \times BN \times \sin \angle MBC} = \frac{BS \times BR}{BM \times BN} = \frac{6 \times 3}{7 \times 4} = \frac{9}{14}$$

So $\dfrac{S_{SRNM}}{S_{\triangle BMN}} == \dfrac{5}{14}$ (1)

We also have $\dfrac{S_{\triangle BMN}}{S_{\triangle ABC}} = \dfrac{MN}{AB} = \dfrac{1}{3}$ (2)

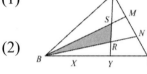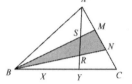

$(1) \times (2)$: $\dfrac{S_{SRNM}}{S_{\triangle ABC}} = \dfrac{\frac{5}{14}}{\frac{1}{3}} = \dfrac{5}{42}$.

The answer is $5 + 42 = 47$.

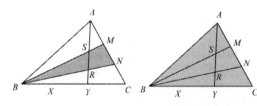

Example 14 (IMO) Let A, B, C, and D be distinct points on a line, in that order. The circles with diameters AC and BD intersect at X and Y. XY meets BC at Z. P is an arbitrary point on the line XY but not on AD. CP intersects the circle with diameter AC again at M, and BP intersects the other circle again at N. Prove that the lines AM, DN, and XY are concurrent.

Solution:
Let E be the point of intersection of AM and XY.
Line EMA intersects the three sides of $\triangle PZC$.
Applying Menelaus' Theorem:

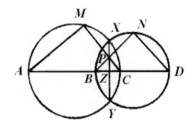

$$1 = \frac{PE}{ZE} \cdot \frac{AZ}{AC} \cdot \frac{CM}{PM} = \frac{PE}{ZE} \cdot \frac{CM}{AC} \cdot \frac{AZ}{PM}. \qquad (1)$$

We know that $\angle AMC = 90° = \angle PZC$, $\angle PZB = 90° = \angle BND$

$\therefore \triangle CAM \sim \triangle CPZ$, $\triangle BDN \sim \triangle BPZ$.

$\therefore \dfrac{CM}{AC} = \dfrac{CZ}{PC}$, $\dfrac{BN}{BD} = \dfrac{BZ}{BP}$.

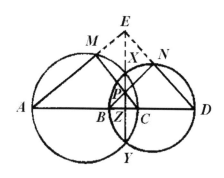

We know that $AZ \cdot CZ = XZ \cdot YZ = BZ \cdot DZ$ and $MP \cdot PC = XP \cdot PY = BP \cdot PN$.

$$\therefore \frac{CM}{AC} \cdot \frac{AZ}{PM} = \frac{AZ}{MP} \cdot \frac{CZ}{PC} = \frac{BZ}{BP} \cdot \frac{DZ}{PN} = \frac{BN}{BD} \cdot \frac{DZ}{PN}. \qquad (2)$$

Substituting (2) into (1): $1 = \dfrac{PE}{EZ} \cdot \dfrac{BN}{BD} \cdot \dfrac{DZ}{PN} = \dfrac{PE}{EZ} \cdot \dfrac{DZ}{BD} \cdot \dfrac{BN}{PN}$.

By the converse of Menelaus' Theorem, we know that E, N, D are collinear. Therefore AM, DN, and XY are concurrent.

Problem Solving Using Menelaus' Or Ceva With Angle Bisect Theorem

Example 15. In triangle ABC, $AB = nAC$. AP is the angle bisector of $\angle A$. $BP \perp AP$. AP and BC meet at Q. Show that $PQ:QA = (n-1):2$.

Proof:
Extend BP and AC to meet at D. Since AP is the angle bisector of $\angle BAC$ and $BP \perp AP$, $\therefore AD = AB$, $PD = PB$.
Applying Menelaus' Theorem to $\triangle DAP$ with the transversal line CQB:
$\dfrac{DC}{AC} \cdot \dfrac{AQ}{PQ} \cdot \dfrac{PB}{DB} = 1$

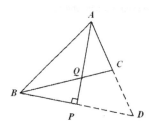

$\therefore \dfrac{PQ}{QA} = \dfrac{PB}{DB} \cdot \dfrac{DC}{AC} = \dfrac{1}{2} \cdot \dfrac{AD - AC}{AC} = \dfrac{1}{2} \cdot \dfrac{AB - AC}{AC} = \dfrac{1}{2} \cdot \dfrac{(n-1)AC}{AC}$

Thus $PQ:QA = (n-1):2$.

Problem Solving Using Menelaus' Or Ceva With Other Theorems

Example 16. As shown in the figure, ABC is a triangle with $\angle B = 90°$, $BC = 3$cm and $AB = 4$cm. D is a point on AC such that $AD = 1$ cm, and E is the midpoint of AB. join D and E, and extend DE to meet CB extended at F. Find BF.

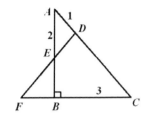

Solution: 001.
Consider $\triangle ABC$. Then E, F and D are, respectively, transversal points on the sides AB, BC, and CA.
By Menelaus' theorem, $\dfrac{AE}{BE} \cdot \dfrac{BF}{CF} \cdot \dfrac{CD}{AD} = 1$. (i)

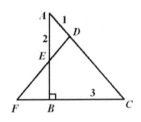

By assumption, $AE = BE = 2$, $AD = 1$, $BC = 3$, and $CF = BF + BC = BF + 3$. By Pythagoras' theorem, $AC = \sqrt{BC^2 + AB^2} = \sqrt{3^2 + 4^2} = 5$. and so $CO = AC - AD = 5 - 1 = 4$. Substituting these data into (i) gives
$\dfrac{2}{2} \cdot \dfrac{BF}{BF+3} \cdot \dfrac{4}{1} = 1$.
Solving for BF yields $BF = 1$.

Example 17. Show that three medians are concurrent of $\triangle ABC$.

Proof:
Suppose the medians BE and CF meet at O and D is the midpoint of BC.
Applying Menelaus' Theorem to $\triangle AFC$ with the transversal points B, O and E:
$\dfrac{AB}{FB} \cdot \dfrac{FO}{CO} \cdot \dfrac{CE}{AE} = 1$ (1)

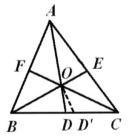

We know that $AB = 2BF$, $CE = EA$. So $2FO = OC$.
Connect AO and extend it to meet BC at D'.
Applying Menelaus' Theorem to $\triangle BCF$ with the transversal points D', O and A:
$\dfrac{BD'}{CD'} \cdot \dfrac{CO}{FO} \cdot \dfrac{FA}{BA} = 1$ (2)

We know that $OC = 2OF$, $AB = 2FA$. Thus (2) becomes: $BD' = CD'$. That is, D and D' are the same point. Therefore three medians are concurrent of $\triangle ABC$.

PROBLEMS

Problem 1. As shown in the figure, $BE = CD$ and $EF = DF$. Show that $\angle B = \angle ACB$.

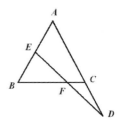

Problem 2. As shown in the figure, in $\triangle ABC$, D is the midpoint of BC. Extend DE to F to meet the extension of CA at F. Show that $\dfrac{AE}{BE} = \dfrac{AF}{CF}$.

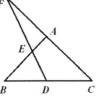

Problem 3. As shown in the figure, E and F are points on BC of triangle ABC such that $BE : EF : FC = 1 : 2 : 3$. The median BD meets AE and AF at M and N respectively and is divided into the lengths of x, y, z. $x:y:z = a:b:c$. Find $a + b + c$.

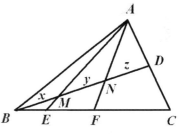

Problem 4. As shown in the figure, there is a convex quadrilateral $ABCD$. The lines DA and CB intersect at K, the lines AB and DC intersect at L, the lines AC and KL intersect at G, the lines DB and KL intersect at F. Prove that $\dfrac{KF}{FL} = \dfrac{KG}{GL}$.

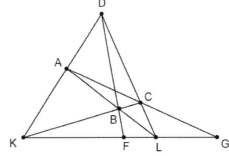

Problem 5. In triangle ABC, B_1 and B_2 are trisection points of AB (with B_1 closer to A), and C_1 and C_2 are trisection points of AC (with C_1 closer to A). Connect B_1C, B_2C, C_1B, and C_2B to form a quadrilateral $PQRS$ as shown in the figure. The area of quadrilateral $PQRS$ can be expressed as $\dfrac{m}{n}$, where m and n are positive integers relatively prime. Find $m + n$.

Problem 6. In $\triangle ABC$, O is a point of the median AD. The extensions of BO and CO meet AC and AB at E and F, respectively. Show that $EF // BC$.

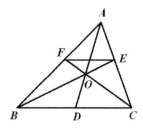

Problem 7. Prove that the altitudes of any triangle are concurrent. The point of intersection is called the orthocenter of the triangle.

Problem 8. (IMO Short List) The incircle of $\triangle ABC$ touches BC, CA, and AB at D, E, and F respectively. X is a point inside $\triangle ABC$ such that the incircle of $\triangle XBC$ touches BC at D also, and touches CX and XB at Y and Z, respectively. Prove that $EFZY$ is a cyclic quadrilateral.

Problem 9. As shown in the figure, the area of parallelogram $ABCD$ is 1. E and F are the

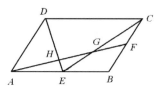

midpoints of *AB* and *BC*, respectively. *AF* meets *CE* at *G* and *DE* at *H*. The area of $\triangle$ *EGH* can be expressed as $\dfrac{m}{n}$, where *m* and *n* are positive integers relatively prime. Find $m + n$.

Problem 10. (2009 AIME) In parallelogram *ABCD*, point *M* is on *AB* so that $\dfrac{AM}{AB} = \dfrac{17}{1000}$, and point *N* is on *AD* so that $\dfrac{AN}{AD} = \dfrac{17}{2009}$. Let *P* be the point of intersection of *AC* and *MN*. Find $\dfrac{AC}{AP}$.

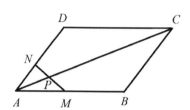

Problem 11. (USAMO) Let *ABC* be a triangle. A circle passing through *A* and *B* intersects segments *AC* and *BC* at *D* and *E*, respectively. Lines *AB* and *DE* intersect at *F* while lines *BD* and *CF* intersect at *M*. Prove that $MF = MC$ if and only if $MB \cdot MD = MC^2$.

Problem 12. (IMO) The diagonals *AC* and *CE* of the regular hexagon *ABCDEF* are divided by the inner points *M* and *N*, respectively, so that $AM / AC = CN / CE = r$. Determine *r* if *B*, *M*, *N* are collinear.

Problem 13. As shown in the figure, $\triangle ABC$ is divided into six smaller triangles with the areas of 40, 30, and 35 for three of them as indicated in the figure. Find the area of $\triangle ABC$.

Problem 14. In $\triangle ABC$, F, D, E are points on AB, BC, CA respectively such that $\frac{BD}{DC} = \frac{CE}{EA} = \frac{AF}{FB} = k > 1$. M, N, and P are the intersection points of the lines AD and BE, BE and CF, AD and CF, respectively. Suppose that the area of $\triangle ABC$ is $S_{\triangle ABC} = 1$, find the area of $\triangle MNP$.

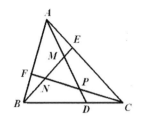

Problem 15. (1983 China High School Math Contest) The diagonals AC and BD of the quadrilateral $ABCD$ divide the quadrilateral $ABCD$ such that $S_{\triangle ABD} : S_{\triangle BCD} : S_{\triangle ABC} = 3:4:1$. M and N are points on AC and CD respectively, so that $AM / AC = CN / CD$. Show that M and N are midpoints of AC and CD respectively if B, M, N are collinear.

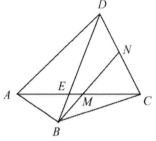

Problem 16. In $\triangle ABC$, CD is the altitude to AB and P is any point on DC, AP meets CB at Q, and BP meets CA at R. Prove that $m\angle RDC = m\angle QDC$.

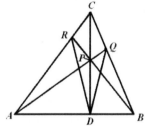

Problem 17. As shown in the figure, in $\triangle ABC$, the angle bisector of $\angle B$ meets CA at Q. The angle bisector of $\angle C$ meet AB at R. The exterior angle bisector of $\angle A$ meet the extension of BC at P. Show that P, Q, R are collinear.

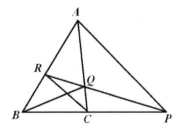

Problem 18. (IMO List) $\triangle ABC$ is an equilateral triangle. P is a point inside $\triangle ABC$. AP, BP, CP meet BC, CA, AB at A_1, B_1, C_1, respectively. Show that
$A_1 B_1 \cdot B_1 C_1 \cdot C_1 A_1 \geq A_1 B \cdot B_1 C \cdot C_1 A$.

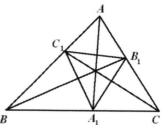

Problem 19. As shown in the figure, M is the midpoint of side BC of triangle ABC. $AB = 15$, and $AC = 20$. Points E and F are taken on AC and AB, respectively, and lines EF and AM intersect at G. $EG/GF = m/n$, where m and n are relatively prime integers. Find $m + n$ if $AE = 2AF$.

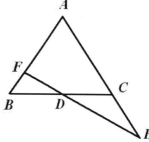

Problem 20. The length of a side of equilateral triangle ABC is a. D is the midpoint of BC. Through D we draw a line to meet AC and the extension of AC at F, and E, respectively. Find $\dfrac{1}{FA} + \dfrac{1}{EA}$ in terms of a.

SOLUTIONS

Problem 1. Proof:

Applying Menelaus' Theorem to $\triangle AED$ with the transversal points B, F and C:

$$\frac{AB}{EB} \cdot \frac{EF}{DF} \cdot \frac{DC}{AC} = 1 \quad (1)$$

We know that $BE = CD$, $EF = DF$.

(1) becomes: $\frac{AB}{AC} = 1 \quad \Rightarrow \quad AB = AC \quad \Rightarrow \angle B = \angle ACB.$

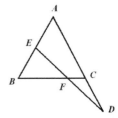

Problem 2. Proof:

Applying Menelaus' Theorem to $\triangle ABC$ with the transversal points at E, D, and F:

$$\frac{AE}{BE} \cdot \frac{BD}{CD} \cdot \frac{CF}{AF} = 1.$$

Since, $BD/CD = 1$. Thus $\frac{AE}{BE} \cdot \frac{CF}{AF} = 1 \quad \Rightarrow \quad \frac{AE}{BE} = \frac{AF}{CF}.$

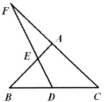

Problem 3. Solution: 021.

Applying Menelaus' Theorem to $\triangle BCD$ with the transversal points E, A, and M:

$\frac{BE}{CE} \cdot \frac{CA}{DA} \cdot \frac{DM}{BM} = 1$, or $\frac{1}{5} \cdot \frac{2}{1} \cdot \frac{y+z}{x} = 1 \quad \Rightarrow \quad 5x = 2y + 2z \quad (1)$

Applying Menelaus' Theorem to $\triangle BCD$ with the transversal points F, A, and N:

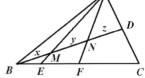

$\frac{BF}{CF} \cdot \frac{CA}{DA} \cdot \frac{DN}{BN} = 1$, or $\frac{3}{3} \cdot \frac{2}{1} \cdot \frac{z}{x+y} = 1 \quad \Rightarrow \quad 2z = x + y \quad (2)$

Solving (1) and (20: $x: y = 3: 4$ and $y:z = 8:7$.
Therefore $x : y : z = 6 : 8 : 7$. $a + b + c = 21$.

Problem 4. Proof:

Apply Ceva's theorem to triangle DKL and the point B, we have

$$\frac{DA}{AK} \cdot \frac{KF}{FL} \cdot \frac{LC}{CD} = 1 \quad (1)$$

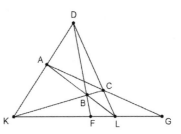

Apply Menelaus's theorem to triangle DKL and the line ACG,

we have $\frac{DA}{AK} \cdot \frac{KG}{GL} \cdot \frac{LC}{CD} = 1 \quad (2)$

146

Divide (1) by (2), the result follows.

Problem 5. Solution: 079.

Applying Menelaus' Theorem to $\triangle ABC_2$ with the transversal points B_1, S, and C:

$$\frac{AB_1}{BB_1} \times \frac{BS}{C_2S} \times \frac{C_2C}{AC} = 1 \Rightarrow \frac{1}{2} \times \frac{BS}{C_2S} \times \frac{1}{3} = 1 \Rightarrow \frac{BS}{C_2S} = 6 \quad (1)$$

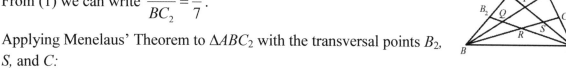

From (1) we can write $\dfrac{BS}{BC_2} = \dfrac{6}{7}$.

Applying Menelaus' Theorem to $\triangle ABC_2$ with the transversal points B_2, S, and C:

$$\frac{AB_2}{BB_2} \times \frac{BR}{C_2R} \times \frac{C_2C}{AC} = 1 \Rightarrow \frac{2}{1} \times \frac{BR}{C_2R} \times \frac{1}{3} = 1 \Rightarrow \frac{BR}{C_2R} = \frac{3}{2} \quad (2)$$

From (2) we can write $\dfrac{BR}{C_2B} = \dfrac{3}{5}$.

Applying Menelaus' Theorem to $\triangle ABC_1$ with the transversal points B_2, Q, and C:

$$\frac{AB_2}{BB_2} \times \frac{BQ}{C_1Q} \times \frac{C_1C}{CA} = 1 \Rightarrow \frac{2}{1} \times \frac{BQ}{C_1Q} \times \frac{2}{3} = 1 \Rightarrow \frac{BQ}{C_1Q} = \frac{3}{4} \quad (3)$$

From (3) we can write $\dfrac{BQ}{BC_1} = \dfrac{3}{7}$.

Applying Menelaus' Theorem to $\triangle ABC_1$ with the transversal points B_1, P, and C:

$$\frac{AB_1}{BB_1} \times \frac{BP}{C_1P} \times \frac{C_1C}{CA} = 1 \Rightarrow \frac{1}{2} \times \frac{BP}{C_1P} \times \frac{2}{3} = 1 \Rightarrow \frac{BP}{C_1P} = \frac{3}{1} \quad (4)$$

From (4) we can write $\dfrac{BP}{BC_1} = \dfrac{3}{4}$.

$$S_{PQRS} = S_{\triangle BPS} - S_{\triangle BQR} = \left(\frac{BP}{BC_1} \times \frac{BS}{BC_2} - \frac{BQ}{BC_1} \times \frac{BR}{BC_2}\right) \times S_{\triangle BC_1C_2} = \frac{9}{70}. \; m + n = 79.$$

Problem 6. Solution:

Since AD, BE, CF are concurrent, by Cevas Theorem,

$$\frac{AF}{FB} \cdot \frac{BD}{DC} \cdot \frac{CE}{EA} = 1.$$

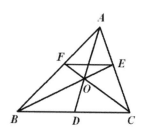

We know that $BD = CD$. $\therefore \dfrac{AF}{FB} = \dfrac{AE}{CE}$, $\therefore EF // BC$

Problem 7. Solution:

Case I (the orthocenter is inside the triangle):

$\triangle ANC \sim \triangle AMB$, and $\dfrac{AN}{MA} = \dfrac{AC}{AB}$. (1)

$\triangle BLA \sim \triangle BNC$, and $\dfrac{BL}{NB} = \dfrac{AB}{BC}$. (2)

$\triangle CMB \sim \triangle CLA$, and $\dfrac{CM}{LC} = \dfrac{BC}{AC}$. (3)

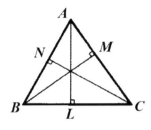

By multiplying (1), (2), and (3),

$$\dfrac{AN}{MA} \cdot \dfrac{BL}{NB} \cdot \dfrac{CM}{LC} = \dfrac{AC}{AB} \cdot \dfrac{AB}{BC} \cdot \dfrac{BC}{AC} = 1.$$

Thus, by Ceva's Theorem, altitudes *AL, BM,* and *CN* are concurrent.

Case II (the orthocenter is outside the triangle):
In $\triangle ABC$, *AL, BM,* and *CN* are altitudes.
$\triangle ANC \sim \triangle AMB$, and $AN/MA = AC/AB$ (1)
$\triangle BLA \sim \triangle BNC$, and $BL/NB = AB/BC$ (2)
$\triangle CMB \sim \triangle CLA$, and $CM/LC = BC/AC$ (3)

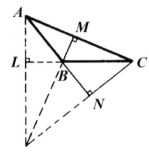

By multiplying (1), (2), and (3),
$(AN/MA)(BL/NB)(CM/LC) = (AC/AB)(AB/BC)(BC/AC) = 1$.
Thus, by Ceva's Theorem, altitudes *AL, BM,* and *CN* are concurrent.

Problem 8. Solution:

If *EF* is parallel to *BC*, *ABC* must be isosceles and *E, Y* are symmetric to *F, Z* with respect to *AD*, so the result follows. Now suppose that *EF* meets *BC* at *P*. By Menelaus's theorem, $\dfrac{AF}{FB} \cdot \dfrac{BP}{CP} \cdot \dfrac{CE}{EA} = 1$.

We know that
$AF = AE$, $XZ = XY$,
$CE = CD = CY$,
$BF = BD = BZ$,

So $1 = \dfrac{AF}{BF} \cdot \dfrac{BP}{CP} \cdot \dfrac{CE}{AE}$

$= \dfrac{BP}{BF} \cdot \dfrac{CE}{CP} = \dfrac{BP}{BZ} \cdot \dfrac{CY}{CP} = \dfrac{XZ}{BZ} \cdot \dfrac{BP}{CP} \cdot \dfrac{CY}{XY}$.

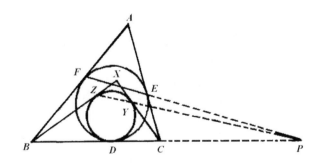

By the converse of Menelaus' Theorem, *Z, Y, P* are collinear.
Therefore $PE \cdot PF = PD^2 = PY \cdot PZ$, from which it follows that *EFZY* is a cyclic quadrilateral.

Problem 9. Solution: 031.
We have three methods solving this problem in the area method chapter. Here we are giving the 4th solution.
Extend *AF* and *DC* such that they meet at *P*. Connect *AC*.
We know that *AE* // *CP*. *G* is the centroid of $\triangle ABC$.
$AE : CP = EG : GC = 1 : 2$.

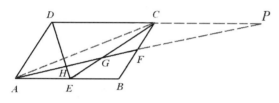
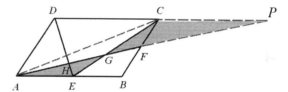

We know that $AE = \frac{1}{2} AB = \frac{1}{2} DC$.

So $CP = DC$.

Applying Menelaus' Theorem to $\triangle CDE$ with the transversal points *P, H,* and *G*:
$\frac{CP}{DP} \times \frac{DH}{EH} \times \frac{EG}{CG} = 1 \Rightarrow \frac{1}{2} \times \frac{DH}{EH} \times \frac{1}{2} = 1 \Rightarrow DH = 4HE$.

So we get $DE = 5HE$. $\frac{S_{\triangle EGH}}{S_{\triangle ECD}} = \frac{EG \times HE}{EC \times DE} = \frac{EG \times HE}{3EG \times 5HE} = \frac{1}{15}$.

We know that $S_{\triangle ECD} = \frac{1}{2} S_{ABCD} = \frac{1}{2}$. Thus $S_{\triangle EGH} = \frac{1}{30}$. $m + n = 31$.

Problem 10. Solution: (our new solution) 177.
Extend *CD* through *D* to meet the extension of *MN* at *Q*.
Triangle *QDN* is similar to triangle *MAN*. So
$\frac{DN}{AN} = \frac{QD}{AM} \Rightarrow \frac{1992y}{17y} = \frac{QD}{17x} \Rightarrow QD = 1992x$.

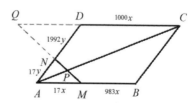

Applying Menelaus' Theorem to $\triangle CAD$ with the transversal points *P, N,* and *Q*:

$$\frac{CP}{AP} \times \frac{AN}{DN} \times \frac{DQ}{CQ} = 1 \Rightarrow \frac{CP}{AP} \times \frac{17y}{1992y} \times \frac{1992x}{2992x} = 1 \Rightarrow$$

$$\frac{CP}{AP} = \frac{2992}{17} = 176$$

or $76 = \dfrac{CP}{AP} = \dfrac{AC - AP}{AP} = \dfrac{AC}{AP} - 1 = 176 \Rightarrow$

$$\frac{AC}{AP} = 176 + 1 = 177.$$

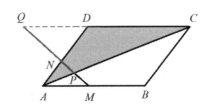

Problem 11. Solution:

Since quadrilateral $ABED$ is cyclic, $\angle CBD = \angle EAD$.

We now that AC, BM, FE meet at D. Applying Ceva's Theorem to triangle BCF and cevians BM, CA, FE gives

$$\frac{FA}{AB} \times \frac{BE}{EC} \times \frac{CM}{MF} = 1.$$

Therefore $MF = MC \Leftrightarrow \dfrac{FA}{AB} \times \dfrac{BE}{EC} = 1 \Leftrightarrow AE \parallel CF \Leftrightarrow \angle FCA =$

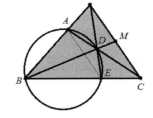

$\angle EAC = \angle MBC \Leftrightarrow \triangle MCD \sim \triangle MBC \Leftrightarrow$

$\dfrac{MB}{MC} = \dfrac{MC}{MD} \Leftrightarrow MB \cdot MD = MC^2.$

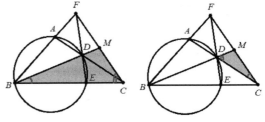

Problem 12. Solution: $r = \dfrac{\sqrt{3}}{3}$.

Join BE which intersects AC at P. Apply Menelaus' Theorem to the triangle EPC and the line BMN, one has

$$\frac{EB}{PB} \cdot \frac{PM}{CM} \cdot \frac{CN}{EN} = 1 \qquad (1)$$

Note that

(i) $\dfrac{CM}{MP} = \dfrac{1-r}{r - \dfrac{1}{2}} = \dfrac{2-2r}{2r-1};$

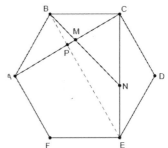

(ii) $PB = AB \cos \angle ABP = \dfrac{1}{2} AB = \dfrac{1}{4} BE \Rightarrow \dfrac{PB}{BE} = \dfrac{1}{4};$

(iii) $\dfrac{EN}{NC} = \dfrac{1-r}{r}$.

Substitute (i), (ii), (iii) into (1), $\dfrac{2-2r}{2r-1} \cdot \dfrac{1}{4} \cdot \dfrac{1-r}{r} = 1$, which implies $r = \dfrac{\sqrt{3}}{3}$.

Problem 13. Solution: 315.

$\dfrac{AF}{FB} = \dfrac{4}{3},\ \dfrac{DO}{OA} = \dfrac{1}{2}$

Applying Menelaus' Theorem to $\triangle ABD$ with the transversal line FCO:

$\dfrac{AF}{BF} \cdot \dfrac{BC}{DC} \cdot \dfrac{DO}{AO} = 1 \Rightarrow \dfrac{4}{3} \cdot \dfrac{BC}{DC} \cdot \dfrac{1}{2} = 1$.

$\therefore \dfrac{BC}{CD} = \dfrac{3}{2} \Rightarrow \dfrac{BC}{BD} = 3$.

$\therefore S_{\triangle ABC} = 3 S_{\triangle ABD} = 3(40 + 30 + 35) = 315$.

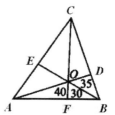

Problem 14. Solution:

We have $\dfrac{S_{\triangle ABD}}{S_{\triangle ABC}} = \dfrac{BD}{BC}$, $S_{\triangle ABC} = 1$, $\dfrac{S_{\triangle ABM}}{S_{\triangle ABD}} = \dfrac{AM}{AD}$.

So $S_{\triangle ABM} = \dfrac{AM}{AD} \cdot \dfrac{BD}{BC} = \dfrac{k}{k+1} \cdot \dfrac{AM}{AD}$ \hfill (1)

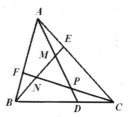

Applying Menelaus' Theorem to $\triangle ACD$ with the transversal points E, B and M:

$\dfrac{AE}{CE} \cdot \dfrac{CB}{DB} \cdot \dfrac{DM}{AM} = 1$.

Therefore $\dfrac{DM}{MA} = \dfrac{EC}{AE} \cdot \dfrac{BD}{BC} = \dfrac{k^2}{k+1}$.

$\dfrac{AD}{AM} = 1 + \dfrac{DM}{AM} = \dfrac{k^2 + k + 1}{k+1}$

Substituting this to (1): $S_{\triangle ABM} = \dfrac{k}{k^2 + k + 1}$

Similarly, we have $S_{\triangle BCN} = S_{\triangle ACP} = \dfrac{k}{k^2 + k + 1}$.

Therefore $S_{\triangle MNP} = S_{\triangle ABC} - (S_{\triangle ABM} + S_{\triangle BCN} + S_{\triangle ACP}) = \dfrac{(k-1)^2}{k^2 + k + 1}$.

Problem 15. Solution:

Let that $AM/AC = CN/CD = r$.

We know that $S_{\triangle ABD} : S_{\triangle BCD} : S_{\triangle ABC} = 3:4:1$. So we have

$\dfrac{BE}{BD} = \dfrac{1}{7}$ and $\dfrac{AE}{AC} = \dfrac{3}{7}$.

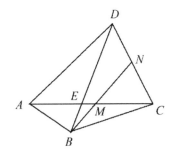

$\dfrac{EM}{MC} = \dfrac{AM - AE}{MC} = \dfrac{r - \dfrac{3}{7}}{1 - r}$.

Applying Menelaus' Theorem to $\triangle CDE$ with the transversal points N, B, and M:

$\dfrac{CN}{DN} \times \dfrac{DB}{EB} \times \dfrac{EM}{CM} = 1 \quad \Rightarrow \quad \dfrac{r}{1-r} \times \dfrac{7}{1} \times \dfrac{r - \dfrac{3}{7}}{1-r} = 1 \quad \Rightarrow \quad 6r^2 - r - 1 = 0$.

Solving we get: $r = \dfrac{1}{2}$ and $r = -\dfrac{1}{3}$ (ignored).

So $AM/AC = CN/CD = 1/2$ and that M and N are midpoints of AC and CD respectively.

Problem 16. Solution:

Extend DR and DQ through R and Q, respectively, to meet a line through C, parallel to AB, at points G and H, respectively

$\triangle CGR \sim \triangle ADR$, and $\dfrac{CR}{RA} = \dfrac{GC}{AD}$ \quad (1)

Similarly, $\triangle BDQ \sim \triangle CHQ$, and $\dfrac{BQ}{QC} = \dfrac{DB}{CH}$ \quad (2)

However, by Ceva's Theorem, in $\triangle ABC$, $\dfrac{CR}{RA} \cdot \dfrac{AD}{DB} \cdot \dfrac{BQ}{QC} = 1$ \quad (3)

By substituting (1) and (2) into (3), we get

$\dfrac{GC}{AD} \cdot \dfrac{AD}{DB} \cdot \dfrac{DB}{CH} = 1$, or $\dfrac{GC}{CH} = 1$. Thus, $GC = CH$.

Since CD is the perpendicular bisector of GH, $\triangle GCD \cong \triangle HCD$, and $m\angle GDC = m\angle HDC$, or $m\angle RDC = m\angle QDC$.

Problem 17. Proof:

We know that AP is the exterior angle bisector of $\angle BAC$.

Therefore $\dfrac{BP}{PC} = \dfrac{AB}{CA}$. (1)

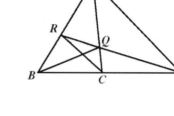

BQ is the angle bisector of $\angle ABC$. So $\dfrac{CQ}{QA} = \dfrac{BC}{AB}$. (2)

CR is the angle bisector of $\angle ACB$. So $\dfrac{AR}{RB} = \dfrac{CA}{BC}$. (3)

$(1) \times (2) \times (3)$: $\dfrac{BP}{PC} \cdot \dfrac{CQ}{QA} \cdot \dfrac{AR}{RB} = \dfrac{AB}{CA} \cdot \dfrac{BC}{AB} \cdot \dfrac{CA}{BC} = 1$.

Since R is on AB, Q is on CA, P is on the extension of BC, by the converse of Menelaus' Theorem, we know that P, Q, and R are collinear.

Problem 18. Proof:

By the Cosine Law we have

$(A_1B_1)^2 = (A_1C)^2 + (B_1C)^2 - A_1C \cdot B_1C$

$\geq 2A_1C \cdot B_1C - A_1C \cdot B_1C = A_1C \cdot B_1C$.

Similarly we have $(B_1C_1)^2 \geq B_1A \cdot C_1A$, $(C_1A_1)^2 \geq C_1B \cdot A_1B$.

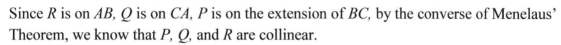

By Ceva's Theorem, we have $\dfrac{A_1C}{A_1B} \cdot \dfrac{B_1A}{B_1C} \cdot \dfrac{C_1B}{C_1A} = 1$.

So $A_1B_1 \cdot B_1C_1 \cdot C_1A_1 \geq \sqrt{A_1B_1 \cdot B_1C_1 \cdot C_1A_1} \geq \overline{A_1C \cdot B_1C \cdot B_1A \cdot C_1A \cdot C_1B \cdot A_1B}$

$= A_1B \cdot B_1C \cdot C_1A \cdot \sqrt{\dfrac{A_1C \cdot B_1A \cdot C_1B}{A_1B \cdot B_1C \cdot C_1A}} = A_1B \cdot B_1C \cdot C_1A$.

Problem 19. Solution: 005.

Extend BC and FE to meet at H. Applying Menelaus' theorem on $\triangle HFB$ with the transversal points G, A, and M:

$\dfrac{HG}{FG} \cdot \dfrac{FA}{BA} \cdot \dfrac{BM}{HM} = 1$ (1)

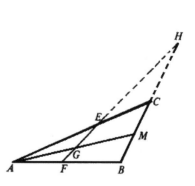

Using Menelaus' theorem on $\triangle HEC$ with the transversal points G, A, and M: $\dfrac{HG}{EG} \cdot \dfrac{EA}{CA} \cdot \dfrac{CM}{HM} = 1$ (2)

(1) ÷ (2) with $CM = BM$ and $EA = 2FA$: $\dfrac{EG}{FG} = 2\dfrac{BA}{CA} = 2 \cdot \dfrac{12}{16} = \dfrac{3}{2}$. $m + n = 5$.

Problem 20. Solution: $2/a$.

Applying Menelaus' Theorem to $\triangle BFD$ with the transversal points A, E and C:
$\dfrac{BA}{FA} \cdot \dfrac{FE}{DE} \cdot \dfrac{DC}{BC} = 1$

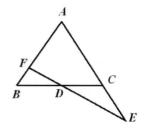

Since D is the midpoint of BC, $\quad \dfrac{BA}{FA} = \dfrac{2DE}{EF} \quad$ (1)

Applying Menelaus' Theorem to $\triangle CED$ with the transversal points A, F and B:
$\dfrac{CA}{EA} \cdot \dfrac{EF}{DF} \cdot \dfrac{DB}{CB} = 1 \quad \Rightarrow \quad \dfrac{CA}{EA} = \dfrac{2DF}{EF} \quad$ (2)

(1) + (2): $\dfrac{BA}{FA} + \dfrac{CA}{EA} = \dfrac{2DE + 2DF}{EF} = 2$. We know that $AB = AC = a$. So $\dfrac{1}{FA} + \dfrac{1}{EA} = \dfrac{2}{a}$.

Chapter 7 Algebraic Manipulation

BASIC KNOWLEDGE

Below is a list of useful equations to be aware of and know. They can all be derived through expanding or factoring.

Perfect square

$(x+y+z)^2 = x^2 + y^2 + z^2 + 2xy + 2xz + 2yz$

$x^2 + y^2 + z^2 - xy - yz - zx = \dfrac{1}{2}[(x-y)^2 + (y-z)^2 + (z-x)^2]$

$(x+y+z+w)^2 = x^2 + y^2 + z^2 + w^2 + 2xy + 2xz + 2xw + 2yz + 2yw + 2zw$

$(a_1 + a_2 + \cdots + a_n)^2$
$= a_1^2 + a_2^2 + \cdots + a_n^2 + 2a_1a_2 + 2a_1a_3 + \cdots + 2a_1a_n + 2a_2a_3 + \cdots + 2a_2a_n + \cdots + 2a_{n-1}a_n$

Difference and sum of two squares

$x^2 + y^2 = (x+y)^2 - 2xy$ $\qquad\qquad x^2 + y^2 = (x-y)^2 + 2xy$

$x^2 - y^2 = (x-y)(x+y)$

$x^4 + 4y^4 = (x^2 + 2xy + 2y^2)(x^2 - 2xy + 2y^2)$

Difference and sum of two cubes

$x^3 + y^3 = (x+y)(x^2 - xy + y^2)$

$x^3 - y^3 = (x-y)(x^2 + xy + y^2)$

$x^3 + y^3 + z^3 = (x+y+z)(x^2 + y^2 + z^2 - xy - yz - zx) + 3xyz$

$(x+y)^3 = x^3 + 3x^2y + 3xy^2 + y^3 = x^3 + y^3 + 3xy(x+y)$

$(x-y)^3 = x^3 - 3x^2y + 3xy^2 - y^3 = x^3 - y^3 - 3xy(x-y)$

$x^n - y^n = (x-y)(x^{n-1} + x^{n-2}y + \cdots + y^{n-1})$ for all n.

$x^n - y^n = (x+y)(x^{n-1} - x^{n-2}y + \ldots - y^{n-1})$ for all even n.

$x^n + y^n = (x+y)(x^{n-1} - x^{n-2}y + \ldots + y^{n-1})$ for all odd n.

Two Theorems

Theorem 1. Let $a_n = Ax^n + By^n$. Then $a_{n+2} = (x+y)a_{n+1} - xya_n$, n is positive integer.

Proof:

$$a_{n+2} = Ax^{n+2} + By^{n+2}$$
$$= (x+y)(Ax^{n+1} + By^{n+1}) - Ayx^{n+1} - Bxy^{n+1}$$
$$= (x+y)a_{n+1} - xy(Ax^n + By^n)$$
$$= (x+y)a_{n+1} - xya_n$$

Theorem 2. Let $a_n = Ax^n + By^n + Cz^n$. Then
$a_{n+3} = (x+y+z)a_{n+2} - (xy+yz+zx)a_{n+1} + xyza_n$, n is positive integer.

Proof:

$$a_{n+3} = Ax^{n+3} + By^{n+3} + Cz^{n+3}$$
$$= (x+y+z)(Ax^{n+2} + By^{n+2} + Cz^{n+2}) - Azx^{n+2} - Bxy^{n+2} - Cyz^{n+2} - Cxz^{n+2} - Bzy^{n+2} - Ayx^{n+2}$$
$$= (x+y+z)a_{n+2} - xy(Ax^{n+1} + By^{n+1}) - yz(By^{n+1} + Cz^{n+1}) - zx(Ax^{n+1} + Cz^{n+1})$$
$$= (x+y+z)a_{n+2} - (xy+yz+zx)(Ax^{n+1} + By^{n+1} + Cz^{n+1}) + Cxyz^{n+1} + Ayzx^{n+1} + Bzxy^{n+1}$$
$$= (x+y+z)a_{n+2} - (xy+yz+zx)a_{n+1} + xyza_n$$

EXAMPLES

Example 1. Find the value of $a^2 + b^2 + c^2 + d^2$ if
$(a+b+c-d)^2 + (a+b-c+d)^2 + (a-b+c+d)^2 + (-a+b+c+d)^2 = 2016$.

Solution: 504.

$$(a+b+c-d)^2 + (a+b-c+d)^2 + (a-b+c+d)^2 + (-a+b+c+d)^2$$
$$= [(a+b)+(c-d)]^2 + [(a+b)-(c-d)]^2 + [(c+d)+(a-b)]^2 + [(c+d)-(a-b)]^2$$
$$= 2(a+b)^2 + 2(c-d)^2 + 2(c+d)^2 + 2(a-b)^2$$
$$= 2[(a+b)^2 + (a-b)^2] + 2[(c+d)^2 + (c-d)^2]$$
$$= 2(2a^2 + 2b^2) + 2(2c^2 + 2d^2)$$
$$= 4(a^2 + b^2 + c^2 + d^2)$$

So we have $4(a^2 + b^2 + c^2 + d^2) = 2016 \quad \Rightarrow \quad a^2 + b^2 + c^2 + d^2 = 2016/4 = 504$.

Example 2. Find the value of $a^2+b^2+c^2-ab-bc-ca$ if $a = 2015x + 2016$, $b = 2015x + 2017$, $c = 2015x + 2018$.

Solution: 003.
$a - b = -1$, $b - c = -1$, $c - a = 2$.
$$a^2 + b^2 + c^2 - ab - bc - ca = \frac{1}{2}[(a-b)^2 + (b-c)^2 + (c-a)^2]$$
$$= \frac{1}{2}[(-1)^2 + (-1)^2 + (2)^2] = 3$$

Example 3. a, b, and c are real numbers. Show that $a = b = c$ if $(a+b+c)^2 = 3(a^2+b^2+c^2)$.

Proof:
We know that $(a+b+c)^2 = a^2 + b^2 + c^2 + 2ab + 2bc + 2ca$. So we have
$3(a^2 + b^2 + c^2) = a^2 + b^2 + c^2 + 2ab + 2bc + 2ca$ or $2a^2 + 2b^2 + 2c^2 - 2ab - 2bc - 2ca = 0$.
By completing the squares: $(a-b)^2 + (b-c)^2 + (c-a)^2 = 0$.
We know that a, b, and c are real numbers. Thus $a - b = 0$, $b - c = 0$, $c - a = 0$.
that is, $a = b = c$.

Example 4. a, b, and c are real numbers such that $a^2 + b^2 + c^2 = 9$. Find the maximum value of $(a-b)^2 + (b-c)^2 + (c-a)^2$.

Solution: 027.
$$(a-b)^2 + (b-c)^2 + (c-a)^2 = 2(a^2 + b^2 + c^2) - 2(ab + bc + ca)$$
$$= 3(a^2 + b^2 + c^2) - [a^2 + b^2 + c^2 + 2(ab + bc + ca)]$$
$$= 3(a^2 + b^2 + c^2) - (a+b+c)^2 = 27 - (a+b+c)^2 \leq 27.$$
The maximum value of $(a-b)^2 + (b-c)^2 + (c-a)^2$ is 27 when $a + b + c = 0$.

Example 5. Find the value of a so that $a^2 - b^2 - c^2 + ab = 2019$ and $a^2 + 3b^2 + 3c^2 - 3ab - 2ac - 2bc = -2005$. a, b, and c be positive integers with $a \geq b \geq c$.

Solution: 254.

$a^2 - b^2 - c^2 + ab = 2019$ (1)

$a^2 + 3b^2 + 3c^2 - 3ab - 2ac - 2bc = -2005$ (2)

(1) + (2): $2a^2 + 2b^2 + 2c^2 - 2ab - 2bc - 2ac = 14$ (3)

(3) can be rearranged to: $(a^2 - 2ab + b^2) + (b^2 - 2bc + c^2) + (a^2 - 2ac + c^2) = 14$.
Or $(a-b)^2 + (b-c)^2 + (a-c)^2 = 14$.

There is one way to express 14 as the sum of three squares of positive integers:
$14 = 3^2 + 2^2 + 1^2$.

We know that $a \geq b \geq c$.
Case 1: $a - c = 3$ and $a - b = 2$ and $b - c = 1$.

Case 2: $a - b = 1$ and $b - c = 2$.

We get: $(a, b, c) = (c + 3, c + 1, c)$ or $(a, b, c,) = (c + 3, c + 2, c)$.

In case 1, $2019 = a^2 - c^2 + ab - b^2 = (a-c)(a+c) + (a-b)b = 3(2c+3) + 2(c+1)$ or $8c + 11 = 2019$ $\Rightarrow$ $c = 251$.

Solving we get $(a,b,c) = (254, 252, 251)$. The second case has no integer solution. Therefore $a = 254$.

Example 6. Find the last three digits of the greatest positive integer not exceeding $(\sqrt{7} + \sqrt{3})^6$.

Solution: 039.

Let $x = \sqrt{7} + \sqrt{3}$ and $y = \sqrt{7} - \sqrt{3}$.

$x + y = (\sqrt{7} + \sqrt{3}) + (\sqrt{7} - \sqrt{3}) = 2\sqrt{7}$.

$xy = (\sqrt{7}+\sqrt{3})(\sqrt{7}-\sqrt{3}) = 7-3 = 4$.

$x^2+y^2 = (x+y)^2 - 2xy = 20$

$x^6+y^6 = (x^2+y^2)^3 - 3(x^2+y^2)\cdot x^2\cdot y^2 = 7040$.

$(\sqrt{7}+\sqrt{3})^6 + (\sqrt{7}-\sqrt{3})^6 = 7040$.

$(\sqrt{7}+\sqrt{3})^6 = 7040 - (\sqrt{7}-\sqrt{3})^6$.

We know that $0 < \sqrt{7}-\sqrt{3} < 1$, so $0 < (\sqrt{7}-\sqrt{3})^6 < 1$.

The greatest positive integer not exceeding $(\sqrt{7}+\sqrt{3})^6$ is $7040 - 1 = 7039$. The answer is 039.

☆**Example 7.** Calculate: $\dfrac{(7^4+64)(15^4+64)(23^4+64)(31^4+64)(39^4+64)}{(3^4+64)(11^4+64)(19^4+64)(27^4+64)(35^4+64)}$.

Solution: 337.

Method 1:

We know that $x^4+4y^4 = (x^2-2xy+2y^2)(x^2+2xy+2y^2)$.

$n^4+4\times 2^4 = (n^2-2(n)\times 2+2\times 2^2)(n^2+2(n)\times 2+2\times 2^2)$

$= (n^2-4n+8)(n^2+4n+8) = [(n-4)n+8][n(n+4)+8]$

$\dfrac{(7^4+64)(15^4+64)(23^4+64)(31^4+64)(39^4+64)}{(3^4+64)(11^4+64)(19^4+64)(27^4+64)(35^4+64)}$

$= \dfrac{(3\times 7+8)(7\times 11+8)(11\times 15+8)(15\times 19+8)\cdots(35\times 39+8)(39\times 43+8)}{(-1\times 3+8)(3\times 7+8)(7\times 11+8)(11\times 15+8)\cdots(31\times 35+8)(35\times 39+8)}$

$= \dfrac{39\times 43+8}{-1\times 3+8} = \dfrac{1685}{5} = 337$

Method 2:

We know that $x^4+4y^4 = (x^2-2xy+2y^2)(x^2+2xy+2y^2)$.

$n^4+4\times 2^4 = (n^2-2(n)\times 2+2\times 2^2)(n^2+2(n)\times 2+2\times 2^2)$

$= (n^2-4n+8)(n^2+4n+8) = [(n-2)^2+4][(n+2)^2+4]$

$\dfrac{(7^4+64)(15^4+64)(23^4+64)(31^4+64)(39^4+64)}{(3^4+64)(11^4+64)(19^4+64)(27^4+64)(35^4+64)}$

159

$$= \frac{(5^2+4)(9^2+4)(13^2+4)(17^2+4)\cdots(37^2+4)(41^2+4)}{(1^2+4)(5^2+4)(9^2+4)(13^2+4)\cdots(33^2+4)(37^2+4)}$$

$$= \frac{41^2+4}{1^2+4} = \frac{1685}{5} = 337.$$

☆**Example 8.** Compute: $\dfrac{(2^4+\frac{1}{4})(4^4+\frac{1}{4})(6^4+\frac{1}{4})(8^4+\frac{1}{4})(10^4+\frac{1}{4})}{(1^4+\frac{1}{4})(3^4+\frac{1}{4})(5^4+\frac{1}{4})(7^4+\frac{1}{4})(9^4+\frac{1}{4})}$.

Solution: 221.

Method 1:

$$\frac{(2^4+\frac{1}{4})(4^4+\frac{1}{4})(6^4+\frac{1}{4})(8^4+\frac{1}{4})(10^4+\frac{1}{4})}{(1^4+\frac{1}{4})(3^4+\frac{1}{4})(5^4+\frac{1}{4})(7^4+\frac{1}{4})(9^4+\frac{1}{4})} = \frac{(4^4+4)(8^4+4)(12^4+4)(16^4+4)(20^4+4)}{(2^4+4)(6^4+4)(10^4+4)(14^4+4)(18^4+4)}.$$

We know that

$$n^4+4\times(1)^4 = (n^2-2n+2)(n^2+2n+2) = [(n-1)^2+1][(n+1)^2+1].$$

So $\dfrac{(4^4+4)(8^4+4)(12^4+4)(16^4+4)(20^4+4)}{(2^4+4)(6^4+4)(10^4+4)(14^4+4)(18^4+4)}$

$$= \frac{(3^2+1)(5^2+1)(7^2+1)(9^2+1)\cdots(19^2+1)(21^2+1)}{(1^2+1)(3^2+1)(5^2+1)(7^2+1)\cdots(17^2+1)(19^2+1)}$$

$$= \frac{21^2+1}{1^2+1} = 221.$$

Method 2:

$$n^4+4\times(\frac{1}{2})^4 = [n^2-2(n)\times\frac{1}{2}+2\times(\frac{1}{2})^2][n^2+2(n)\times\frac{1}{2}+2\times(\frac{1}{2})^2]$$

$$= [(n-\frac{1}{2})^2+\frac{1}{4}][(n+\frac{1}{2})^2+\frac{1}{4}].$$

$$\frac{(2^4+\frac{1}{4})(4^4+\frac{1}{4})(6^4+\frac{1}{4})(8^4+\frac{1}{4})(10^4+\frac{1}{4})}{(1^4+\frac{1}{4})(3^4+\frac{1}{4})(5^4+\frac{1}{4})(7^4+\frac{1}{4})(9^4+\frac{1}{4})} =$$

$$\frac{[(2-\frac{1}{2})^2+\frac{1}{4}][(2+\frac{1}{2})^2+\frac{1}{4}][(4-\frac{1}{2})^2+\frac{1}{4}][(4+\frac{1}{2})^2+\frac{1}{4}]\cdots[(10-\frac{1}{2})^2+\frac{1}{4}][(10+\frac{1}{2})^2+\frac{1}{4}]}{[(1-\frac{1}{2})^2+\frac{1}{4}][(1+\frac{1}{2})^2+\frac{1}{4}][(3-\frac{1}{2})^2+\frac{1}{4}][(3+\frac{1}{2})^2+\frac{1}{4}]\cdots[(9-\frac{1}{2})^2+\frac{1}{4}][(9+\frac{1}{2})^2+\frac{1}{4}]}$$

$$= \frac{(10+\frac{1}{2})^2+\frac{1}{4}}{(1-\frac{1}{2})^2+\frac{1}{4}} = \frac{\frac{21^2+1}{4}}{\frac{2}{4}} = \frac{442}{2} = 221.$$

General case: $\dfrac{(a_2^4+4d^4)(a_4^4+4d^4)\cdots(a_{2n}^4+4d^4)}{(a_1^4+4d^4)(a_3^4+4d^4)\cdots(a_{2n-1}^4+4d^4)}$, $a_{2n}-a_{2n-1}=\cdots=a_2-a_1=2d$.

can be simplified into $\dfrac{a_{2n}a_{2n+1}+2d^2}{a_0 a_1+2d^2}$, or $\dfrac{(a_{2n}+d)^2+d^2}{(a_1-d)^2+d^2}$, where $a_0=a_1-2d$.

Example 9. What is the value of $(4+2\sqrt{3})^{3/2}-(4-2\sqrt{3})^{3/2}$?

Solution: 020.
Method 1:
Let $a=(4+2\sqrt{3})^{1/2}=[(\sqrt{3})^2+2\times\sqrt{3}\times 1+1^2]^{1/2}=\sqrt{3}+1$ and $b=(4-2\sqrt{3})^{1/2}=\sqrt{3}-1$.
We would like to find the value of $(4+2\sqrt{3})^{3/2}-(4-2\sqrt{3})^{3/2}$
Note that $a^3-b^3=(a-b)(a^2+ab+b^2)$
$=(a-b)(a^2-2ab+b^2+2ab+ab)=(a-b)[(a-b)^2+3ab]$.

$(4+2\sqrt{3})^{3/2}-(4-2\sqrt{3})^{3/2}=2[2^2+3(\sqrt{3}+1)(\sqrt{3}-1)]=2[4+3(3-1)]=20.$

Method 2:
Let $a=(4+2\sqrt{3})^{1/2}$ and $b=(4-2\sqrt{3})^{1/2}$.
We wish to find $a^3-b^3=(a-b)(a^2+ab+b^2)$.

We can easily calculate the values of the expressions of $a^2 + b^2$ and ab:
$a^2 + b^2 = (4 + 2\sqrt{3}) + (4 - 2\sqrt{3}) = 8$.
$ab = [(4 + 2\sqrt{3})]^{1/2}[(4 - 2\sqrt{3})]^{1/2} = (4^2 - 2^2 \times 3)^{1/2} = 4^{1/2} = 2$.

Now we wish to find the value of $a - b$.
We know that $(a - b)^2 = a^2 - 2ab + b^2 = (a^2 + b^2) - 2ab = 8 - 2 \times 2 = 4 \Rightarrow a - b = 2$.
Therefore $a^3 - b^3 = (a - b)(a^2 + ab + b^2) = 2 \times (8 + 2) = 20$.

Example 10. $m = a/b$ is the largest real number z such that
$x + y + z = 5$
$xy + yz + xz = 3$
and x, y are also real. Find $a + b$ if a and b are positive integers relatively prime.

Solution: 016.
Since $x + y + z = 5$, we have $x + y = 5 - z$.
Squaring both sides gives us $(x + y)^2 = (5 - z)^2$.
Since $xy + yz + xz = 3$, we have $xy = 3 - xz - yz = 3 - z(x + y) = 3 - z(5 - z)$.
$(x - y)^2 = (x + y)^2 - 4xy = (5 - z)^2 - 4[3 - z(5 - z)]$
$= -3z^2 + 10z + 13 = (13 - 3z)(1 + z)$

Since $(x - y)^2 \geq 0$, this means that
$(13 - 3z)(1 + z) \geq 0$.
Solving the inequality gives us
$-1 \leq z \leq \dfrac{13}{3}$.

The largest real number z is $\dfrac{13}{3}$ when $x = y = \dfrac{1}{3}$. The answer is $13 + 3 = 16$.

☆**Example 11.** x, y, and z are positive numbers satisfying $xyz = 1$, $x + \frac{1}{z} = 10$, and $y + \frac{1}{x} = 17$. If $z + \frac{1}{y} = \frac{m}{n}$, where m and n are relatively prime positive integers. Find $m + n$.

Solution: 198.

$$10 \times 17 \times \frac{m}{n} = (x + \frac{1}{z})(y + \frac{1}{x})(z + \frac{1}{y})$$

$$= xyz + x + \frac{1}{z} + y + \frac{1}{x} + z + \frac{1}{y} + \frac{1}{xyz}$$

$$= 1 + 10 + 17 + 1 + \frac{m}{n} = 29 + \frac{m}{n}$$

So we have $10 \times 17 \times \frac{m}{n} = 29 + \frac{m}{n}$ $\Rightarrow$ $\frac{169m}{n} = 29$ $\Rightarrow$ $\frac{m}{n} = \frac{29}{169}$.

The answer is $29 + 169 = 198$.

☆**Example 12.** What is the value of m such that $x^2 - x - 1$ is a factor of $mx^7 + nx^6 + 1$? m and n are integers.

Solution: 008.

Using the quadratic formula, we solve the quadratic equation $x^2 - x - 1 = 0$ to get the roots

$$x_1 = \frac{1+\sqrt{5}}{2} \text{ and } x_2 = \frac{1-\sqrt{5}}{2}.$$

We can observe that $x_1 + x_2 = 1$ and $x_1 x_2 = -1$.

Thus, $(x_1 + x_2)^2 = x_1^2 + x_2^2 + 2x_1 x_2 = 1$ and

$$x_1^2 + x_2^2 = 3 \qquad (1)$$

We know that $x^2 - x - 1$ is a factor of $mx^7 + nx^6 + 1$, so x_1 and x_2 are also the roots of $mx^7 + nx^6 + 1 = 0$.

Therefore we have $mx_1^7 + nx_1^6 = -1$ \qquad (2)

and $mx_2^7 + nx_2^6 = -1$ \qquad (3)

(2) $\times x_2^6$ $\Rightarrow$ $m x_1^7 x_2^6 + n x_1^6 x_2^6 = -x_2^6$ $\Rightarrow$ $mx_1(-1)^6 + n(-1)^6 = -x_2^6$

163

$\Rightarrow \quad mx_1 + n = -x_2^6$ \hfill (4)

$(3) \times x_1^6$: $mx_2 + n = -x_1^6$ \hfill (5)

$(4) - (5)$: $m(x_1 - x_2) = x_1^6 - x_2^6$.

So $m = \dfrac{x_1^6 - x_2^6}{x_1 - x_2} = \dfrac{(x_1^3 - x_2^3)(x_1^3 + x_2^3)}{x_1 - x_2} = \dfrac{(x_1 - x_2)(x_1^2 + x_1x_2 + x_2^2)(x_1^3 + x_2^3)}{x_1 - x_2}$

$= (x_1^2 + x_1x_2 + x_2^2)(x_1^3 + x_2^3) = (x_1^2 + x_1x_2 + x_2^2)(x_1 + x_2)(x_1^2 - x_1x_2 + x_2^2)$

$= (3-1)(1)(3+1) = 8.$

☆**Example 13.** The real numbers a, b, x, y satisfy $ax + by = 3$, $ax^2 + by^2 = 7$, $ax^3 + by^3 = 16$, $ax^4 + by^4 = 42$. Find $ax^5 + by^5$.

Solution: 020.

By **Theorem 1**, $ax^3 + by^3 = (ax^2 + by^2)(x+y) - (ax+by)xy \Rightarrow 16 = 7(x+y) - 3xy$ \hfill (1)

$ax^4 + by^4 = (ax^3 + by^3)(x+y) - (ax^2 + by^2)xy \Rightarrow 42 = 16(x+y) - 7xy$ \hfill (2)

Solving (1) and (2) we get: $x + y = -14$ and $xy = -38$.

Therefore $ax^5 + by^5 = (ax^4 + by^4)(x+y) - (ax^3 + by^3)xy = 42 \times (-14) - 16 \times (-38) = 20$.

Example 14. For $x < 0$, $x - \dfrac{1}{x} = \sqrt{5}$. $\dfrac{x^{12} - x^{10} + x^6 + x^4 - x^0 + x^{-2}}{x^{12} - x^{10} + x^8 + x^2 - x^0 + x^{-2}} = m/n$, where m and n are relatively prime positive integers. Find $m + n$.

Solution: 487.

We divided both the numerator and denominator of $\dfrac{x^{12} - x^{10} + x^6 + x^4 - x^0 + x^{-2}}{x^{12} - x^{10} + x^8 + x^2 - x^0 + x^{-2}}$ by x^5:

$\dfrac{x^{12} - x^{10} + x^6 + x^4 - x^0 + x^{-2}}{x^{12} - x^{10} + x^8 + x^2 - x^0 + x^{-2}} = \dfrac{x^7 - x^5 + x^1 + x^{-1} - x^{-5} + x^{-7}}{x^7 - x^5 + x^3 + x^{-3} - x^{-5} + x^{-7}} =$

$\dfrac{(x^7 + x^{-7}) - (x^5 + x^{-5}) + (x^1 + x^{-1})}{(x^7 + x^{-7}) - (x^5 + x^{-5}) + (x^3 + x^{-3})}.$

Let $a_n = x^n + (\dfrac{1}{x})^n$. We know that $x < 0$, $x - \dfrac{1}{x} = \sqrt{5}$.

So $a_1 = x + \dfrac{1}{x} = -\sqrt{(x-\dfrac{1}{x})^2 + 4x \times \dfrac{1}{x}} = -3$.

$a_2 = x^2 + (\dfrac{1}{x})^2 = (x+\dfrac{1}{x})^2 - 2x \times \dfrac{1}{x} = (-3)^2 - 2 = 7$.

By **Theorem 1**, $a_{n+2} = (x+\dfrac{1}{x})a_{n+1} - x \times \dfrac{1}{x} a_n = (x+\dfrac{1}{x})a_{n+1} + a_n = -3a_{n+1} - a_n$.

$a_3 = -3a_2 - a_1 = -3 \times 7 - (-3) = -18$.
$a_4 = -3a_3 - a_2 = -3 \times (-18) - 7 = 47$
$a_5 = -3a_4 - a_3 = -3 \times 47 - (-18) = -123$
$a_6 = -3a_5 - a_4 = -3 \times (-123) - 47 = 322$
$a_7 = -3a_6 - a_5 = -3 \times 322 - (-123) = -843$.

$$\dfrac{(x^7+x^{-7}) - (x^5+x^{-5}) + (x^1+x^{-1})}{(x^7+x^{-7}) - (x^5+x^{-5}) + (x^3+x^{-3})} = \dfrac{a_7 - a_5 + a_1}{a_7 - a_5 + a_3} = \dfrac{-843+123-3}{-843+123-18} = \dfrac{241}{246}.$$

The answer is $241 + 246 = 487$.

Example 15. The real numbers x, y, z satisfy $x + y + z = 1$, $x^2 + y^2 + z^2 = 2$, and $x^3 + y^3 + z^3 = 3$. Find $x^5 + y^5 + z^5$.

Solution: 006.

Let $a_n = x^n + y^n + z^n$.

$a_1 = x + y + z = 1$
$a_2 = x^2 + y^2 + z^2 = 2$
$a_3 = x^3 + y^3 + z^3 = 3$

$xy + yz + zx = \dfrac{(x+y+z)^2 - (x^2+y^2+z^2)}{2} = -\dfrac{1}{2}$

$3xyz = x^3 + y^3 + z^3 - (x+y+z)(x^2+y^2+z^2 - xy - yz - zx)$

$= 3xyz = 3 - (1)[(2-(-\dfrac{1}{2})] = \dfrac{1}{2}$ $\quad \Rightarrow \quad xyz = \dfrac{1}{6}$.

By **Theorem 2**, $a_n = x^n + y^n + z^n$ can be written as
$a_{n+3} = (x+y+z)a_{n+2} - (xy+yz+zx)a_{n+1} + xyz a_n$, n is positive integer.

$$a_{n+3} = a_{n+2} + \frac{1}{2}a_{n+1} + \frac{1}{6}a_n$$

So $a_4 = a_3 + \frac{1}{2}a_2 + \frac{1}{6}a_1 = 3 + \frac{1}{2} \times 2 + \frac{1}{6} = \frac{25}{6}$.

$a_5 = a_4 + \frac{1}{2}a_3 + \frac{1}{6}a_2 = \frac{25}{6} + \frac{1}{2} \times 3 + \frac{1}{6} \times 2 = 6$.

$x^5 + y^5 + z^5 = 6$.

50 AIME Lectures — Chapter 7 Algebraic Manipulation

PROBLEMS

Problem 1. $a(b+c-a)^2 + b(c+a-b)^2 + c(a+b-c)^2 + (b+c-a)(c+a-b)(a+b-c) = 2016$. Find the value of abc.

Problem 2. Find the value of $a^4 + b^4 + c^4 - a^2b^2 - b^2c^2 - c^2a^2$ if $a^2 - b^2 = 1 + \sqrt{2}$, and $b^2 - c^2 = 1 - \sqrt{2}$.

Problem 3. a, b, and c are the lengths of three sides of $\triangle ABC$. Find the area of $\triangle ABC$ if $\dfrac{2a^2}{1+a^2} = b$, $\dfrac{2b^2}{1+b^2} = c$, and $\dfrac{2c^2}{1+c^2} = a$. The area of $\triangle ABC$ can be expressed as $\dfrac{\sqrt{m}}{n}$. Find the value of $m + n$ if m and n are positive integers relatively prime.

Problem 4. a, b, and c are real numbers such that $a+b+c=0$, $a^2+b^2+c^2 = 0.1$. Find the value of $100{,}000(a^4+b^4+c^4)$.

Problem 5. $(a+b)(b+c)(c+a) + abc = 66$, a, b, and c are positive integers. Find the value of $a^2+b^2+c^2$.

Problem 6. $(ab+bc+ca)(a+b+c) - abc = 140$, a, b, and c are positive integers. Find the value of $a^2+b^2+c^2$.

Problem 7. Find the smallest integer greater than $(\sqrt{3}+\sqrt{2})^6$.

Problem 8 Find the last three digits of $\left\lfloor \left(\sqrt{7}+\sqrt{5}\right)^6 \right\rfloor$.

☆Problem 9. Calculate: $\dfrac{(7^4+324)(19^4+324)(31^4+324)(43^4+324)\cdots(103^4+324)}{(1^4+324)(13^4+324)(25^4+324)(37^4+324)\cdots(97^4+324)}$.

Problem 10. Find the smallest $m + n$ if $\dfrac{(5^4 + \frac{1}{4})(7^4 + \frac{1}{4})(9^4 + \frac{1}{4})(11^4 + \frac{1}{4})(13^4 + \frac{1}{4})}{(4^4 + \frac{1}{4})(6^4 + \frac{1}{4})(8^4 + \frac{1}{4})(10^4 + \frac{1}{4})(12^4 + \frac{1}{4})} = \dfrac{m}{n}$.

Problem 11. (1990 AIME) Find the value of $(52 + 6\sqrt{43})^{3/2} - (52 - 6\sqrt{43})^{3/2}$.

Problem 12. Find $x^6 + y^6$ if $x = \sqrt{5+\sqrt{5}}$ and $y = \sqrt{5-\sqrt{5}}$.

Problem 13. (2010 NC Math Contest) Let x, y, and z be positive real numbers such that $x + y + z = 1$ and $xy + yz + xz = 1/3$. Find the number of possible values of the expression $\dfrac{x}{y} + \dfrac{y}{z} + \dfrac{z}{x}$.

☆**Problem 14.** Find the last three digits of $m = \dfrac{(x+y)(y+z)(z+x)}{xyz}$ if $\dfrac{x+y}{z} + \dfrac{y+z}{x} + \dfrac{z+x}{y} = 2015$.

☆**Problem 15.** $x^2 - x - 1$ is a factor of $ax^{17} + bx^{16} + 1$ for some integers a and b. Find a

Problem 16. The real numbers a, b, x, y, z satisfy $ax + by + cz = 1$, $ax^2 + by^2 + cz^2 = 0$, $ax^3 + by^3 + cz^3 = 2$, $ax^4 + by^4 + cz^4 = 3$, $ax^5 + by^5 + cz^5 = 4$, $ax^6 + by^6 + cz^6 = 5$. $ax^7 + by^7 + cz^7 = m/n$, where m and n are relatively prime positive integers. Find $m + n$.

Problem 17. The real nonzero numbers a, b, and c satisfy $a + b + c = 0$. $\dfrac{(a^7 + b^7 + c^7)^2}{(a^2 + b^2 + c^2)(a^3 + b^3 + c^3)(a^4 + b^4 + c^4)(a^5 + b^5 + c^5)} = m/n$, where m and n are relatively prime positive integers. Find $m + n$.

Problem 18. (1973 USAMO modified) Find $x^{2015} + y^{2016} + z^{2017}$ if x, y, and z are the real roots of the system of simultaneous equations:
$$\begin{cases} x + y + z = 3, & (1) \\ x^2 + y^2 + z^2 = 3, & (2) \\ x^5 + y^5 + z^5 = 3 & (3) \end{cases}$$

Problem 19. The real numbers x, y, z satisfy $x + y + z = 1$, $x^2 + y^2 + z^2 = 2$, $x^3 + y^3 + z^3 = 3$, and $x^4 + y^4 + z^4 = m/n$, where m and n are relatively prime positive integers. Find $m + n$.

50 AIME Lectures — Chapter 7 Algebraic Manipulation

SOLUTIONS

Problem 1. Solution: 504.

Let $b+c-a=x$, $c+a-b=y$, $a+b-c=z$.

So $a=\frac{1}{2}(y+z)$, $b=\frac{1}{2}(x+z)$, $c=\frac{1}{2}(x+y)$.

$a(b+c-a)^2 + b(c+a-b)^2 + c(a+b-c)^2 + (b+c-a)(c+a-b)(a+b-c)$

$= \frac{1}{2}[(y+z)x^2 + (x+z)y^2 + (x+y)z^2 + 2xyz]$

$= \frac{1}{2}[(y+z)x^2 + zy(y+z) + xy(y+z) + xz(y+z)]$

$= \frac{1}{2}(y+z)[x(x+y) + z(x+y)]$

$= \frac{1}{2}(x+y)(y+z)(x+z) = \frac{1}{2}(2c)(2a)(2b) = 4abc$

So $4abc = 2016$ $\Rightarrow$ $abc = 2016/4 = 504$.

Problem 2. Solution: 005

$a^2 - c^2 = (a^2 - b^2) + (b^2 - c^2) = 2$. $(a^2 - c^2)^2 = 4$.

$(a^2 - b^2)^2 = 3 + 2\sqrt{2}$, $(b^2 - c^2)^2 = 3 - \sqrt{2}$,

$a^4 + b^4 + c^4 - a^2b^2 - b^2c^2 - c^2a^2 = \frac{1}{2}[(a^2 - b^2)^2 + (b^2 - c^2)^2 + (c^2 - a^2)^2]$

$= \frac{1}{2}(3 + 2\sqrt{2} + 3 - 2\sqrt{2} + 4) = 5$.

Problem 3. Solution: 007.

$\dfrac{2a^2}{1+a^2} = b \quad \Rightarrow \quad 1 + \dfrac{1}{a^2} = \dfrac{2}{b}$ \hfill (1)

$\dfrac{2b^2}{1+b^2} = c \quad \Rightarrow \quad 1 + \dfrac{1}{b^2} = \dfrac{2}{c}$ \hfill (2)

$\dfrac{2c^2}{1+c^2} = a \quad \Rightarrow \quad 1 + \dfrac{1}{c^2} = \dfrac{2}{a}$ \hfill (3)

(1) + (2) + (3): $1+\dfrac{1}{a^2}+1+\dfrac{1}{b^2}+1+\dfrac{1}{c^2}=\dfrac{2}{a}+\dfrac{2}{b}+\dfrac{2}{c}$ ⇒

$(1-\dfrac{1}{a})^2+(1-\dfrac{1}{b})^2+(1-\dfrac{1}{c})^2=0$.

Thus $a = b = c = 1$. The area of $\triangle ABC$ is $\dfrac{\sqrt{3}}{4}$. The answer is $3 + 4 = 7$.

Problem 4. Solution: 500.
$(a+b+c)^2 = a^2+b^2+c^2+2ab+2bc+2ca$ ⇒ $0 = 0.1 + 2ab + 2bc + 2ca$
⇒ $-0.1 = 2ab+2bc+2ca$ ⇒ $ab+bc+ca = -0.05$ ⇒
$(ab+bc+ca)^2 = (-0.05)^2 = 0.05^2$.
We know that $(ab+bc+ca)^2 = a^2b^2+b^2c^2+c^2a^2+2abc(a+b+c) = a^2b^2+b^2c^2+c^2a^2$

$a^4+b^4+c^4 = (a^2+b^2+c^2)^2 - 2(a^2b^2+b^2c^2+c^2a^2) = 0.1^2 - 2\times 0.05^2 = 0.005$.
$100{,}000(a^4+b^4+c^4) = 500$.

Problem 5. Solution: 014.
$(a+b)(b+c)(c+a)+abc$
$= (b+c)a^2+(b+c)^2 a+abc+bc(b+c) = (b+c)a^2+(b^2+3bc+c^2)a+bc(b+c)$

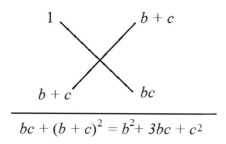

$bc + (b+c)^2 = b^2 + 3bc + c^2$

$(a+b)(b+c)(c+a)+abc = (a+b+c)[(b+c)a+bc] = (a+b+c)(ab+bc+ca) = 66$.
So $(a+b+c)(ab+bc+ca) = 66$ ⇒ $a+b+c = 6$ and $ab+bc+ca = 11$.
$a^2+b^2+c^2 = (a+b+c)^2 - (2ab+2bc+2ca) = 6^2 - 2\times 11 = 36 - 22 = 14$.

Problem 6. Solution: 026.
$(ab+bc+ca)(a+b+c) - abc$

$= (b+c)a^2 + (b+c)^2 a - abc + bc(b+c) = (b+c)a^2 + (b^2 + 2bc + c^2)a + bc(b+c)$
$= (b+c)[a^2 + a(b+c) + bc] = (b+c)(a+b)(c+a)$.

Let $a+b \le b+c \le c+a$.

So $(a+b)(b+c)(c+a) = 140 = 2 \times 7 \times 10 = 2 \times 5 \times 10 = 4 \times 5 \times 7$

Only $(a+b)(b+c)(c+a) = 4 \times 5 \times 7$ yields the positive integers solution.

So $a = 3$, $b = 1$, and $c = 4$.

$a^2 + b^2 + c^2 = 3^2 + 1^2 + 4^2 = 26$.

Problem 7. Solution: 970.

Construct $a_n = (\sqrt{3} + \sqrt{2})^{2n} + (\sqrt{3} - \sqrt{2})^{2n}$

Or $a_n = (5 + 2\sqrt{6})^n + (5 - 2\sqrt{6})^n$

$a_{n+2} = [(5 + 2\sqrt{6}) + (5 - 2\sqrt{6})]a_{n+1} - (5 + 2\sqrt{6})(5 - 2\sqrt{6})a_n = 10a_{n+1} - a_n$

$a_1 = 10$, $a_2 = 98$.

$a_3 = 10 \times 98 - 10 = 970$.

$a_3 = 10 \times 98 - 10 = 970 = (5 + 2\sqrt{6})^3 + (5 - 2\sqrt{6})^3$

$(5 + 2\sqrt{6})^3 = 970 - (5 - 2\sqrt{6})^3$

Since $0 < (5 - 2\sqrt{6})^3 < 1$

The smallest integer greater than $(5 + 2\sqrt{6})^3$ is 970.

Problem 8 Solution: 535.

Let $x = \sqrt{7} + \sqrt{5}$ and $y = \sqrt{7} - \sqrt{5}$.

$x + y = (\sqrt{7} + \sqrt{5}) + (\sqrt{7} - \sqrt{5}) = 2\sqrt{7}$.

$xy = (\sqrt{7} + \sqrt{5})(\sqrt{7} - \sqrt{5}) = 7 - 5 = 2$.

$x^2 + y^2 = (x+y)^2 - 2xy = 24$

$x^6 + y^6 = (x^2 + y^2)^3 - 3(x^2 + y^2) \cdot x^2 \cdot y^2 = 13536$.

$(\sqrt{7} + \sqrt{5})^6 + (\sqrt{7} - \sqrt{5})^6 = 13536$.

$(\sqrt{7} + \sqrt{5})^6 = 13536 - (\sqrt{7} - \sqrt{5})^6$.

We know that $0 < \sqrt{7} - \sqrt{5} < 1$. So $0 < (\sqrt{7} - \sqrt{5})^6 < 1$.

The greatest positive integer not exceeding $(\sqrt{7} + \sqrt{5})^6$ is $13536 - 1 = 13535$.

☆**Problem 9.** Solution: 865.

We know that $x^4 + 4y^4 = (x^2 - 2xy + 2y^2)(x^2 + 2xy + 2y^2)$.

$n^4 + 4 \times 3^4 = (n^2 - 2 \times n \times 3 + 2 \times 3^2)(n^2 + 2 \times n \times 3 + 2 \times 3^2)$

$= (n^2 + 6n + 18)(n^2 - 6n + 18) = [(n-6)n + 18][n(n+6) + 18]$

$\dfrac{(7^4 + 324)(19^4 + 324)(31^4 + 324)(43^4 + 324) \cdots (103^4 + 324)}{(1^4 + 324)(13^4 + 324)(25^4 + 324)(37^4 + 324) \cdots (97^4 + 324)}$

$= \dfrac{(1 \times 7 + 18)(7 \times 13 + 18)(13 \times 19 + 18)(19 \times 25 + 18) \cdots (97 \times 103 + 18)(103 \times 109 + 18)}{(-5 \times 1 + 18)(1 \times 7 + 18)(7 \times 13 + 18)(13 \times 19 + 18) \cdots (91 \times 97 + 18)(97 \times 103 + 18)}$

$= \dfrac{103 \times 109 + 18}{-5 \times 1 + 18} = \dfrac{11245}{13} = 865$.

Problem 10. Solution: 078.

$n^4 + 4 \times (\dfrac{1}{2})^4 = [n^2 - 2(n) \times \dfrac{1}{2} + 2 \times (\dfrac{1}{2})^2][n^2 + 2(n) \times \dfrac{1}{2} + 2 \times (\dfrac{1}{2})^2]$

$= [(n - \dfrac{1}{2})^2 + \dfrac{1}{4}][(n + \dfrac{1}{2})^2 + \dfrac{1}{4}]$.

$\dfrac{(5^4 + \dfrac{1}{4})(7^4 + \dfrac{1}{4})(9^4 + \dfrac{1}{4})(11^4 + \dfrac{1}{4})(13^4 + \dfrac{1}{4})}{(4^4 + \dfrac{1}{4})(6^4 + \dfrac{1}{4})(8^4 + \dfrac{1}{4})(10^4 + \dfrac{1}{4})(12^4 + \dfrac{1}{4})} =$

$\dfrac{[(5 - \dfrac{1}{2})^2 + \dfrac{1}{4}][(5 + \dfrac{1}{2})^2 + \dfrac{1}{4}][(7 - \dfrac{1}{2})^2 + \dfrac{1}{4}][(7 + \dfrac{1}{2})^2 + \dfrac{1}{4}] \cdots [(13 - \dfrac{1}{2})^2 + \dfrac{1}{4}][(13 + \dfrac{1}{2})^2 + \dfrac{1}{4}]}{[(4 - \dfrac{1}{2})^2 + \dfrac{1}{4}][(4 + \dfrac{1}{2})^2 + \dfrac{1}{4}][(6 - \dfrac{1}{2})^2 + \dfrac{1}{4}][(6 + \dfrac{1}{2})^2 + \dfrac{1}{4}] \cdots [(12 - \dfrac{1}{2})^2 + \dfrac{1}{4}][(12 + \dfrac{1}{2})^2 + \dfrac{1}{4}]}$

$= \dfrac{(13 + \dfrac{1}{2})^2 + \dfrac{1}{4}}{(4 - \dfrac{1}{2})^2 + \dfrac{1}{4}} = \dfrac{\dfrac{27^2 + 1}{4}}{\dfrac{50}{4}} = \dfrac{730}{50} = \dfrac{73}{5}$. So $m + n = 73 + 5 = 78$.

Problem 11. Solution: 828.

Method 1:

Let $a = (52 + 6\sqrt{43})^{1/2} = [(\sqrt{43})^2 + 2 \times \sqrt{43} \times 3 + 3^2]^{1/2} = \sqrt{43} + 3$ and $b = (52 - 6\sqrt{43})^{1/2} = \sqrt{43} - 3$.

173

We would like to find the value of $(52+6\sqrt{43})^{3/2} - (52-6\sqrt{43})^{3/2}$.

Note that $a^3 - b^3 = (a-b)(a^2+ab+b^2) = (a-b)(a^2-2ab+b^2+2ab+ab)$
$= (a-b)[(a-b)^2 + 3ab]$

$(52+6\sqrt{43})^{3/2} - (52-6\sqrt{43})^{3/2} = 6[6^2 + 3(\sqrt{43}+3)(\sqrt{43}-3)] = 6[36+3(43-9)] = 828$.

Method 2:

Let $a = (52+6\sqrt{43})^{1/2}$ and $b = (52-6\sqrt{43})^{1/2}$.

We wish to find $a^3 - b^3 = (a-b)(a^2+ab+b^2)$.

We can easily calculate the values of the expressions of $a^2 + b^2$ and ab:

$a^2 + b^2 = (52+6\sqrt{43}) + (52-6\sqrt{43}) = 104$.

$ab = [(52+6\sqrt{43})]^{1/2}[(52-6\sqrt{43})]^{1/2} = (52^2 - 6^2 \times 43)^{1/2} = 1156^{1/2} = 34$.

Now we wish to find the value of $a - b$.

We know that $(a-b)^2 = a^2 - 2ab + b^2 = (a^2+b^2) - 2ab = 104 - 2 \times 34 = 36 \Rightarrow a - b = 6$.

Therefore $a^3 - b^3 = (a-b)(a^2+ab+b^2) = 6 \times (104+34) = 828$.

Problem 12. Solution: 400.

Since $x = \sqrt{5+\sqrt{5}}$ and $y = \sqrt{5-\sqrt{5}}$, $x^2 \cdot y^2 = (5+\sqrt{5})(5-\sqrt{5}) = 25 - 5 = 20$.

$x^2 + y^2 = (5+\sqrt{5}) + (5-\sqrt{5}) = 10$

$x^6 + y^6 = (x^2+y^2)^3 - 3(x^2+y^2) \cdot x^2 \cdot y^2 = 10^3 - 3 \times 10 \times 20 = 400$

(If you are confused about the equation above, expand out $(x^2+y^2)^3 - 3(x^2+y^2) \cdot x^2 \cdot y^2$)

Problem 13. Solution: 001.

Since $1 = (x+y+z)^2 = x^2+y^2+z^2 + 2(xy+yz+xz) = x^2+y^2+z^2 + 2/3$, we get
$x^2+y^2+z^2 = 1/3$. Then $x^2+y^2+z^2 - xy - yz - xz = 0$.

We know that $x^2+y^2+z^2 - xy - yz - zx = \dfrac{1}{2}[(x-y)^2 + (y-z)^2 + (z-x)^2]$.

Therefore $\dfrac{1}{2}[(x-y)^2 + (y-z)^2 + (z-x)^2] = 0$.

Since x, y, and z are positive real numbers, we have $x = y = z$, which implies that $\frac{x}{y} + \frac{y}{z} + \frac{z}{x} = 3$. 3 is the only value for $\frac{x}{y} + \frac{y}{z} + \frac{z}{x}$.

☆**Problem 14.** Solution: 017.
$$\frac{(x+y)(y+z)(z+x)}{xyz} = \frac{(x^2y + xy^2) + (x^2z + xz^2) + (y^2z + yz^2) + 2xyz}{xyz}$$
$$= \frac{xy(x+y) + xz(x+z) + yz(y+z) + 2xyz}{xyz}$$
$$= \frac{x+y}{z} + \frac{y+z}{x} + \frac{z+x}{y} + 2 = 2015 + 2 = 2017.$$

☆**Problem 15.** Solution: 187.
Using the quadratic formula, we see that the quadratic equation $x^2 - x - 1 = 0$ has the solutions: $p = \frac{1+\sqrt{5}}{2}$ and $q = \frac{1-\sqrt{5}}{2}$.

We can observe that $p + q = 1$ and $pq = -1$.
Since $x^2 - x - 1$ is a factor of $ax^{17} + bx^{16} + 1$, p and q are also the roots of $ax^{17} + bx^{16} + 1 = 0$.

Therefore we have $ap^{17} + bp^{16} = -1$ \hfill (1)

and $aq^{17} + bq^{16} = -1$ \hfill (2)

(1) × $q^{16} \Rightarrow ap^{17}q^{16} + bp^{16}q^{16} = -q^{16} \Rightarrow ap(-1)^{16} + b(-1)^{16} = -q^{16}$

$\Rightarrow \quad ap + b = -q^{16}$ \hfill (3)

(2) × p^{16}: $aq + b = -p^{16}$ \hfill (4)

(3) − (4): $a(p - q) = p^{16} - q^{16}$.

So
$$a = \frac{p^{16} - q^{16}}{p - q} = \frac{(p^8 + q^8)(p^8 - q^8)}{p - q} = \frac{(p^8 + q^8)(p^4 + q^4)(p^4 - q^4)}{p - q}$$
$$= \frac{(p^8 + q^8)(p^4 + q^4)(p^2 + q^2)(p^2 - q^2)}{p - q} = \frac{(p^8 + q^8)(p^4 + q^4)(p^2 + q^2)(p+q)(p-q)}{p - q}.$$
$$= (p^8 + q^8)(p^4 + q^4)(p^2 + q^2)(p + q)$$

Since $(p+q)^2 = p^2 + q^2 + 2pq$, we can calculate that:
$p^2 + q^2 = (p+q)^2 - 2pq = 1 + 2 = 3$.
Similarly, $p^4 + q^4 = (p^2 + q^2)^2 - 2(pq)^2 = 9 - 2 = 7$
and $p^8 + q^8 = (p^4 + q^4)^2 - 2(pq)^4 = 49 - 2 = 47$.
Therefore $a = 47 \times 7 \times 3 \times 1 = 987$.

Problem 16. Solution: 041.

By **Theorem 2**, $a_n = Ax^n + By^n + Cz^n$ can be written as

$a_{n+3} = (x+y+z)a_{n+2} - (xy+yz+zx)a_{n+1} + xyz\,a_n$, n is positive integer.

Let $A_1 = x+y+z$, $A_2 = -(xy+yz+zx)$, and $A_3 = xyz$.

Then we have $a_{n+3} = A_1 a_{n+2} + A_2 a_{n+1} + A_3 a_n$ $\hspace{2em}$ (1)

We know that $a_1 = 1$, $a_2 = 0$, $a_3 = 2$, $a_4 = 3$, $a_5 = 4$, $a_6 = 5$.

Substituting these values into (1):

$A_1 + 0 \times A_2 + 2A_3 = 3$ $\hspace{2em}$ (2)

$3A_1 + 2 \times A_2 + 0 \times A_3 = 4$ $\hspace{2em}$ (3)

$4A_1 + 3A_2 + 2A_3 = 5$ $\hspace{2em}$ (4)

Solving the system of equations (2), (3), and (4):

$A_1 = \dfrac{8}{3}$, $A_2 = -2$, $A_3 = \dfrac{1}{6}$.

Thus we get $a_{n+3} = \dfrac{8}{3} a_{n+2} - 2a_{n+1} + \dfrac{1}{6} a_n$, $n \geq 4$.

When $n = 4$, we get $a_7 = \dfrac{8}{3} a_6 - 2a_5 + \dfrac{1}{6} a_4 = \dfrac{8}{3} \times 5 - 2 \times 4 + \dfrac{1}{6} \times 3 = \dfrac{35}{6}$.

The answer is $35 + 6 = 41$.

Problem 17. Solution: 109.

Let $a_n = a^n + b^n + c^n$.

$a_1 = a + b + c = 0$

$a_2 = a^2 + b^2 + c^2 = (a+b+c)^2 - 2(ab+bc+ca) = -2(ab+bc+ca)$.

$a_3 = a^3 + b^3 + c^3 = (a+b+c)(a^2+b^2+c^2 - bc - ca - ab) + 3abc = 3abc$

By **Theorem 2**, $a_n = a^n + b^n + c^n$ can be written as
$$a_{n+3} = (a+b+c)a_{n+2} - (ab+bc+ca)a_{n+1} + abc\, a_n$$
$$= -(ab+bc+ca)a_{n+1} + abc\, a_n = \frac{1}{2}a_2 a_{n+1} + \frac{1}{3}a_3 a_n$$

Then we have
$$a_4 = \frac{1}{2}a_2 a_2 + \frac{1}{3}a_3 a_1 = \frac{1}{2}a_2^2$$
$$a_5 = \frac{1}{2}a_2 a_3 + \frac{1}{3}a_3 a_2 = \frac{5}{6}a_2 a_3$$
$$a_7 = \frac{1}{2}a_2 a_5 + \frac{1}{3}a_3 a_4 = \frac{1}{2}a_2 \times \frac{5}{6}a_2 a_3 + \frac{1}{3}a_3 \times \frac{1}{2}a_2^2 = \frac{7}{12}a_2^2 a_3.$$

Therefore $\dfrac{(a^7+b^7+c^7)^2}{(a^2+b^2+c^2)(a^3+b^3+c^3)(a^4+b^4+c^4)(a^5+b^5+c^5)}$

$$= \frac{(a_7)^2}{a_2 a_3 a_4 a_5} = \frac{(\frac{7}{12}a_2^2 a_3)^2}{a_2 a_3 \cdot \frac{1}{2}a_2^2 \cdot \frac{5}{6}a_2 a_3} = \frac{49}{60}.$$

The answer is $49 + 60 = 109$.

Problem 18. Solution: 003.
$(2) - (1) \times 2$:
$x^2 + y^2 + z^2 - 2x - 2y - 2z = -3$
Completing the square: $(x-1)^2 + (y-1)^2 + (z-1)^2 = 0$

$\therefore x = 1, y = 1, z = 1$. $x^{2015} + y^{2016} + z^{2017} = 3$.

Problem 19. Solution: 031.
$$xy + yz + xz = \frac{1}{2}[(x+y+z)^2 - (x^2+y^2+z^2)] = \frac{1}{2}(1^2 - 2) = -\frac{1}{2}.$$
$$x^4 + y^4 + z^4 = (x^2+y^2+z^2)^2 - 2(x^2 y^2 + y^2 z^2 + z^2 x^2)$$
$$= 2^2 - 2[(xy+yz+zx)^2 - 2xyz(x+y+z)]$$
$$= 4 - 2[(-\frac{1}{2})^2 - 2xyz] = \frac{7}{2} + 4xyz$$

We also know that $x^3 + y^3 + z^3 = (x+y+z)(x^2+y^2+z^2-xy-yz-zx) + 3xyz$.

So $3 - 3xyz = 2 - (-\frac{1}{2}) \quad \Rightarrow xyz = \frac{1}{6}$.

Thus $x^4 + y^4 + z^4 = \frac{7}{2} + 4xyz = \frac{7}{2} + 4 \times \frac{1}{6} = \frac{25}{6}$.

The answer is $25 + 6 = 31$.

1. DEFINITION

If a and x are positive real numbers and $a \neq 1$, then y is the logarithm to the base a of x.
This can be written as $y = \log_a x$ \hfill (1.1)
if and only if $\quad x = a^y$ \hfill (1.2)

A quick way to convert the logarithm to the exponent:

$$\log_a x = y \Rightarrow a^y = x$$

Notes:
(1) The logarithm base 10 is called the **common logarithm.** $\log x$ always refers to log base 10, i.e., $\log x = \log_{10} x$.

(2) The logarithm base e is called the **natural logarithm.** $\ln x = \log_e x$.

(3) $\log_{10} x$ is always written as $\log x$.

(4) Zero and negative numbers have no logarithm expressions. The following expressions are undefined: $\log_a 0$, $\log_a(-3)$, or $\log_{-10} x$.

The graphs of logarithmic functions $f(x) = \log_a x$ all have an x-intercept of 1, and are increasing when $a > 1$ and decreasing when $a < 1$.

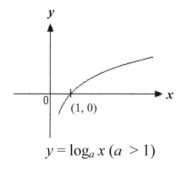
$y = \log_a x \; (a > 1)$

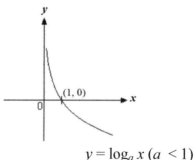
$y = \log_a x \; (a < 1)$

2. PROPERTIES OF LOGARITHMS:

If a, b, x and y are positive real numbers, $a \neq 1$, $b \neq 1$, and r is any real number, we have

$$\log_a 1 = 0 \qquad (2.1)$$

$$\log_a a = 1 \qquad (2.2)$$

$$a^{\log_a x} = x \qquad (2.3)$$

$$\log_a a^r = r \qquad (2.4)$$

$$\log_a b \log_b c = \log_a c \qquad (2.5)$$

3. THE LAWS OF LOGARITHMS:

Law 1: the Product Identity

$$\log_a xy = \log_a x + \log_a y \qquad (3.1)$$

Proof:
Let $m = \log_a x$ and $n = \log_a y$.
The exponential form of the equations is $a^m = x$ and $a^n = y$.
Multiplying these two equations, we get $a^m a^n = xy \implies a^{m+n} = xy$
Transforming the exponential form to the logarithmic form, we have $\log_a xy = m + n$.
Since $m = \log_a x$ and $n = \log_a y$, $\log_a xy = \log_a x + \log_a y$.

Law 2: the Quotient Identity

$$\log_a\left(\frac{x}{y}\right) = \log_a x - \log_a y \qquad (3.2)$$

Proof:
Let $m = \log_a x$ and $n = \log_a y$.
The exponential form of the equations is $a^m = x$ and $a^n = y$
Dividing these two equations, we get $a^m / a^n = x/y \implies a^{m-n} = x/y$
Use the definition of the logarithm, we get $\log_a\left(\frac{x}{y}\right) = m - n$.

Since $m = \log_a x$ and $n = \log_a y$, $\log_a\left(\frac{x}{y}\right) = \log_a x - \log_a y$.

When we apply **Law 1 the Product Identity** $\log_a xy = \log_a x + \log_a y$ or **Law 2: the Quotient Identity** $\log_a\left(\frac{x}{y}\right) = \log_a x - \log_a y$, we need to know that both x and y in the expressions $\log_a xy$ and $\log_a(\frac{x}{y})$, can be negative. However, in the expressions $\log_a x + \log_a y$ or $\log_a x - \log_a y$, neither of them can be negative.

$\log_a (-2)(-3) \neq \log_a(-2) + \log_a(-3)$ (undefined).
$\log_a(\frac{-2}{-3}) \neq \log_a(-2) - \log_a(-3)$ (undefined).

Law 3: the Power Identity

Formula 1: $\log_a x^r = r \log_a x$ (3.3)

Proof:
Since $x = a^{\log_a x}$, $\log_a x^r = \log_a (a^{\log_a x})^r \rightarrow \log_a x^r = (r \log_a x) \log_a a$.
Recall that $\log_a a = 1$. Substituting this value into the equation, we have $\log_a x^r = r \log_a x$.

Formula 2: $\log_{a^m} b^n = \frac{n}{m} \log_a b$ $(a, b > 0, a \neq 1)$ (3.4)

Proof:
Let $\log_{a^m} b^n = c$.

The exponential form of the equations is $(a^m)^c = b^n$.

Taking the logarithm of both sides yields $c \log_a a^m = n \log_a b$ or $cm = n \log_a b$.

$c = \frac{n}{m} \log_a b \quad \Rightarrow \quad \log_{a^m} b^n = \frac{n}{m} \log_a b$.

When we apply **Law 3: the Power Identity** $\log_a x^r = r \log_a x$, we need to be sure that in the expressions $\log_a x^r$, x can be negative if r is even. However, x must be positive in the expression $r \log_a x$.
$\log_a (-2)^2 \neq 2 \log_a (-2)$, (undefined).

4. CHANGE-OF-BASE THEOREM:

Formula 1: $\quad \log_a x = \dfrac{\log_b x}{\log_b a}$ (4.1)

Proof:
Let $y = \log_a x$. The exponential form of this equation is $a^y = x$.
Taking the logarithm on both sides, we get $\log_b a^y = \log_b x \Rightarrow y \log_b a = \log_b x$
Dividing both sides by $\log_b b$, we obtain $y = \dfrac{\log_b x}{\log_b a} \Rightarrow \log_a x = \dfrac{\log_b x}{\log_b a}$.

Formula 2: $\quad \log_a N = \log_{a^m} N^m, \quad m \neq 0$ (4.2)

Proof:
$\log_a N = \dfrac{\log_b N}{\log_b a} = \dfrac{m \log_b N}{m \log_b a} = \dfrac{\log_b N^m}{\log_b a^m} = \log_{a^m} N^m$.

Formula 3: $\quad \log_a N = \dfrac{1}{\log_N a}, \quad N \neq 1$ (4.3)

Proof:
$\log_a N = \dfrac{\log_N N}{\log_N a} = \dfrac{1}{\log_N a}$.

Formula 4: $\quad \log_a N = -\log_a \dfrac{1}{N}$ (4.4)

Proof:
$\log_a N = \log_a (\dfrac{1}{N})^{-1} = -\log_a \dfrac{1}{N}$

Formula 5: $\quad \log_a N = -\log_{\frac{1}{a}} N$ (4.5)

Proof:

$$\log_a N = \log_{a^{-1}} N^{-1} = -\log_{\frac{1}{a}} N$$

Formula 6: $\log_a N = m \log_{a^m} N$, $m \neq 0$ \hfill (4.6)

Proof:

$\log_a N = \log_{a^m} N^m = m \log_{a^m} N$

Formula 7: $\dfrac{\log_a M}{\log_a N} = \dfrac{\log_b M}{\log_b N}$ $\quad (a > 0, a \neq 1, b > 0, b \neq 1, M, N > 0, N \neq 1)$ \hfill (4.7)

Proof :

By the Change-of-Base Theorem, we have $\dfrac{\log_a M}{\log_a N} = \log_N M$, and $\dfrac{\log_b M}{\log_b N} = \log_N M$.

Therefore $\dfrac{\log_a M}{\log_a N} = \dfrac{\log_b M}{\log_b N}$.

Formula 8: $\log_a \sqrt[n]{N} = \dfrac{1}{n} \log_a N$, N is integer greater than 1. \hfill (4.8)

5. SOLVING LOGARITHM EQUATIONS

If x, y and $a \neq 1$ are positive real numbers, $x = y$ if and only if $\log_a x = \log_a y$. Similarly $x^a = y^a$ if and only if $x = y$.

6. EXAMPLES

Example 1. (ARML) Compute all real values of x such that $\log_2(\log_2 x) = \log_4(\log_4 x)$.

Solution:

By the formula (4.6), we have $\log_2(\log_2 x) = 2\log_4(2\log_4 x) = \log_4(2\log_4 x)^2$.
Therefore $\log_4(2\log_4 x)^2 = \log_4(\log_4 x)$ $\quad \Rightarrow \quad (2\log_4 x)^2 = \log_4 x \quad \Rightarrow$
$4(\log_4 x)^2 - \log_4 x = 0 \quad\quad \Rightarrow (\log_4 x)(4\log_4 x - 1) = 0$

We have $\log_4 x = 0 \Rightarrow x = 4^0 = 1$ (extraneous because $\log_2 x$ will be zero and $\log_2(\log_2 x)$ will be undefined).

Or $4\log_2 x - 1 = 0 \Rightarrow \log_4 x = \dfrac{1}{4} \Rightarrow x = 4^{1/4} = \sqrt{2}$.

Example 2 (ARML) Given $\dfrac{\log(xy)}{\log(\dfrac{x}{y})} = \dfrac{1}{2}$, increasing y by 50% decreases x by a factor of k. Compute k.

Solution:
Method 1 (official solution):

Step 1: $\log(xy) = \dfrac{1}{2}\log(\dfrac{x}{y}) = \log\sqrt{\dfrac{x}{y}}$ \hfill (1)

Step 2: $xy = \sqrt{\dfrac{x}{y}}$ \hfill (2)

Step 3: $\sqrt{x} = \dfrac{1}{y^{\frac{3}{2}}}$ \hfill (3)

Step 4: $x = \dfrac{1}{y^3}$ \hfill (4)

Increasing by 50% gives $\dfrac{1}{(\dfrac{3}{2}y)^3} = \left(\dfrac{8}{27} \cdot \dfrac{1}{y^3}\right) = \dfrac{8}{27}x$. Thus $k = \dfrac{8}{27}$.

Note: The given equation is valid for $x, y < 0$. From step 2 to step 3 in the official solution, they separated $\sqrt{\dfrac{x}{y}}$ to $\dfrac{\sqrt{x}}{\sqrt{y}}$, which is incorrect for the case $x, y < 0$.

The correct way should be: squaring both sides of (2): $(xy)^2 = \dfrac{x}{y} \Rightarrow x = \dfrac{1}{y^3}$.

Method 2 (solution given by Intermediate Algebra from Art of Problem Solving):
Multiplying both sides by $2 \log (x/y)$, the equation becomes

$$2\log(xy) = \log\frac{x}{y} \quad (1)$$

So $2\log x + 2\log y = \log x - \log y$ (2)

Rearranging this gives $\log x + 3\log y = 0$ (3)

Applying logarithm identities to the left sides gives
$\log x + 3\log y = \log x + \log y^3 = \log(xy^3)$, so $\log(xy^3) = 0$, which mean $xy^3 = 1$. Hence if y increases by 50%, meaning that y is multiplied by 3/2, then x must be multiplied by a factor of $(2/3)^3 = 8/27$.

Note: The original equation is valid for $x, y < 0$ as well. But from equation (1) to equation (2), it was incorrectly assumed that $x, y > 0$. We cannot apply the product identity if $x, y < 0$.

Method 3 (our solution):

The given equation can be written as: $\log(xy) = \frac{1}{2}\log(\frac{x}{y})$ (1)

When we increase y by 50% and decrease x by a factor of k, we have

$\log(kx \times 1.5y) = \frac{1}{2}\log(\frac{kx}{1.5y}) \Rightarrow \log(1.5k) + \log(xy) = \frac{1}{2}[\log(\frac{k}{1.5}) + \log(\frac{x}{y})]$ (2)

Substituting (1) into (2): $\log(1.5k) = \frac{1}{2}\log(\frac{k}{1.5}) \Rightarrow 2\log(1.5k) = \log(\frac{k}{1.5})$

$\Rightarrow \log(1.5k)^2 = \log(\frac{k}{1.5}) \Rightarrow (1.5k)^2 = \frac{k}{1.5} \Rightarrow k = \frac{1}{1.5^3} = \frac{8}{27}$.

Example 3. (ARML) For integers x and y with $1 < x, y \le 100$, compute the number of ordered pairs (x, y) such that $\log_x y + \log_y x^2 = 3$.

Solution: 108.

$\log_x y + \log_y x^2 = 3 \Rightarrow \log_x y + 2\log_y x = 3 \Rightarrow \log_x y + \frac{2}{\log_x y} = 3$

$\Rightarrow (\log_x y)^2 + 2 = 3\log_x y \Rightarrow (\log_x y)^2 - 3\log_x y + 2 = 0$

$\Rightarrow (\log_x y - 1)(\log_x y - 2) = 0$.

Thus $\log_x y - 1 = 0$ or $\log_x y - 2 = 0$.

The solutions to the first equation are the 99 ordered pairs from (2, 2) to (100, 100); the solutions to the second equation are the 9 ordered pairs (2, 4), (3, 9), (4, 16),…,(10, 100). Thus there are 99 + 9 = 108 ordered pairs of solutions.

Example 4. Solve $\log x^2 + \log x^8 = 10$.

Solution:
Method 1 (incorrect way):
By **Law 3: the Power Identity,** $\log_a x^r = r \log_a x$, the given equation can be written as
$$2\log x + 8 \log x = 10 \Rightarrow 10 \log x = 10 \Rightarrow \log x = 1.$$
Therefore, the solution is $x = 10$. We can plug this back into the given equation to check and see that it is a solution.

However, we missed one solution because we misused the law 3, since we are not allowed to move "r" to the front if $x > 0$.

Method 2 (correct way):
We know that x^2 and x^8 are positive, so by **Law 1: the Product Identity** $\log_a x + \log_a y = \log_a xy$, the given equation becomes $\log(x^2 \cdot x^8) = 10 \Rightarrow x^{10} = 10^{10} \Rightarrow x = \pm 10$. Plugging these values back into the given equation, we can check and see that both values of x are the solutions.

Example 5. For the equation $2\log[\frac{1}{2}(a-b)] = \log a + \log b$, a/b can be expressed as $m + n\sqrt{t}$ in the simplest radical form. Find $m + n + t$.

Solution: 007.

For $\log a$, $\log b$, and $\log[\frac{1}{2}(a-b)]$ to be defined, the following statement must be true: $a > b > 0$.

The given equation can be written as $\log[\frac{1}{2}(a-b)]^2 = \log(ab)$.

So $[\frac{1}{2}(a-b)]^2 = ab \quad \Rightarrow a^2 - 6ab + b^2 = 0$.

Since that $b > 0$, we can divide both sides of the equation by b^2 and obtain:

$\left(\frac{a}{b}\right)^2 - 6\left(\frac{a}{b}\right) + 1 = 0$.

Solving for a/b, we get $\frac{a}{b} = 3 + 2\sqrt{2}$ or $\frac{a}{b} = 3 - 2\sqrt{2}$. The latter answer is extraneous since $3 - 2\sqrt{2} < 1$. The answer is $3 + 2 + 2 = 7$.

☆**Example 6.** (2000 AIME I) The system of equations
$$\log_{10}(2000xy) - (\log_{10} x)(\log_{10} y) = 4$$
$$\log_{10}(2yz) - (\log_{10} y)(\log_{10} z) = 1$$
$$\log_{10}(zx) - (\log_{10} z)(\log_{10} x) = 0$$
has two solutions (x_1, y_1, z_1) and (x_2, y_2, z_2). Find $y_1 + y_2$.

Solution: 025.
Method 1 (official solution):
Let $u = \log_{10} x$, $v = \log_{10} y$, $w = \log_{10} z$.
We rewrite the given system of equations as

$\begin{cases} uv - u - v + 1 = \log_{10} 2, \\ vw - v - w + 1 = \log_{10} 2, \\ wu - w - u + 1 = 1. \end{cases}$ or $\begin{cases} (u-1)(v-1) = \log_{10} 2, \\ (v-1)(w-1) = \log_{10} 2, \\ (w-1)(u-1) = 1. \end{cases}$

From the first two equations, we get $u = w$.
From the third equation we have two cases: $u = v = 2$ or $u = v = 0$.
Case I: $v = \log_{10} 20$. This gives us $x_1 = 100$, $y_1 = 20$, $z_1 = 100$.
Case II: $v = \log_{10} 5$. This gives us $x_2 = 1$, $y_2 = 5$, $z_2 = 1$.
Therefore $y_1 + y_2 = 25$.

Method 2 (our solution):
$\log_{10}(2000xy) - (\log_{10} x)(\log_{10} y) = 4 \quad \Rightarrow$
$\quad \log 2 + 3 + \log x + \log y - (\log x)(\log y) = 4$
or $\log 2 + \log x + \log y - (\log x)(\log y) = 1$ \hfill (1)

$\log_{10}(2yz) - (\log_{10} y)(\log_{10} z) = 1 \Rightarrow \log 2 + \log y + \log z - (\log y)(\log z) = 1$ \hfill (2)

$\log_{10}(zx) - (\log_{10} z)(\log_{10} x) = 0 \Rightarrow \log z + \log x - (\log z)(\log x) = 0$ \hfill (3)

(1) – (2): $\log x + (\log x)(\log y) - [\log z - (\log y)(\log z)] = 0 \Rightarrow$

$\log x(1 + \log y) - \log z(1 + \log y) = 0 \Rightarrow (1 + \log y)(\log x - \log z) = 0$ \hfill (4)

We know that $1 + \log y \neq 0$. So we have $\log x - \log z = 0 \Rightarrow x = z$.

Substituting $x = z$ into (3): $\log x + \log x - (\log x)(\log x) = 0$

$\Rightarrow \quad 2\log x - (\log x)^2 = 0 \Rightarrow \quad (\log x)(2 - \log x) = 0$.

We have either $\log x = 0 \Rightarrow x = 1$, and $y = 5$, $z = 1$.

or $2 - \log x = 0 \Rightarrow \quad x = 100$, and $y = 20$, $z = 100$.

Therefore $y_1 + y_2 = 25$.

☆**Example 7.** Find $(\log_3 x)^2$ if $\log_3(\log_{27} x) = \log_{27}(\log_3 x)$.

Solution: 027.

Since $\log_{27} x = \dfrac{1}{\log_x 27} = \dfrac{1}{3\log_x 3} = \dfrac{1}{3}\log_3 x = \log_3 x^{\frac{1}{3}}$,

$\log_3(\log_{27} x) = \log_3(\log_3 x^{\frac{1}{3}}) = \dfrac{1}{3}\log_3(\log_3 x)$.

So $\log_{27}(\log_3 x) = \dfrac{1}{3}\log_3(\log_3 x)$ \hfill (1)

Let $y = \log_3 x$.

By the formula (4.2), (1) becomes: $\log_3 \dfrac{y}{3} = \dfrac{1}{3}\log_3 y \quad \Rightarrow \quad \log_3(\dfrac{y}{3})^3 = \log_3 y \Rightarrow$

$(\dfrac{y}{3})^3 = y$

Rearranging the terms, we get $y(y^2 - 27) = 0$. Since $y \neq 0$, $y^2 = (\log_3 x)^2 = 27$.

☆**Example 8.** a, b, and c are positive integers forming an increasing geometric sequence and $b - a$ is the square of an integer. Find $a + b + c$ if $\log_8 a + \log_8 b + \log_8 c = 5$.

Solution: 112.

Note that $\log_8 a + \log_8 b + \log_8 c = 5 = \log_8 abc$. Then $8^5 = abc = b^3$, so $b = 2^5 = 32$ and $ac = 2^{10}$. Because $b \neq a$ and $b - a$ is the square of an integer, the only possibilities for a are 7, 16, 23, 28, and 31. Of these, only 16 is a divisor of 2^{10}.
Thus $a + b + c = 16 + 32 + 64 = 112$.

Example 9. α and β are two distinct roots of the equation $(\log 3x)(\log 5x) = k$. The product of α and β can be expressed as $\dfrac{m}{n}$, where m and n are positive integers relatively prime. Find $m + n$.

Solution: 016.
Since α and β are two distinct roots, we have
$$\log 3\alpha \cdot \log 5\alpha = k \qquad (1)$$
$$\log 3\beta \cdot \log 5\beta = k \qquad (2)$$
(1) − (2): $\log 3\alpha \cdot \log 5\alpha - \log 3\beta \cdot \log 5\beta = 0$.
$(\log 3 + \log \alpha)(\log 5 + \log \alpha) - (\log 3 + \log \beta)(\log 5 + \log \beta) = 0$.
$\log 15(\log \alpha - \log \beta) + (\log^2 \alpha - \log^2 \beta) = 0$.
$(\log \alpha - \log \beta)[(\log 15 + (\log \alpha + \log \beta)] = 0$
Since $\alpha \neq \beta$, and $\log \alpha - \log \beta \neq 0$, $\log 15 + (\log \alpha + \log \beta) = 0 \Rightarrow \log 15 = -\log \alpha\beta$
Therefore $\alpha\beta = \dfrac{1}{15}$. The answer is $m + n = 1 + 15 = 16$.

Example 10. The value of y can be expressed as $m\sqrt{n}$, where m and n are relatively prime positive integers. Find $m + n$ if
$$\begin{cases} \log_5(x^2 + 2x - 2) = 0, & (1) \\ 2\log_5(x+2) - \log_5 y + \dfrac{1}{2} = 0. & (2) \end{cases}$$

Solution: 014.
Simplifying (1), we get $x^2 + 2x - 2 = 1$. Solving this quadratic for x, we get $x = 1, x = -3$. $x = -3$ is extraneous, since it yields a negative value that we must take the logarithm of when we substitute x into equation (2).

Simplifying (2), we get $\dfrac{\sqrt{5}(x+2)^2}{y}=1$.

Substituting $x = 1$ into the above equation: $y=\sqrt{5}(1+2)^2=9\sqrt{5}$. The answer is 14.

☆**Example 11.** (AIME) Let x, y and z all exceed 1 and let w be a positive number such that $\log_x w = 24$, $\log_y w = 40$ and $\log_{xyz} w = 12$. Find $\log_z w$.

Solution: 060.
Method 1:
Changing the given logarithms into exponential forms, we get
$x^{24}=w$, $y^{40}=w$, $(xyz)^{12}=w$.

$z^{12}=\dfrac{w}{x^{12}y^{12}}=\dfrac{w}{w^{\frac{1}{2}}w^{\frac{3}{10}}}=w^{\frac{1}{5}}$.

Therefore $w=z^{60}$ and $\log_z w = 60$.

Method 2:

Let $\log_z w = t$. We then have $\log z = \dfrac{\log w}{t}$, $\log x = \dfrac{\log w}{24}$, and $\log y = \dfrac{\log w}{40}$.

$\log_{xyz} w = \dfrac{\log w}{\log x + \log y + \log z} = \dfrac{\log w}{\dfrac{\log w}{24}+\dfrac{\log w}{40}+\dfrac{\log w}{t}} = 12$

Or $\dfrac{1}{24}+\dfrac{1}{40}+\dfrac{1}{t}=\dfrac{1}{12}$. Solving for t, we get $t = 60$. Thus $\log_z w = 60$.

Method 3:

$\log_w z = \log_w \dfrac{zxy}{xy} = \log_w xyz - \log_w x - \log_w y = \dfrac{1}{12}-\dfrac{1}{24}-\dfrac{1}{40}=\dfrac{1}{60}$. $\therefore \log_z w = 60$.

Method 4:

By (4.3), we have $\log_{xyz} w = 12$ $\Rightarrow$ $\log_w xyz = \dfrac{1}{12}$ \qquad (1)

By (4.1): (1) becomes $\dfrac{\log x}{\log w} + \dfrac{\log y}{\log w} + \dfrac{\log z}{\log w} = \dfrac{1}{12} \Rightarrow \dfrac{1}{\log_x w} + \dfrac{1}{\log_y w} + \dfrac{1}{\log_z w} = \dfrac{1}{12}$

$\dfrac{1}{\log_z w} = \dfrac{1}{12} - \dfrac{1}{24} - \dfrac{1}{40} = \dfrac{1}{60} \Rightarrow \log_z w = 60$.

Example 12. $xy^2 = 100$ with $1 \le x \le 10$. The smallest value of $(\log x)^2 + (\log y)^2$ can be expressed as $\dfrac{m}{n}$, where m and n are relatively prime positive integers. Find $m + n$.

Solution: 009.

We know that $y > 0$ and $y = \dfrac{10}{\sqrt{x}}$.

$(\log x)^2 + (\log y)^2 = (\log x)^2 + \left(\log \dfrac{10}{\sqrt{x}}\right)^2 = (\log x)^2 + (1 - \dfrac{1}{2}\log x)^2$

$= \dfrac{5}{4}(\log x)^2 - \log x + 1 = \dfrac{5}{4}\left(\log x - \dfrac{2}{5}\right)^2 + \dfrac{4}{5}$

Since $1 \le x \le 10$, then $0 \le \log x \le 1$.

When $\log x = \dfrac{2}{5}$, or $x = 10^{\frac{2}{5}}$, $(\log x)^2 + (\log y)^2$ has the smallest value of $\dfrac{4}{5}$. The answer is $4 + 5 = 9$.

50 AIME Lectures   Chapter 8 Logarithms

PROBLEMS

Problem 1. Solve for x: $2\log_{25} x + \log_x 25 = 3$. What is the sum of the solutions?

Problem 2. (ARML) Compute the largest real value of b such that the solutions to the following equation are integers: $(\log_{2^{10}} x^{2b})^2 = \log_{2^{10}} x^4$.

☆**Problem 3.** Determine the number of ordered pairs (a, b) of integers such that $\log_a b + 12 \log_b a = 7$, $2 \le a \le 2015$, and $2 \le b \le 2015$.

Problem 4. (NEAML) Determine the numerical value of: $(\log_{x^2}(y^5))(\log_y(x^4))$.

☆**Problem 5.** (AIME) Determine the value of ab if $\log_8 a + \log_4 b^2 = 5$ and $\log_8 b + \log_4 a^2 = 7$.

Problem 6. The solution to the system of equations can be expressed as $(x, y, z) = (\frac{a}{b}, \frac{c}{d}, \frac{e}{f})$. Find $a + c + e$.

$$\begin{cases} \log_2 x + \log_4 y + \log_4 z = 2 & (1) \\ \log_3 y + \log_9 z + \log_9 x = 2 & (2) \\ \log_4 z + \log_{16} x + \log_{16} y = 2 & (3). \end{cases}$$

☆**Problem 7.** Find $(\log_2 x)^3$ if $\log_2(\log_{16} x) = \log_{16}(\log_2 x)$.

Problem 8. Find the value of $x + y + z$ if $\log_2(\log_3 x) = \log_3(\log_4 y) = \log_4(\log_2 z) = 1$.

☆**Problem 9.** Find the last three digits of the product of the positive roots of $\sqrt{2015} x^{\log_{2015} x} = x^2$.

☆**Problem 10.** The solutions to the system of equations $\log_{225} x + \log_{729} y = 4$ and $\log_x 225 - \log_y 729 = 1$ are (x_1, y_1) and (x_2, y_2). Find $\log_{45}(x_1 y_1 x_2 y_2)$.

Problem 11. a, b, c form a geometric sequence and $\log_c a$, $\log_b c$, $\log_a b$ form an arithmetic sequence. The common difference of the arithmetic sequence can be expressed as $\dfrac{m}{n}$, where m and n are relatively prime positive integers. Find $m + n$.

Problem 12. For positive numbers x and y, if $xy = 490$ and $(\log x - \log 7)(\log y - \log 7) = -\dfrac{143}{4}$, how many digits are there of the integer part of the greater of x and y?

☆Problem 13. (2009 AIME II) Suppose that a, b, and c are positive real numbers such that $a^{\log_3 7} = 27$, $b^{\log_7 11} = 49$, and $c^{\log_{11} 25} = \sqrt{11}$. Find $a^{(\log_3 7)^2} + b^{(\log_7 11)^2} + c^{(\log_{11} 25)^2}$.

SOLUTIONS

Problem 1. Solution: 030.

We may rewrite $2\log_{25} x + \log_x 25 = 3$ as

$$2\log_{25} x + \frac{1}{\log_{25} x} = 3 \quad \Rightarrow \quad 2\log_{25}^2 x - 3\log_{25} x + 1 = 0 \quad \Rightarrow$$

$$(2\log_{25} x - 1)(\log_{25} x - 1) = 0$$

So $\log_{25} x = \frac{1}{2}$, $x_1 = 25^{\frac{1}{2}} = 5$; $\log_{25} x = 1$, $x_2 = 25$.

We can check to see that these two values are both solutions by plugging them into the given equation. The answer is $5 + 25 = 30$.

Problem 2. Solution: $b = \sqrt{10}$.

Method 1 (from the book "Intermediate Algebra" by Art of Problem Solving):
We remove the exponents from the arguments, x^{2b} and x^4:

$$(2b\log_{2^{10}} x)^2 = 4\log_{2^{10}} x \tag{1}$$

Noting that $\log_{2^{10}} x = \log_2 x^{1/10} = \frac{1}{10}\log_2 x$, our expression becomes:

$$(\frac{b}{5}\log_2 x)^2 = \frac{2}{5}\log_2 x \tag{2}$$

Multiplying both sides of (2) by 25 gives us:

$$b^2 (\log_2 x)^2 = 10\log_2 x \quad \Rightarrow \quad (b^2 \log_2 x - 10)\log_2 x = 0.$$

We have $\log_2 x = 0$ or $b^2 \log_2 x - 10 = 0$.

The first equation gives us $x = 1$ no matter what b is. The second equation gives us $x = 2^{10/b^2}$.

In order for x to be an integer, the expression $10/b^2$ must be a positive integer. The largest value is $b = \sqrt{10}$.

Note: Equation (1) is correct only when $x > 0$. However, the original equation $(\log_{2^{10}} x^{2b})^2 = \log_{2^{10}} x^4$ is true for $x < 0$ as well.

Method 2 (official solution):

$$(\log_{2^{10}} x^{2b})^2 = 4\log_{2^{10}} x \tag{1}$$

$$\Rightarrow \quad 4b^2 (\log_{2^{10}} x)^2 - 4\log_{2^{10}} x = 0 \tag{2}$$

$$(\log_{2^{10}} x)(b^2 \log_{2^{10}}(x) - 1) = 0$$

If $\log_{2^{10}} x = 0$, then $x = 1$.

If $b^2 \log_{2^{10}} x - 1 = 0$, then $\log_{2^{10}} x = \dfrac{1}{b^2}$, giving $x = (2^{10})^{\frac{1}{b^2}} = 2^{\frac{10}{b^2}}$.

There are several values that b can hold so that x an integer. If $b = \pm 1$, the $x = 2^{10}$. If $b = \pm\dfrac{\sqrt{10}}{3}$, the $x = 2^9$. But the largest value of b such that the second solution an integer is $b = \sqrt{10}$, which gives us $x = 2$.

Note: Both equations (1) and (2) are correct only if $x > 0$. The given equation is valid whether $x > 0$ or $x < 0$ but (2) and (3) will not be true if $x < 0$, so (2) and (3) are not equivalent to the given equation.

Method 3 (our solution):
$(\log_{2^{10}} x^{2b})^2 = \log_{2^{10}} x^4 \quad \Rightarrow \quad (b\log_{2^{10}} x^2)^2 = 2\log_{2^{10}} x^2$ (We should make sure that the argument is still positive even when $x < 0$).

Taking b^2 out, the equation becomes

$b^2 (\log_{2^{10}} x^2)^2 = 2\log_{2^{10}} x^2 \quad \Rightarrow \quad b^2 (\log_{2^{10}} x^2)^2 - 2\log_{2^{10}} x^2 = 0$

$\Rightarrow \quad (b^2 \log_{2^{10}} x^2 - 2)\log_{2^{10}} x^2 = 0$.

This gives us $\log_{2^{10}} x^2 = 0$ or $b^2 \log_{2^{10}} x^2 - 2 = 0$.

The first equation results in $x^2 = 1$. Solving for x, we get $x = 1$ or $x = -1$. We can see that both values of x are the solutions to the given equation. Under these values of x, b can be any value. So there is no largest value of b possible.

Solving the second equation, we get $b^2 \log_{2^{10}} x^2 = 2$.

Since we want the largest value of b and we can assume that $b \neq 0$, we have

$\log_{2^{10}} x^2 = \dfrac{2}{b^2} \quad \Rightarrow \quad x^2 = (2^{10})^{\frac{2}{b^2}} = 2^{\frac{20}{b^2}}$

Therefore $x_1 = (2^{\frac{20}{b^2}})^{\frac{1}{2}} = 2^{\frac{10}{b^2}}$ or $x_2 = -(2^{\frac{20}{b^2}})^{\frac{1}{2}} = -2^{\frac{10}{b^2}}$.

In order for x to be an integer, the expression $10/b^2$ must be a positive integer. Since b is real number, there are many values that b can hold such that x is an integer for example, $b = \pm 1$, $b = \pm\sqrt{2}$, $b = \pm\sqrt{5}$, $b = \pm\frac{\sqrt{10}}{n}$, where n can be any positive integer. The largest such value is $b = \sqrt{10}$.

Problem 3. Solution: 048.
Let $x = \log_a b$. Because $\log_b a = 1/\log_a b$, the given equation can be written as $x + (12/x) = 7$, and because $x \neq 0$, this is equivalent to $x^2 - 7x + 12 = 0$, whose solutions are 3 and 4.

If $3 = x = \log_a b$, then $a^3 = b$. Because $12^3 = 1728$ and $13^3 = 2197$, there are $12 - 1 = 11$ ordered pairs (a, b) such that $a^3 = b$ and a and b satisfy the given conditions.

If $4 = x = \log_a b$, then $a^4 = b$. Now $6^4 = 1296$ and $7^4 = 2401$, so there are $6 - 1 = 5$ ordered pairs (a, b) such that $a^4 = b$ and a and b satisfy the given conditions.

Thus there are $43 + 5 = 48$ of the requested ordered pairs.

Problem 4. Solution: 010.
Method 1 (official solution):
$$\left(\log_{x^2}(y^5)\right)\left(\log_y(x^4)\right)$$
$$= \left(\frac{1}{2}\log_x(y^5)\right)\left(\log_y(x^4)\right) \quad \text{(Step 1)}$$
$$= \left(\frac{1}{2}\right)(5 \cdot 4)\left(\log_x y\right)\left(\log_y x\right) \quad \text{(Step 2)}$$
$$= 10\left(\frac{\log y}{\log x}\right)\left(\frac{\log x}{\log y}\right) = 10.$$

Note: Step 1 of this solution is incorrect. In the given expression $(\log_{x^2}(y^5))(\log_y(x^4))$, x can be either positive or negative. In step 1, x was forced to be positive in $\left(\frac{1}{2}\log_x(y^5)\right)$. However, it is okay to set $(\log_{x^2}(y^5)) = 5\log_{x^2}(y)$ because y must be positive since y is the base in the expression $(\log_y(x^4))$.

Method 2 (our solution):
$(\log_{x^2}(y^5))(\log_y(x^4))$
$= (5\log_{x^2} y)(\log_y(x^4)) = 5 \times \dfrac{\log y}{\log x^2} \times \dfrac{\log x^4}{\log y}$ (note that log y is not zero since y is not 1).
$= 5 \times \dfrac{\log x^4}{\log x^2} = 5 \times \dfrac{\log(x^2)^2}{\log x^2} = 2 \times 5 \times \dfrac{\log x^2}{\log x^2} = 10$.

Problem 5. Solution: 512.
Method 1:
Adding the two given equations, we get: $\log_8 ab + \log_4 a^2 b^2 = 12$
By the Change-of-Base formula, we can change the two logarithms from base 8 and 4, respectively into base 2: $\dfrac{\log_2 ab}{3} + \log_2 ab = 12$.

So $\dfrac{4}{3}\log_2 ab = 12$, $\log_2 ab = 9$ and $ab = 2^9 = 512$.

Method 2:
$\log_8 a + \log_8 b + \log_4 a^2 + \log_2 b^2 = \log_8 ab + \log_4 a^2 b^2 = 12$
$= \log_{2^3}(\sqrt[3]{ab})^3 + \log_{2^2}(ab)^2 = \log_2 \sqrt[3]{ab} + \log_2 ab = \log_2(ab)^{\frac{4}{3}}$

Therefore $\log_2(ab)^{\frac{4}{3}} = 12 \Rightarrow (ab)^{\frac{4}{3}} = 2^{12} \Rightarrow ab = 2^9 = 512$.

Problem 6. Solution: 061.
We know that $x > 0$, $y > 0$, and $z > 0$.

Use the Change-of-Base formula, we can change the bases to 2, 3, and 4 in (1), (2), and (3), respectively:

$$\begin{cases} \log_2 x + \dfrac{1}{2}\log_2 y + \dfrac{1}{2}\log_2 z = \log_2 4, \\ \log_3 y + \dfrac{1}{2}\log_3 z + \dfrac{1}{2}\log_3 x = \log_3 9, \\ \log_4 z + \dfrac{1}{2}\log_4 x + \dfrac{1}{2}\log_4 y = \log_4 16. \end{cases} \Rightarrow \begin{cases} x\sqrt{yz} = 4 & (4), \\ y\sqrt{zx} = 9 & (5), \\ z\sqrt{xy} = 16 & (6). \end{cases}$$

Multiplication of all three equations together gives $(xyz)^2 = 24^2$.
Since $x > 0, y > 0, z > 0$, $xyz = 24$ \hfill (7)
Square both sides of (4): $x^2 yz = 16$ \hfill (8)

Dividing equation (8) by equation (7), we get $x = \dfrac{2}{3}$.

Similarly, we can obtain the values of y and z: $y = \dfrac{27}{8}$ and $z = \dfrac{32}{3}$.

Plugging these values back into the given equation, we can check and see that the values $x = \dfrac{2}{3}$, $y = \dfrac{27}{8}$, $z = \dfrac{32}{3}$ are the solutions. $a + c + e = 2 + 27 + 32 = 61$.

Problem 7. Solution: 256.

Since $\log_{16} x = \dfrac{1}{\log_x 16} = \dfrac{1}{4\log_x 2} = \dfrac{1}{4}\log_2 x$, $\log_2(\log_{16} x) = \dfrac{1}{4}\log_2(\log_2 x)$.

So $\log_{16}(\log_2 x) = \dfrac{1}{4}\log_2(\log_2 x)$ \hfill (1)

Let $y = \log_2 x$.

By the formula (4.2), (1) becomes: $\log_2 \dfrac{y}{4} = \dfrac{1}{4}\log_2 y \Rightarrow \log_2 \dfrac{y}{4} = \log_2 y^{\frac{1}{4}} \Rightarrow$

$\dfrac{y}{4} = y^{\frac{1}{4}} \Rightarrow (\dfrac{y}{4})^4 = y \Rightarrow (\dfrac{y}{4})^4 = y \Rightarrow y^4 = 256y$.

Rearranging the terms, we get $y(y^3 - 256) = 0$. Since $y \neq 0$, $y^3 = (\log_2 x)^3 = 256$.

Problem 8. Solution: 089

Since for any base $b \neq 0$, $\log_b N = 0$ only if $N = 1$, the given equations yield

$\log_3 x = 2 \quad \Rightarrow \quad x = 3^2$

$\log_4 y = 3 \quad \Rightarrow \quad y = 4^3$

$\log_2 z = 4 \quad \Rightarrow \quad z = 2^4$

Adding these results gives $x + y + z = 3^2 + 4^3 + 2^4 = 9 + 64 + 16 = 89$.

Problem 9. Solution: 225.

Taking logarithm of both sides of the equation, we find that

$\log_{2015}(\sqrt{2015} x^{\log_{2015} x}) = \log_{2015} x^2$.

$\log_{2015} \sqrt{2015} + (\log_{2015} x)^2 = 2 \log_{2015} x,$

$(\log_{2015} x)^2 - 2 \log_{2015} x + \dfrac{1}{2} = 0 \qquad (1)$

Let $y = \log_{2015} x$.

(1) becomes: $y^2 - 2y + \dfrac{1}{2} = 0$. The sum of the roots is $y_1 + y_2 = -\dfrac{(-2)}{1} = 2$.

That is $\log_{2015} x_1 + \log_{2015} x_2 = 2 \quad \Rightarrow \quad \log_{2015}(x_1 \times x_2) = 2 \Rightarrow x_1 \times x_2 = 2015^2$.

The last 3 digits of 2015^2 is $2015^2 \equiv 15^2 = 225 \mod 1000$.

Problem 10. Solution: 012.

Let $m = \log_{225} x$ and $n = \log_{729} y$. Then we have

$m + n = 4 \quad \Rightarrow \quad m = 4 - n \qquad (1)$

$\dfrac{1}{m} - \dfrac{1}{n} = 1 \quad \Rightarrow \quad n - m = mn \qquad (2)$

Substituting (1) into (2): $n - (4 - n) = (4 - n)n \quad \Rightarrow \quad 2n - 4 = 4n - n^2$

$\Rightarrow \quad n^2 - 2n - 4 = 0$.

So $n_1 = 1 - \sqrt{5}$ and $n_2 = 1 + \sqrt{5}$ Then $m_1 = 4 - n_1 = 4 - (1 - \sqrt{5}) = 3 - \sqrt{5}$, $m_2 = 3 + \sqrt{5}$.

Thus $x_1 x_2 = 225^{m_1} 225^{m_2} = 225^{m_1 + m_2} = 225^6$, $y_1 y_2 = 729^{n_1 + n_2} = 729^2$, and

$\log_{45}(x_1 y_1 x_2 y_2) = \log_{45}(225^6 729^2) = \log_{45}(15^{12} 3^{12}) = \log_{45} 45^{12} = 12$.

Problem 11. Solution: 005.

Let $\log_c a + d = \log_b c = \log_a b - d$.

$$\frac{\log a}{\log c} + d = \frac{\log c}{\log b} = \frac{\log b}{\log a} - d$$

$$\frac{\log a + d\log c}{\log c} = \frac{\log b - d\log a}{\log a} = \frac{\log c}{\log b}$$

$$\therefore \frac{\log a + d\log c + \log b - d\log a}{\log c + \log a} = \frac{\log c}{\log b}.$$

$$\frac{\log ab + d\log\frac{c}{a}}{\log ac} = \frac{\log c}{\log b} \qquad (1)$$

Substituting $b^2 = ac$ into (1) yields $\log ab + d\log\frac{c}{a} = 2\log c = \log c^2$.

Therefore $d = \dfrac{\log\frac{c^2}{ab}}{\log\frac{c}{a}} = \dfrac{\log\frac{c^2}{a\sqrt{ac}}}{\log\frac{c}{a}} = \dfrac{\log(\frac{c}{a})^{\frac{3}{2}}}{\log(\frac{c}{a})} = \dfrac{3}{2}$. The answer is $3 + 2 = 5$.

Problem 12. Solution: 008.
$xy = 490, x > 0, y > 0$ \qquad (1)
$\therefore \log x + \log y = 2\log 7 + 1$

$(\log x - \log 7) + (\log y - \log 7) = 1$ \qquad (2)

We also have $(\log x - \log 7) + (\log y - \log 7) = -\dfrac{143}{4}$ \qquad (3)

From (2) and (3), we know that $\log x - \log 7$ and $\log y - \log 7$ are the two roots of

$t^2 - t - \dfrac{143}{4} = 0$.

$(t + \dfrac{11}{2})(t - \dfrac{13}{2}) = 0$.

Let $x > y$, $t = \log x - \log 7 = \dfrac{13}{2}$.

$\therefore \log x = \log 7 + \dfrac{13}{2} = \log 7 + 6.5$ \qquad (4)

Since $10^{\frac{1}{2}} < 7 < 10$, then $0.5 < \log 7 < 1$. From (4) we have $7 < \log x < 7.5$, so the integer part is 8.

Problem 13. Solution: 469.
Method 1 (official solution):
It follows from the properties of exponents that
$$a^{(\log_3 7)^2} + b^{(\log_7 11)^2} + c^{(\log_{11} 25)^2}$$
$$= (a^{\log_3 7})^{\log_3 7} + (b^{\log_7 11})^{\log_7 11} + (c^{\log_{11} 25})^{\log_{11} 25} = 27^{\log_3 7} + 49^{\log_7 11} + \sqrt{11}^{\log_{11} 25}$$
$$= 3^{3\log_3 7} + 7^{2\log_7 11} + 11^{\frac{1}{2}\log_{11} 25} = 7^3 + 11^2 + \sqrt{25} = 343 + 121 + 5 = 469.$$

Method 2 (our solution):
Taking the logarithm of both sides of $a^{\log_3 7} = 27$ yields $(\log_3 7)(\log_3 a) = \log_3 27 = 3$ (1)
Multiplying both sides of (1) by $\log_3 7$: $(\log_3 7)^2 (\log_3 a) = 3\log_3 7 \Rightarrow$
$$\log_3 a^{(\log_3 7)^2} = \log_3 7^3 \Rightarrow \qquad a^{(\log_3 7)^2} = 7^3.$$

Similarly, we get $b^{(\log_7 11)^2} = 11^2$ and $c^{(\log_{11} 25)^2} = 25^{\frac{1}{2}}$.
Therefore $a^{(\log_3 7)^2} + b^{(\log_7 11)^2} + c^{(\log_{11} 25)^2} = 7^3 + 11^2 + \sqrt{25} = 343 + 121 + 5 = 469.$

1. SYSTEM OF LINEAR EQUATIONS

A group (two or more) of equations is called a system of equations. The solutions of a system of equations should satisfy all the equations.

A system of two equations is as follows:
$$\begin{cases} a_1 x + b_1 y = c_1 \\ a_2 x + b_2 y = c_2 \end{cases}$$
(1)
(2)

Case I: When $\dfrac{a_1}{a_2} \neq \dfrac{b_1}{b_2}$, the system of equations has one solution:

Case II: When $\dfrac{a_1}{a_2} = \dfrac{b_1}{b_2} = \dfrac{c_1}{c_2}$, the system of equations has infinitely many solutions.

Case III: When $\dfrac{a_1}{a_2} = \dfrac{b_1}{b_2} \neq \dfrac{c_1}{c_2}$, the system of equations has no solution.

The two commonly used methods to solve a system of equations are substitution and elimination methods.

Example 1. Find $3x + 2y + 6z$ if x, y, and z satisfy the system of equations
$$\begin{cases} (x+y):(y+z):(z+x) = 3:4:5 \\ 7x + 3y - 5z = 4 \end{cases}$$
(1)
(2)

Solution: 052.
Let $\quad x + y = 3k$ (3)
$\quad\quad y + z = 4k$ (4)
$\quad\quad z + x = 5k$ (5)
$k \neq 0$.
(3) + (4) + (5): $2(x + y + z) = 12k \quad \Rightarrow \quad x + y + z = 6k$ (6)

(6) – (3), (6) – (4), and (6) – (5), we get $x = 2k$, $y = k$, and $z = 3k$. Substituting these values into (2): $14k + 3k - 15k = 4 \quad \Rightarrow \quad k = 2$
$3x + 2y + 6z = 6k + 2k + 19k = 12 + 4 + 36 = 52$

☆ **Example 2.** Find $3x + 4y + 5z$ if $x, y, z, u,$ and v satisfy the system of equations

$$\begin{cases} 2x + y + z + u + v = 16 & (1) \\ x + 2y + z + u + v = 17 & (2) \\ x + y + 2z + u + v = 18 & (3) \\ x + y + z + 2u + v = 19 & (4) \\ x + y + z + u + 2v = 20 & (5) \end{cases}$$

Solution: 026.

$(1) + (2) + (3) + (4) + (5)$: $6(x + y + z + u + v) = 90 \Rightarrow x + y + z + u + v = 15$ (6)
$(1) - (6)$: $x = 1$.
$(2) - (6)$: $y = 2$.
$(3) - (6)$: $z = 3$.
$3x + 4y + 5z = 3 + 8 + 15 = 26$.

☆**Example 3.** Find $16 x_1 + 25 x_2 + 36 x_3 + 49 x_4 + 64 x_5 + 81 x_6 + 100 x_7$ given that:
$x_1 + 4 x_2 + 9 x_3 + 16 x_4 + 25 x_5 + 36 x_6 + 49 x_7 = 1$ (1)
$4 x_1 + 9 x_2 + 16 x_3 + 25 x_4 + 36 x_5 + 49 x_6 + 64 x_7 = 12$ (2)
$9 x_1 + 16 x_2 + 25 x_3 + 36 x_4 + 49 x_5 + 64 x_6 + 81 x_7 = 123$ (3)

Solution: 334.
Method 1:
$3 \times (2)$: $12 x_1 + 27 x_2 + 48 x_3 + 75 x_4 + 108 x_5 + 147 x_6 + 192 x_7 = 36$ (4)
$3 \times (3)$: $27 x_1 + 48 x_2 + 75 x_3 + 108 x_4 + 147 x_5 + 192 x_6 + 243 x_7 = 369$ (5)
$(5) - (4)$: $15 x_1 + 21 x_2 + 27 x_3 + 33 x_4 + 39 x_5 + 45 x_6 + 51 x_7 = 333$ (6)
$(6) + (1)$: $16 x_1 + 25 x_2 + 36 x_3 + 49 x_4 + 64 x_5 + 81 x_6 + 100 x_7 = 334$

Method 2 (by Anthony Cheng):
$(2) - (1)$: $3x_1 + 5x_2 + 7x_3 + 9x_4 + 11x_5 + 13x_6 + 15x_7 = 11$ (4)
$(3) - (2)$: $5x_1 + 7x_2 + 9x_3 + 11x_4 + 13x_5 + 15x_6 + 17x_7 = 111$ (5)
$(5) - (4)$: $2x_1 + 2x_2 + 2x_3 + 2x_4 + 2x_5 + 2x_6 + 2x_7 = 100$ (6)
$(5) + (6)$: $7x_1 + 9x_2 + 11x_3 + 13x_4 + 15x_5 + 17x_6 + 19x_7 = 211$ (7)
$(7) + (3)$: $16 x_1 + 25 x_2 + 36 x_3 + 49 x_4 + 64 x_5 + 81 x_6 + 100 x_7 = 334$

Example 4. Find $\sum_{100}^{i=1} x_i^2$ if $x_1, x_2, x_3, x_4, \cdots, x_{100}$ satisfy the system of equations

$$\begin{cases} x_1 + 2x_2 + 2x_3 + 2x_4 + 2x_5 + \cdots + 2x_{100} = 1 & (1) \\ x_1 + 3x_2 + 4x_3 + 4x_4 + 4x_5 + \cdots + 4x_{100} = 2 & (2) \\ x_1 + 3x_2 + 5x_3 + 6x_4 + 6x_5 + \cdots + 6x_{100} = 3 & (3) \\ x_1 + 3x_2 + 5x_3 + 7x_4 + 8x_5 + \cdots + 8x_{100} = 4 & (4) \\ \cdots \quad \cdots \quad \cdots \quad \cdots \quad \cdots \\ x_1 + 3x_2 + 5x_3 + 7x_4 + 9x_5 + \cdots + 199x_{100} = 100 & (100) \end{cases}$$

Solution: 100.

$(2) - (1), (3) - (1), \ldots (100) - (1)$, we get

$$\begin{cases} x_2 + 2x_3 + 2x_4 + 2x_5 + \cdots + 2x_{100} = 1 \\ x_2 + 3x_3 + 4x_4 + 4x_5 + \cdots + 4x_{100} = 2 \\ x_2 + 3x_3 + 5x_4 + 6x_5 + \cdots + 6x_{100} = 3 \\ \cdots \quad \cdots \quad \cdots \quad \cdots \\ x_2 + 3x_3 + 5x_4 + 7x_5 + \cdots + 197x_{100} = 99 \end{cases}$$

We repeat the same procedure and we will get 100 systems of equations. We then create a new system of equations by using the first equation in each of the 100 systems of equations:

$$\begin{cases} x_1 + 2x_2 + 2x_3 + 2x_4 + 2x_5 + \cdots + 2x_{100} = 1 \\ x_2 + 2x_3 + 2x_4 + 2x_5 + \cdots + 2x_{100} = 1 \\ x_3 + 2x_4 + 2x_5 + \cdots + 2x_{100} = 1 \\ \cdots \quad \cdots \quad \cdots \quad \cdots \\ x_{99} + 2x_{100} = 1 \\ x_{100} = 1 \end{cases}$$

So we get the solutions: $x_1 = -1$, $x_2 = 1$, $x_3 = -1$, $x_4 = 1, \ldots, x_{99} = -1$, $x_{100} = 1$.

$\sum_{100}^{i=1} x_i^2 = 100$.

2. SOME SKILLS FOR SOLVING NONLINEAR EQUATIONS

2.1. Method of Constructing the Variance

Let $\bar{x}$ be the mean of $x_1, x_2, x_3, \ldots, x_n$.
The variance is:
$$s^2 = \frac{1}{n}[(x_1 - \bar{x})^2 + (x_2 - \bar{x})^2 + \cdots + (x_n - \bar{x})^2]$$
$$= \frac{1}{n}[(x_1^2 + x_2^2 + \cdots + x_n^2) - \frac{1}{n}(x_1 + x_2 + \cdots + x_n)^2].$$

It is clear that $s \geq 0$ (with equality if and only if $x_1 = x_2 = x_3 = \ldots = x_n = \bar{x}$).

Example 5: Find $100x$ if x and y are real numbers satisfying
$$\begin{cases} x + y = 2, \\ xy - z^2 = 1 \end{cases}$$

Solution: 100.
Rewrite the given equations as
$$\begin{cases} x + y = 2, \\ xy = 1 + z^2 \end{cases}$$
The variance is of x and y is:
$$s^2 = \frac{1}{2}[(x^2 + y^2) - \frac{1}{2}(x+y)^2] = \frac{1}{2}[\frac{1}{2}(x+y)^2 - 2xy] = \frac{1}{2}[2 - 2(1+z^2)] \geq 0 \Rightarrow z^2 \leq 0.$$
Thus, z must be 0.

Substituting $z = 0$ into the given equations, we find: $x = 1, y = 1$.
The solutions for (x, y, z) are $(1, 1, 0)$; thus, our answer is $100 \times 1 = 100$.

Example 6. (USAMO Modified) Find $100x$ if x and y are real numbers satisfying the system of equations
$$\begin{cases} x + y + z = 3 & (1) \\ x^2 + y^2 + z^2 = 3 & (2) \\ x^3 + y^3 + z^3 = 3 & (3) \end{cases}$$

Solution: 100.

From (1) and (2): $x + y = 3 - z$ \hfill (4)

Squaring both sides of (4):

$x^2 + 2xy + y^2 = 9 - 6z + z^2 \Rightarrow 2xy = 9 - 6z + z^2 - (x^2 + y^2)$ \hfill (5)

From (2) we get: $x^2 + y^2 = 3 - z^2$ \hfill (6)

Substituting (6) into (5) and simplifying: $xy = z^2 - 2z + 3$.

$$S^2 = \frac{1}{2}[(x^2+y^2)-\frac{1}{2}(x+y)^2] = \frac{1}{2}[\frac{1}{2}(x+y)^2 - 2xy] = -\frac{3}{4}(z-1)^2 \geq 0,$$

$z = 1$, and $x + y = 2$, $xy = 1$. So $x = y = 1$.

Substituting $x = y = z = 1$ into (3): $x = y = z = 1$. The answer is $100 \times 1 = 100$.

2.2. Method of Completing The Squares

Example 7. Find $m^2 + n^2$ if the value of y can be expressed as $\frac{m}{n}$, where m and n are positive integers relatively prime and y and z are real numbers satisfying the equation $5y^2 + 5z^2 + 8yz - 6y - 6z + 2 = 0$.

Solution: 010.

The given equation can be written as $(9y^2 - 6y + 1) + (9z^2 - 6z + 1) = 4y^2 + -8yz + 4z^2$ or

$(3y-1)^2 + (3z-1)^2 = 4(y-z)^2$ \hfill (1)

Let $u = 3y - 1$, $v = 3z - 1$.

Then (1) becomes $5u^2 + 8uv + 5v^2 = 0$.

Note that $\Delta = (8v)^2 - 4 \times 5 \times 5v^2 = -36v^2$.

We know that and y and z are real numbers, so we have $v = 0$, and $u = 0$.

$u = 3y - 1 \quad \Rightarrow \quad y = \frac{1}{3}$.

$v = 3z - 1 \quad \Rightarrow \quad z = \frac{1}{3}$.

$m^2 + n^2 = 1^2 + 3^2 = 10$.

Example 8. Find $100(x+y-z)$ if x, y, and z are real numbers satisfying the system of equations
$$x^2 + y^2 + z^2 - 9x - 8y - 5z + 11 = 0 \tag{1}$$
$$x + 2y + 3z + 1 = 0 \tag{2}$$

Solution: 600.

$(1) + (2) \times 3$: $x^2 + y^2 + z^2 - 6x - 2y + 4z + 14 = 0 \quad \Rightarrow$
$(x^2 - 6x + 9) + (y^2 - 2y + 1) + (z^2 + 4z + 4) = 0 \Rightarrow (x-3)^2 + (y-1)^2 + (z+2)^2 = 0$

We know that x, y, and z are real numbers, so we have
$x - 3 = 0 \quad \Rightarrow \quad x = 3$.
$y - 1 = 0 \quad \Rightarrow \quad y = 1$.
$z + 2 = 0 \quad \Rightarrow \quad z = -2$.

$100(x + y - z) = 100 \times 6 = 600$.

2.3. Solving System Of Equations Using Vieta's Theorem

Example 9. Find the number of distinct ordered triples (x, y, z) satisfying the equations
$$x + 2y + 4z = 12$$
$$xy + 4yz + 2xz = 22$$
$$xyz = 6.$$

Solution: 006.
Let $a = x$, $b = 2y$, and $c = 4z$.
$x + 2y + 4z = 12 \quad \Rightarrow \quad a + b + c = 12$
$xy + 4yz + 2xz = 22 \quad \Rightarrow \quad ab + bc + ca = 44 \quad\quad\quad (4)$
$xyz = 6 \quad \Rightarrow \quad abc = 48$
a, b, and c are the solutions of the equation: $t^3 - 12t^2 + 44t - 48 = 0 \quad \Rightarrow$
$(t - 2)(t - 4)(t - 6) = 0$

The triple (2, 4, 6) and each of its permutations satisfies the system (4). Since there is a one-to-one correspondence between (a, b, c) and (x, y, z), the original system has 6 distinct solutions (x, y, z): (2, 2, $\frac{3}{2}$), (2, 3, 1), (4, 1, $\frac{3}{2}$), (4, 3, $\frac{1}{2}$), (6, 1, 1), (6, 2, $\frac{1}{2}$).

3. RATIONAL EQUATIONS

Example 10. Find the largest value of x satisfying $\frac{2x^2}{x^2-4} \times (x^2+6) = \frac{10x^2}{x^2-4}$.

Solution: 003.

$$\frac{2x^2}{x^2-4} \times (x^2+6) = \frac{10x^2}{x^2-4} \Rightarrow \frac{2x^2}{x^2-4} \times (x^2+6) - \frac{10x^2}{x^2-4} = 0 \Rightarrow$$

$$\frac{2x^2}{x^2-4}[(x^2+6) - 5x] = 0 \Rightarrow \frac{2x^2(x-2)(x-3)}{(x-2)(x+2)} = 0.$$

We know that $x - 2 \neq 0$, so we simplify the above equation into: $\frac{2x^2(x-3)}{(x+2)} = 0$.

The solutions are $x = 0$ and $x = 3$. We can check that both are the solutions of the equation. The answer is 3.

Example 11. Find the positive value of x satisfying $x^2 + 6 - \frac{1}{x-2} = \frac{5x^2 - 10x - 1}{x-2}$.

Solution: 003.

The given equation can be written as $x^2 + 6 - \frac{1}{x-2} = 5x - \frac{1}{x-2} \Rightarrow x^2 - 5x + 6 = 0$

$\Rightarrow (x-2)(x-3) = 0$

Thus $x = 3$ or $x = 2$, but it is obvious that $x \neq 2$. Thus $x = 3$.

☆**Example 12.** Find abc if $\frac{3}{a+3} + \frac{3}{b+3} + \frac{3}{c+3} = 1$ and $a + b + c = 43$.

Solution: 441.

$$\frac{3}{a+3}+\frac{3}{b+3}+\frac{3}{c+3}=1 \quad \Rightarrow \quad \frac{3(b+3)(c+3)+3(a+3)(c+3)+3(a+3)(b+3)}{(a+3)(b+3)(c+3)}=1$$

$$\Rightarrow \quad 3(b+3)(c+3)+3(a+3)(c+3)+3(a+3)(b+3)=(a+3)(b+3)(c+3)$$

$$\Rightarrow 3(ab+bc+ca)+18(a+b+c)+81=abc+3(ab+bc+ca)+9(a+b+c)+27$$

$$\Rightarrow 9(a+b+c)+54=abc \quad \Rightarrow abc=9\times 43+54=441.$$

☆**Example 13.** Let m be the largest real solution to the equation

$$\frac{1}{x-1}+\frac{3}{x-3}+\frac{5}{x-5}+\frac{7}{x-7}=x^2-4x-4$$

There are positive integers a, b and c such that $m=a+\sqrt{b+\sqrt{c}}$. Find $a+b+c$.

Solution: 031.

$$\frac{1}{x-1}+\frac{3}{x-3}+\frac{5}{x-5}+\frac{7}{x-7}=x^2-4x-4 \quad \Rightarrow$$

$$\frac{-(x-1)+x}{x-1}+\frac{-(x-3)+x}{x-3}+\frac{-(x-5)+x}{x-5}+\frac{-(x-7)+x}{x-7}=x^2-4x-4$$

$$\Rightarrow -4+\frac{x}{x-1}+\frac{x}{x-3}+\frac{x}{x-5}+\frac{x}{x-7}=x^2-4x-4 \Rightarrow \frac{x}{x-1}+\frac{x}{x-3}+\frac{x}{x-5}+\frac{x}{x-7}-x(x-4)$$

$$\Rightarrow \quad x[\frac{1}{x-1}+\frac{1}{x-3}+\frac{1}{x-5}+\frac{1}{x-7}-(x-4)]=0 \qquad (1)$$

We get $x=0$ or $\frac{1}{x-1}+\frac{1}{x-3}+\frac{1}{x-5}+\frac{1}{x-7}-(x-4)=0 \qquad (2)$

Let $y=x-4$ in (2):

$$\frac{1}{y+3}+\frac{1}{y+1}+\frac{1}{y-1}+\frac{1}{y-3}-y=0 \quad \Rightarrow \quad (\frac{1}{y+3}+\frac{1}{y-3})+(\frac{1}{y+1}+\frac{1}{y-1})-y=0$$

$$\Rightarrow \quad \frac{2y}{y^2-9}+\frac{2y}{y^2-1}-y=0 \Rightarrow \quad y(\frac{2}{y^2-9}+\frac{2}{y^2-1}-1)=0 \qquad (3)$$

We get $y=0$ or $\frac{2}{y^2-9}+\frac{2}{y^2-1}-1=0 \qquad (4)$

Let $z=y^2$, (4) becomes: $\frac{2}{z-9}+\frac{2}{z-1}-1=0 \quad \Rightarrow \quad \frac{2(z-1)+2(z-9)}{(z-9)(z-1)}=1$

$$\Rightarrow \quad 4z-20=(z-9)(z-1) \quad \Rightarrow \quad 4z-20=z^2-10z+9 \quad \Rightarrow \quad z^2-14z+29=0$$

Solving we get $z_{1,2}=7\pm 2\sqrt{5}$. Since we want the greatest value, we get $z=7+2\sqrt{5}$

Thus $y = \sqrt{7+2\sqrt{5}}$ and $m = 4 + y = 4 + \sqrt{7+2\sqrt{5}} = 4 + \sqrt{7+\sqrt{20}}$
$a + b + c = 4 + 7 + 20 = 031$.

Example 14. Let m be the smallest real solution to the equation
$$\frac{1}{x+5} + \frac{2}{x+4} + \frac{3}{x+3} - \frac{3}{x+2} + \frac{2}{x+1} + \frac{1}{x} = 0$$
There are positive integers a, b and c such that $m = \dfrac{-a-\sqrt{b}}{c}$ in simplest radical form. Find $a+b+c$.

Solution: 420.
The original equation can be written as
$$(\frac{1}{x+5}+\frac{1}{x})+(\frac{3}{x+3}-\frac{3}{x+2})+(\frac{2}{x+1}+\frac{2}{x+4}) = 0 \Rightarrow$$
$$\frac{2x+5}{(x+5)x} - \frac{3(2x+5)}{(x+3)(x+2)} + \frac{2(2x+5)}{(x+1)(x+4)} = 0 \Rightarrow$$
$$(2x+5)(\frac{1}{x^2+5x} - \frac{3}{x^2+5x+6} + \frac{2}{x^2+5x+4}) = 0 \qquad (1)$$

We have $2x+5 = 0 \Rightarrow x_1 = -5/2$.

We have $\dfrac{1}{x^2+5x} + \dfrac{2}{x^2+5x+4} - \dfrac{3}{x^2+5x+6} = 0 \qquad (2)$

Let $y = x^2 + 5x$. (2) becomes $\dfrac{1}{y} + \dfrac{2}{y+4} - \dfrac{3}{y+6} = 0 \Rightarrow \dfrac{10y+24}{y(y+4)(y+6)} = 0 \Rightarrow y = -\dfrac{12}{5}$.

When $y = -\dfrac{12}{5}$, $x^2 + 5x = -\dfrac{12}{5} \Rightarrow 5x^2 + 25x + 12 = 0 \qquad (3)$

Solving we get $x_2 = \dfrac{-25+\sqrt{385}}{10}$, and $x_3 = \dfrac{-25-\sqrt{385}}{10}$.

Since we want the smallest real solution, we get $m = x_3 = \dfrac{-25-\sqrt{385}}{10}$.

$a + b + c = 25 + 385 + 10 = 420$.

210

☆**Example 15.** (AIME) Find the positive solution
$$\frac{1}{x^2-10x-29}+\frac{1}{x^2-10x-45}-\frac{2}{x^2-10x-69}=0$$

Solution: 013.
Method 1 (official solution):
Let $y = x^2 - 10x$. The equation in the problem then becomes
$$\frac{1}{y-29}+\frac{1}{y-45}-\frac{2}{y-69}=0$$
From which $\frac{1}{y-29}-\frac{1}{y-69}=\frac{1}{y-69}-\frac{1}{y-45}=0$ and
$\frac{-40}{(y-29)(y-69)}=\frac{24}{(y-45)(y-69)}$ follows. This equation has $y = 39$ as its only solution.
We then note that $x^2 - 10x = 39$ is satisfied by the positive number 13.

Method 2 (our solution):
The equation in the problem can be written as
$$\frac{1}{x^2-10x-29}-\frac{1}{x^2-10x-69}=\frac{1}{x^2-10x-69}-\frac{1}{x^2-10x-45}$$
$\Rightarrow \quad \frac{-40}{(x^2-10x-29)(x^2-10x-69)}=\frac{24}{(x^2-10x-69)(x^2-10x-45)}$
$\Rightarrow \quad -5[(x^2-10x-69)(x^2-10x-45)]=3[(x^2-10x-29)(x^2-10x-69)]$
$\Rightarrow \quad 3[(x^2-10x-29)(x^2-10x-69)]+5[(x^2-10x-69)(x^2-10x-45)]=0$
$\Rightarrow \quad (x^2-10x-69)[3(x^2-10x-29)+5(x^2-10x-45)]=0$
$\Rightarrow \quad (x^2-10x-69)(8x^2-80x-312)=0$

We know that $x^2 - 10x - 69 \neq 0$. So $8x^2 - 80x - 312 = 0 \quad \Rightarrow \quad x^2 - 10x - 39 = 0$.
The solutions are $x_1 = 13$ and $x_2 = -3$. The answer is the positive number 13.

Method 3 (our solution):
Let $y = x^2 - 10x - 49$. The equation in the problem then becomes
$$\frac{1}{y+20}+\frac{1}{y+4}-\frac{2}{y-20}=0 \quad \Rightarrow \quad y^2-16y-80+y^2-400-2y^2-48y-160=0$$

$\Rightarrow \quad -64y = 640 \quad \Rightarrow \quad y = -10$.

So $x^2 - 10x - 49 = -10 \quad \Rightarrow \quad x^2 - 10x - 39 = 0$.

The solutions are $x_1 = 13$ and $x_2 = -3$. The answer is the positive number 13.

Method 4 (our solution):

Let $y = x^2 - 10x - 29$. The equation in the problem then becomes $\dfrac{1}{y} + \dfrac{1}{y-16} - \dfrac{2}{y-40} = 0$

$\Rightarrow \quad \dfrac{1}{y} - \dfrac{1}{y-40} = \dfrac{1}{y-40} - \dfrac{1}{y-16} \quad \Rightarrow \quad \dfrac{-40}{y(y-40)} = \dfrac{24}{(y-40)(y-16)}$

$\dfrac{-5}{y} = \dfrac{3}{y-16} \quad \Rightarrow \quad y = 10$.

So $x^2 - 10x - 29 = 10 \quad \Rightarrow \quad x^2 - 10x - 39 = 0$.

The solutions are $x_1 = 13$ and $x_2 = -3$. The answer is 13.

☆**Example 16.** Find the largest solution to the equation

$$\dfrac{1}{x^2 + 11x - 8} + \dfrac{1}{x^2 + 2x - 8} - \dfrac{1}{x^2 - 13x - 8} = 0.$$

Solution: 008.

Let $y = x^2 - 8$. The equation in the problem then becomes $\dfrac{1}{y+11x} + \dfrac{1}{y+2x} + \dfrac{1}{y-13x} = 0$

$\Rightarrow \quad 3y^2 - 147x^2 = 0 \quad \Rightarrow \quad y^2 - 49x^2 = 0$

So we get $y = \pm 7x$.

When $y = 7x$, $x^2 - 8 = 7x \quad \Rightarrow \quad x^2 - 7x - 8 = 0$.

Solving we have $x_1 = 8$ and $x_2 = -1$.

When $y = -7x$, $x^2 - 8 = -7x \quad \Rightarrow \quad x^2 + 7x - 8 = 0$.

Solving we have $x_3 = -8$ and $x_4 = 1$.

The largest solution is $x_1 = 8$. The answer is 8.

4. RADICAL EQUATIONS

☆**Example 17.** Let m be the largest real solution to the equation $\dfrac{\sqrt{22x}}{\sqrt{22x-120}} = \dfrac{x}{10-x}$.

There are positive integers a, and b such that $m = \dfrac{a}{b}$. Find $a+b$.

Solution: 063.

Squaring both sides: $\dfrac{22x}{22x-120} = \dfrac{x^2}{(10-x)^2}$ $\Rightarrow$ $\dfrac{11x}{11x-60} - \dfrac{x^2}{(10-x)^2} = 0$

$\Rightarrow$ $x[\dfrac{11}{11x-60} - \dfrac{x}{(10-x)^2}] = 0$

We get $x = 0$ or $\dfrac{11}{11x-60} - \dfrac{x}{(10-x)^2} = 0$ $\Rightarrow$ $11(10-x)^2 - x(11x-60) = 0$

$\Rightarrow$ $11(100 - 20x + x^2) - 11x^2 + 60x = 0$ $\Rightarrow$ $1100 - 220x + 11x^2 - 11x^2 + 60x = 0$

$\Rightarrow$ $1100 - 160x = 0 \Rightarrow x = \dfrac{55}{8}$.

The largest solution is $x = \dfrac{55}{8}$. $a + b = 55 + 8 = 63$.

Example 18. Find the positive real solution to the equation $x^2 + 4x - 8\sqrt{8x} + 20 = 0$.

Solution: 002.

The original equation can be written as $x^2 - 4x + 4 + 8x - 8\sqrt{8x} + 16 = 0$ $\Rightarrow$
$(x-2)^2 + (\sqrt{8x} - 4)^2 = 0$.

We get $x - 2 = 0$ and $\sqrt{8x} - 4 = 0$. The solution is $x = 2$.

☆**Example 19.** (AIME) What is the product of the real roots of the equation
$x^2 + 18x + 30 = 2\sqrt{x^2 + 18x + 45}$.

Solution: 020.

Method 1:
Substitute to simplify. Define u to be the nonnegative number such that
$u^2 = x^2 + 18x + 45$. So $u^2 - 15 = 2\sqrt{u^2} = 2u$ (since $u \geq 0$).
$u^2 - 2u - 15 = 0 \quad \Rightarrow \quad (u-5)(u+3) = 0$.
Since $u \geq 0$, we have $u = 5$.
$x^2 + 18x + 45 = 5^2 \quad \Rightarrow \quad x^2 + 18x + 20 = 0$.
Since $\Delta = 18^2 - 4 \times 20 > 0$, the equation has real solutions and the product is 20.

Method 2 (our solution):
The original equation can be written as
$x^2 + 18x + 45 - 2\sqrt{x^2 + 18x + 45} - 15 = 0 \Rightarrow (\sqrt{x^2 + 18x + 45} + 3)(\sqrt{x^2 + 18x + 45} - 5) = 0$
So we have $\sqrt{x^2 + 18x + 45} + 3 = 0$ (no real solutions)
$\sqrt{x^2 + 18x + 45} - 5 = 0 \quad \Rightarrow \quad \sqrt{x^2 + 18x + 45} = 5 \quad \Rightarrow \quad x^2 + 18x + 45 = 25$
$\Rightarrow \quad x^2 + 18x + 20 = 0$.
Since $\Delta = 18^2 - 4 \times 20 > 0$, the equation has real solutions and the product is 20.

Method 3:
The original equation can be written as
$x^2 + 18x + 45 - 2\sqrt{x^2 + 18x + 45} + 1 = 16 \Rightarrow (\sqrt{x^2 + 18x + 45} - 1)^2 = 16$.
We have $\sqrt{x^2 + 18x + 45} - 1 = -4 \quad \Rightarrow \quad \sqrt{x^2 + 18x + 45} = -3$ (no real solutions).
or $\sqrt{x^2 + 18x + 45} - 1 = 4 \quad \Rightarrow \quad \sqrt{x^2 + 18x + 45} = 5 \quad \Rightarrow \quad x^2 + 18x + 45 = 25$
$\Rightarrow \quad x^2 + 18x + 20 = 0$.
Since $\Delta = 18^2 - 4 \times 20 > 0$, the equation has real solutions and the product is 20.

50 AIME Lectures — Chapter 9 Solving Equations

PROBLEMS

Problem 1. Find $3x + 2y + 6z$ if x, y, and z satisfy the system of equations

$$\begin{cases} \dfrac{x}{2} = \dfrac{y}{3} = \dfrac{z}{5} & (1) \\ 2x + 3y - z = 16 & (2) \end{cases}$$

☆ **Problem 2.** Find $3u + 2v$ if x, y, z, u, and v satisfy the system of equations

$2x + y + z + u + v = 8$ \hfill (1)
$x + 2y + z + u + v = 16$ \hfill (2)
$x + y + 2z + u + v = 32$ \hfill (3)
$x + y + z + 2u + v = 64$ \hfill (4)
$x + y + z + u + 2v = 126$ \hfill (5)

Problem 3. Find $x_1 + 4x_4$ if x_1, x_2, x_3, x_4, x_5 satisfy the system of equations

$x_1 + 2x_2 + 3x_3 + 4x_4 + 5x_5 = 210$ \hfill (1)
$x_2 + 2x_3 + 3x_4 + 4x_5 + 5x_1 = 185$ \hfill (2)
$x_3 + 2x_4 + 3x_5 + 4x_1 + 5x_2 = 110$ \hfill (3)
$x_4 + 2x_5 + 3x_1 + 4x_2 + 5x_3 = 110$ \hfill (4)
$x_5 + 2x_1 + 3x_2 + 4x_3 + 5x_4 = 135$ \hfill (5)

Problem 4. Find $8x_1 - 4x_2$ if $x_1, x_2, x_3, x_4, \cdots, x_{100}$ satisfy the system of equations

$$\begin{cases} x_1 + 2x_2 + 2x_3 + 2x_4 + 2x_5 + \cdots + 2x_{100} = 1 & (1) \\ 2x_1 + 2x_2 + 2x_3 + 2x_4 + 2x_5 + \cdots + 2x_{100} = 2 & (2) \\ 2x_1 + 2x_2 + 3x_3 + 2x_4 + 2x_5 + \cdots + 2x_{100} = 3 & (3) \\ 2x_1 + 2x_2 + 2x_3 + 4x_4 + 2x_5 + \cdots + 2x_{100} = 4 & (4) \\ \cdots \quad \cdots \quad \cdots \quad \cdots \quad \cdots & \\ 2x_1 + 2x_2 + 2x_3 + 2x_4 + 2x_5 + \cdots + 100x_{100} = 100 & (100) \end{cases}$$

Problem 5: Find $m + n$ if the greatest value of y can be expressed as $\dfrac{m}{n}$, where m and n are positive integers relatively prime and x and y are real numbers satisfying the system of equations
$$\begin{cases} x(x+1)(3x+5y)=144 \\ x^2+4x+5y=24. \end{cases}$$

Problem 6. Find $10x + 100z$. x, y, and z are real numbers satisfying the system of equations
$$\begin{cases} 2x+3y+z=13 & (1) \\ 4x^2+9y^2+z^2-2x+15y+3z=82 & (2) \end{cases}$$

Problem 7. Find $100x^2 + y^2$ if x and y are real numbers satisfying the equation
$5x^2-6xy+2y^2-4x+2y+1=0$.

Problem 8. Find $100(x+y+z)$ if x, y, and z are real numbers satisfying the system of equations
$$\begin{cases} 2x+3y+z=13 & (1) \\ 4x^2+9y^2+z^2-2x+15y+3z=82 & (2) \end{cases}$$

Problem 9. Find $100(x+y)$ if x and y are real numbers satisfying the system of equations:
$$\begin{cases} x+y+\dfrac{9}{x}+\dfrac{4}{y}=10 \\ (x^2+9)(y^2+4)=24xy \end{cases}$$

Problem 10. Find the positive value of n satisfying $\dfrac{1}{1985}=\dfrac{1}{1+(1-\dfrac{1}{n})^2}\times\dfrac{1}{n^2}$.

Problem 11. Find the positive real value of x satisfying $x^2-x+1=\dfrac{6}{x^2-x}$.

☆**Problem 12.** Find $1000 + m + n$ if m and n are two nonzero roots of the equation $\dfrac{a}{x+a} + \dfrac{b}{x+b} + \dfrac{c}{x+c} = 3$ with $a + b + c = 12$, and $ab + cb + ac = 47$.

Problem 13. Let m be the largest real solution to the equation
$$\dfrac{3}{x} + \dfrac{1}{x-1} + \dfrac{4}{x-2} + \dfrac{4}{x-3} + \dfrac{1}{x-4} + \dfrac{3}{x-5} = 0$$
There are positive integers a, b and c such that $m = \dfrac{a+\sqrt{b}}{c}$. Find $a+b+c$.

Problem 14. Let m be the real solution to the equation
$29\left(\dfrac{17-7x}{x+2} + \dfrac{8x+55}{x+3}\right) = 31\left(\dfrac{24-5x}{x+1} + \dfrac{5-6x}{x+4}\right) + 370$. There are positive integers a, and b such that $m = -\dfrac{a}{b}$. Find $a+b$.

Problem 15. Find the largest solution to the equation
$$\dfrac{1}{x^2+2x+10} + \dfrac{1}{x^2+11x+10} - \dfrac{1}{x^2-13x+10} = 0$$

☆**Problem 16.** Find the largest solution to the equation $\dfrac{x-2}{3} + \dfrac{x-3}{2} = \dfrac{3}{x-2} + \dfrac{2}{x-3}$.

☆**Problem 17.** Find the last three digits of the sum of the solutions of the equation $\sqrt[4]{x} = \dfrac{14}{9-\sqrt[4]{x}}$.

Problem 18. Find $800m$ if m is the positive solution to the equation
$$x^2 + \dfrac{1}{x^2} + \sqrt{x^2 + 2 + \dfrac{1}{x^2}} = 4.$$

☆ **Problem 19.** Let $m = \dfrac{a}{b}$ be the positive real solution to the equation $2x^2 - 5x - 2x\sqrt{x^2 - 5x - 3} = 19$. a and b are positive integers relatively prime. Find $a + b$.

Problem 20. How many solutions are there for real x, y, z and u to the system of equations below?
$$\begin{cases} x + y + z + u = 8, & (1) \\ x^2 + y^2 + z^2 + u^2 = 20, & (2) \\ xy + xu + zy + zu = 16, & (3) \\ xyzu = 9. & (4) \end{cases}$$

Problem 21. Given the equation $49(x^2 + 4y^2 + 9z^2) = 36(x + y + z)^2$, $x, y,$ and z are real numbers. $x : y : z$ can be expressed as $a : b : c$, where $a, b,$ and c are positive integers relatively prime. Find $a + b + c$.

SOLUTIONS

Problem 1. Solution: 084.

Let $\dfrac{x}{2} = \dfrac{y}{3} = \dfrac{z}{5} = k$ \hfill (3)

$x = 2k$, $y = 3k$, and $z = 5k$. Substituting these values into (2): $4k + 9k - 5k = 16 \Rightarrow$
$k = 2$
$3x + 2y + 6z = 6k + 6k + 30k = 42k = 84$

☆ **Problem 2.** Solution: 239.

(1) + (2) + (3) + (4) + (5):
$6(x + y + z + u + v) = 246 \Rightarrow x + y + z + u + v = 41$ \hfill (6)
(4) − (6): $u = 23$.
(5) − (6): $v = 85$.
$3u + 2v = 3 \times 23 + 2 \times 85 = 239$.

Problem 3. Solution: 065.

Let $S = x_1 + x_2 + x_3 + x_4 + x_5$.

(1) + (2) + (3) + (4) + (5): $S + 2S + 3S + 4S + 5S = 750 \Rightarrow 15S = 750 \Rightarrow S = 50$

(1) − (2): $-4x_1 + x_2 + x_3 + x_4 + x_5 = 25 \Rightarrow x_1 + x_2 + x_3 + x_4 + x_5 - 5x_1 = 25 \Rightarrow$

$x_1 = \dfrac{50 - 25}{5} = 5$

(5) − (4): $-x_1 - x_2 - x_3 + 4x_4 - x_5 = 25 \Rightarrow -x_1 - x_2 - x_3 - x_4 - x_5 + 5x_4 = 25$

$\Rightarrow -S + 5x_4 = 25 \Rightarrow x_4 = \dfrac{50 + 25}{5} = 15$

$x_1 + 4x_4 = 5 + 4 \times 15 = 5 + 60 = 65$.

Problem 4. Solution: 400.

(2) − (1), (3) − (2), (4) − (3), (5) − (4), ... (100) − (99), we get
$x_1 = 1$
$x_3 = 1$
$-x_3 + 2x_4 = 1$
$-2x_4 + 3x_5 = 1$

$$\cdots \quad \cdots \quad \cdots \quad \cdots$$
$$-97x_{99} + 98x_{100} = 1$$

So we get the solutions: $x_1 = x_3 = x_4 = \ldots = x_{99} = x_{100} = 1$.
Substituting all these values to equation (2) we get $x_2 = 2 - 100 = -98$.
$8x_1 - 4x_2 = 8 \times 1 - 4 \times (-98) = 400$.

Problem 5. Solution: 029.

Rewrite the equations as: $\begin{cases} (x^2 + x)(3x + 5y) = 144, \\ (x^2 + x) + (3x + 5y) = 24. \end{cases}$

Let $x^2 + x = a$, $3x + 5y = b$. $a + b = 24$, $ab = 144$.
The square of the difference of a and b:
$$s^2 = \frac{1}{2}[(a^2 + b^2) - \frac{1}{2}(a+b)^2] = \frac{1}{2}[\frac{1}{2}(a+b)^2 - 2ab] = \frac{1}{2}(\frac{1}{2} \times 24^2 - 2 \times 144) = 0$$
$a = b = 12$.

So $x^2 + x = 3x + 5y = 12$. Solving: $\begin{cases} x_1 = 3, \\ y_1 = \dfrac{3}{5}; \end{cases} \begin{cases} x_2 = -4, \\ y_2 = \dfrac{24}{5}. \end{cases}$

The greatest value of y is 24/5. The answer is $24 + 5 = 29$.

Problem 6. Solution: 430.
From (1): $2x + (3y + 3) = 16 - z$. (3)
(1) + (2): $(2x)^2 + (3y + 3)^2 = -z^2 - 4z + 104$ (4)
The square of the difference of $2x$, $3y + 3$
$$S^2 = \frac{1}{2}[(2x)^2 + (3y+3)^2 - \frac{1}{2}(2x+3y+3)^2] \geq 0 \quad (5)$$

Substituting (3), (4) into (5): $-3(z-4)^2 \geq 0 \quad \Rightarrow \quad z = 4$
Substituting $z = 4$ into (1), (2): $x = 3$, $y = 1$.
The answer is $10x + 100z = 30 + 400 = 430$.

Problem 7. Solution: 101.
The left hand side of the given equation can be written as
$= (x^2 - 2xy + y^2) + (4x^2 - 4xy + y^2) - 4x + 2y + 1$
$= (x-y)^2 + (2x-y)^2 - 2(2x-y) + 1$

$= (x-y)^2 + (2x-y-1)^2$.

So we have $(x-y)^2 + (2x-y-1)^2 = 0$.

We know that x and y are real numbers, so we have

$(x-y)^2 = 0 \quad \Rightarrow \quad x = y$

$(2x-y-1)^2 = 0 \quad \Rightarrow \quad 2x-y-1=0 \Rightarrow \quad 2x-x-1=0 \Rightarrow \quad x=y=1$.

$100x^2 + y^2 = 101$.

Problem 8. Solution: 800.

From (1), we have $2x + 3y = 13 - z$.

Let $2x = \dfrac{13-z}{2} + t$, and $3y = \dfrac{13-z}{2} - t$ \hfill (3)

Substituting (3) into (2): $3(z-4)^2 + 4\left(t - \dfrac{3}{2}\right)^2 = 0$.

So $z = 4$ and $t = \dfrac{3}{2}$ \hfill (4)

Substituting the values in (4) into (3), we get $x = 3$, $y = 1$. The solution is $x = 3$, $y = 1$, $z = 4$.

$100(x+y+z) = 100 \times 8 = 800$.

Problem 9. Solution: 500.

The given system of equations can be written as

$\begin{cases} (x+\dfrac{9}{x}) + (y+\dfrac{4}{y}) = 10 & (1) \\ \left(x+\dfrac{9}{x}\right)\left(y+\dfrac{4}{y}\right) = 24 & (2) \end{cases}$

$x + \dfrac{9}{x} = m$ and $y + \dfrac{4}{y} = n$ are two roots of the quadratic equation: $t^2 - 10t + 24 = 0$.

So $t_1 = 4$ and $t_2 = 6$.

It follows that

Or
$$\begin{cases} x + \dfrac{9}{x} = 6 \\ y + \dfrac{4}{y} = 4 \end{cases} \quad (3)$$

$$\begin{cases} x + \dfrac{9}{x} = 4 \\ y + \dfrac{4}{y} = 6 \end{cases} \quad (4)$$

Solving (3), we get $x = 3$, $y = 2$. There are no real solutions for (4).
The answer is $100(x+y) = 100(2+3) = 500$.

Problem 10. Solution: 032.

$$\dfrac{1}{1985} = \dfrac{1}{1+(1-\dfrac{1}{n})^2} \times \dfrac{1}{n^2} \Rightarrow \dfrac{1}{1985} = \dfrac{1}{1+(\dfrac{n-1}{n})^2} \times \dfrac{1}{n^2} \Rightarrow \dfrac{1}{1985} = \dfrac{1}{1+\dfrac{(n-1)^2}{n^2}} \times \dfrac{1}{n^2}$$

$$\Rightarrow \dfrac{1}{1985} = \dfrac{1}{\dfrac{n^2+(n-1)^2}{n^2}} \times \dfrac{1}{n^2} \Rightarrow \dfrac{1}{1985} = \dfrac{1}{n^2+(n-1)^2}$$

$$\Rightarrow n^2 + (n-1)^2 = 1985 \Rightarrow n^2 + n^2 - 2n + 1 = 1985$$
$$\Rightarrow 2n^2 - 2n - 1984 = 0 \Rightarrow n^2 - n - 992 = 0 \Rightarrow (n-32)(n+31) = 0$$

The positive value of n is 32.

Problem 11. Solution: 002.

Let $y = x^2 - x$. The given equation becomes: $y + 1 = \dfrac{6}{y} \Rightarrow y^2 + y - 6 = 0 \Rightarrow$

$(y-2)(y+3) = 0$
So $y = 2$ or $y = -3$.
So we have $x^2 - x = -3 \Rightarrow x^2 - x + 3 = 0$ (no real solution).
$x^2 - x = 2 \Rightarrow x^2 - x - 2 = 0$.
So $x = 2$ or $x = -1$.
We have checked and both are the solutions. The answer is $x = 2$.

☆**Problem 12.** Solution: 992.

$$\frac{a}{x+a}+\frac{b}{x+b}+\frac{c}{x+c}=3 \quad\Rightarrow\quad (1-\frac{a}{x+a})+(1-\frac{b}{x+b})+(1-\frac{c}{x+c})=0 \quad\Rightarrow$$

$$\frac{x}{x+a}+\frac{x}{x+b}+\frac{x}{x+c}=0 \quad\Rightarrow\quad \frac{x[3x^2+2(a+b+c)x+(ab+bc+ca)]}{(x+a)(x+b)(x+c)}=0.$$

We have $x = 0$ or

$$3x^2+2(a+b+c)x+(ab+bc+ca)=0 \quad\Rightarrow\quad 3x^2+24x+47=0.$$

The sum of the roots is $m+n = -\frac{24}{3} = -8$

The answer is $1000 + m + n = 1000 - 8 = 992$.

Problem 13. Solution: 024.

The original equation can be written as $3(\frac{1}{x}+\frac{1}{x-5})+(\frac{1}{x-1}+\frac{1}{x-4})+4(\frac{1}{x-2}+\frac{1}{x-3})=0$

$$\Rightarrow \quad \frac{3(2x-5)}{x(x-5)}+\frac{2x-5}{(x-1)(x-4)}+\frac{4(2x-5)}{(x-2)(x-3)}=0$$

$$\Rightarrow \quad (2x-5)[\frac{3}{x(x-5)}+\frac{1}{(x-1)(x-4)}+\frac{4}{(x-2)(x-3)}]=0 \quad (1)$$

We have $2x - 5 = 0 \quad\Rightarrow\quad x_1 = 5/2$.

We have $\frac{3}{x(x-5)}+\frac{1}{(x-1)(x-4)}+\frac{4}{(x-2)(x-3)}=0 \quad\Rightarrow$

$$\frac{3}{x^2-5x}+\frac{1}{x^2-5x+4}+\frac{4}{x^2-5x+6}=0 \quad (2)$$

Let $y = x^2 - 5x$. (2) becomes $\frac{3}{y}+\frac{1}{y+4}+\frac{4}{y+6}=0 \Rightarrow \quad 2y^2+13y+18=0$

$$\Rightarrow \quad (y+2)(2y+9)=0$$

We get $y = -2$ or $y = -\frac{9}{2}$.

When $y = -2$, $x^2 - 5x = -2 \quad\Rightarrow\quad x^2 - 5x + 2 = 0$

Solving we get $x_2 = \frac{5+\sqrt{17}}{2}$, and $x_3 = \frac{5-\sqrt{17}}{2}$.

When $y = -\frac{9}{2}$, $x^2 - 5x = -\frac{9}{2} \quad\Rightarrow\quad 2x^2 - 10x + 9 = 0$

Solving we get $x_4 = \dfrac{5+\sqrt{7}}{2}$, and $x_5 = \dfrac{5-\sqrt{7}}{2}$.

Since we want the greatest real solution, we get $m = x_2 = \dfrac{5+\sqrt{17}}{2}$

$a+b+c = 5+17+2 = 24$.

Problem 14. Solution: 007.

The original equation can be written as

$29(\dfrac{31}{x+2} - 7 + \dfrac{31}{x+3} + 8) = 31(\dfrac{29}{x+1} - 5 + \dfrac{29}{x+4} - 6) + 370 \Rightarrow$

$29 \times 31(\dfrac{1}{x+2} + \dfrac{1}{x+3}) = 31 \times 29(\dfrac{1}{x+1} + \dfrac{1}{x+4}) \Rightarrow \dfrac{1}{x+2} + \dfrac{1}{x+3} = \dfrac{1}{x+1} + \dfrac{1}{x+4}$

$\Rightarrow \dfrac{1}{x+1} - \dfrac{1}{x+3} = \dfrac{1}{x+2} - \dfrac{1}{x+4} \Rightarrow \dfrac{2}{(x+1)(x+3)} = \dfrac{2}{(x+2)(x+4)} \Rightarrow$

$(x+1)(x+3) = (x+2)(x+4) \Rightarrow x^2 + 4x + 3 = x^2 + 6x + 8 \Rightarrow$

$x = -\dfrac{5}{2}$. The answer is $5+2 = 7$.

Problem 15. Solution: 005.

Let $y = x^2 + 10$. The equation in the problem then becomes

$\dfrac{1}{y+2x} + \dfrac{1}{y+11x} + \dfrac{1}{y-13x} = 0 \quad\Rightarrow\quad y^2 - 49x^2 = 0$

So we get $y = \pm 7x$.

When $y = 7x$, $x^2 + 10 = 7x \Rightarrow x^2 - 7x + 10 = 0$.

Solving we have $x_1 = 2$ and $x_2 = 5$.

When $y = -7x$, $x^2 + 10 = -7x \Rightarrow x^2 + 7x + 10 = 0$.

Solving we have $x_3 = -2$ and $x_4 = -5$.

The largest solution is $x_2 = 5$. The answer is 5.

☆**Problem 16.** Solution: 005.

Let $u = \dfrac{x-2}{3}$, $v = \dfrac{x-3}{2}$. The equation in the problem then becomes $u + v = \dfrac{1}{u} + \dfrac{1}{v} \Rightarrow$
$(uv - 1)(u + v) = 0$.

So we have $u + v = 0 \Rightarrow \dfrac{x-2}{3} + \dfrac{x-3}{2} = 0 \Rightarrow x = \dfrac{13}{5}$

and $uv = 1 \Rightarrow \dfrac{x-2}{3} \times \dfrac{x-3}{2} = 1 \Rightarrow x = 5$.

The answer is 5.

☆**Problem 17.** Solution: 417.

$$\sqrt[4]{x} = \dfrac{14}{9 - \sqrt[4]{x}} \Rightarrow \sqrt[4]{x}(9 - \sqrt[4]{x}) = 14 \qquad (1)$$

Let $y = \sqrt[4]{x}$. (1) becomes $y(9 - y) = 14 \Rightarrow y^2 - 9y + 14 = 0$.
Solving we get $y = 7$ or $y = 2$. And $x = 7^4$ or $x = 2^4$.

The sum of the solutions is $7^4 + 2^4 = 2401 + 16 = 2417$. The answer is 417.

Problem 18. Solution: 800.

Let $y = \sqrt{x^2 + 2 + \dfrac{1}{x^2}}$. So $y^2 = x^2 + 2 + \dfrac{1}{x^2} \Rightarrow y^2 - 2 = x^2 + \dfrac{1}{x^2}$.

The original equation becomes $y^2 - 2 + y = 4 \Rightarrow y^2 + y - 6 = 0$.
Solving we get $y_1 = -3$, $y_2 = 2$.

When $y_1 = -3$, $\sqrt{x^2 + 2 + \dfrac{1}{x^2}} = -3$ (no real solutions).

When $y_2 = 2$, $\sqrt{x^2 + 2 + \dfrac{1}{x^2}} = 2 \Rightarrow x^2 + 2 + \dfrac{1}{x^2} = 4 \Rightarrow (x + \dfrac{1}{x})^2 = 4 \qquad (1)$

Since we like to find the positive solution, from (1), we have $x + \dfrac{1}{x} = 2 \Rightarrow$

$x^2 - 2x + 1 = 0 \Rightarrow x = 1$.
The answer is $800 \times 1 = 800$.

☆ **Problem 19.** Solution: 032.

Let $y = \sqrt{x^2 - 5x - 3}$. The equation in the problem can be written as $y^2 - 2xy + x^2 = 16$
$\Rightarrow$ $(x - y)^2 = 16$ $\Rightarrow$ $x - y = -4$ or $\Rightarrow$ $x - y = 4$.

For $x - y = -4$, $x - \sqrt{x^2 - 5x - 3} = -4$ $\Rightarrow$ $x + 4 = \sqrt{x^2 - 5x - 3}$ $\Rightarrow$ $(x+4)^2 = x^2 - 5x - 3$
$\Rightarrow$ $x^2 + 8x + 16 = x^2 - 5x - 3$ $\Rightarrow$ $13x = -19$ $\Rightarrow$ $x = -\dfrac{19}{13}$

For $x - y = 4$, $x - \sqrt{x^2 - 5x - 3} = 4$ $\Rightarrow$ $x - 4 = \sqrt{x^2 - 5x - 3}$ $\Rightarrow$ $(x-4)^2 = x^2 - 5x - 3$
$\Rightarrow$ $x^2 - 8x + 16 = x^2 - 5x - 3$ $\Rightarrow$ $-3x = -19$ $\Rightarrow$ $x = \dfrac{19}{13}$.

$a + b = 19 + 13 = 32$.

Problem 20. Solution: 004.
Factoring (3), we have $(x + z) \cdot (y + u) = 16$.   (5)

From (1), (5) we have $\begin{cases} (x+z)+(y+u)=8 \\ (x+z)\cdot(y+u)=16 \end{cases}$

Taking $x + z$, $y + u$ as unknowns, based on the Vieta formula, we have
$\begin{cases} x + z = 4, \quad (6) \\ y + u = 4. \quad (7) \end{cases}$

We complete the square for (2): $(x + z)^2 - 2xz + (y + u)^2 - 2yu = 20$.
Or $16 - 2xz + 16 - 2yu = 20$.
So $xz + yu = 6$ (8)

From (8), (4), we have $\begin{cases} xz + yu = 6 \\ (xz)\cdot(yu) = 9 \end{cases}$.

Taking xz, yu as unknowns, based on the Vieta formula, we have
$\begin{cases} xz = 3, \quad (9) \\ yu = 3. \quad (10) \end{cases}$

We know from (6), (9) and (7), (10) that x, z or y, u are two roots of $t^2 - 4t + 3 = 0$, so the solutions are $(x, y, z, u) = (1, 1, 3, 3), (3, 1, 1, 3), (1, 3, 3, 1), (3, 3, 1, 1)$.

Problem 21. Solution: 014.
Expanding the equation and cancelling the like terms, we get
$13x^2 + 160y^2 + 405z^2 - 72((xy + yz + zx) = 0$.

Completing the squares: $(3x-12y)^2 +(4y-9z)^2 +(18z-2x)^2 =0$.

Since x, y, and z are real numbers, we have

$3x-12y=0 \quad \Rightarrow \quad x:y = 3:12 = 1:4$

$4y-9z=0 \quad \Rightarrow \quad y:z = 4:9$

So $x:y:z = 1:4:9$.

The answer is $1 + 4 + 9 = 14$.

Chapter 10 Cauchy's Inequalities

BASIC KNOWLEDGE

1.1. Cauchy's Inequality

Let $a_1, a_2, a_3, \ldots, a_n$ and $b_1, b_2, b_3, \ldots, b_n$ be real numbers. Then

$$(a_1^2 + a_2^2 + \ldots + a_n^2) \cdot (b_1^2 + b_2^2 + \ldots + b_n^2) \geq (a_1 b_1 + a_2 b_2 + \ldots + a_n b_n)^2 \qquad (1.1.1)$$

Equality occurs if and only if $b_i = 0 \, (i = 1, 2, \ldots, n)$ or $a_i = k b_i \, (i = 1, 2, \ldots, n)$.

Note:

(1). $a_i = k b_i \, (i = 1, 2, \ldots, n)$ is equivalent to: $\dfrac{a_1}{b_1} = \dfrac{a_2}{b_2} = \cdots = \dfrac{a_n}{b_n}$.

(2). An easy way to memorize the Cauchy's inequality is in the form

$\sum a^2 \sum b^2 \geq (\sum ab)^2$, which actually means $\sum_{i=1}^{n} a_i^2 \sum_{i=1}^{n} b_i^2 \geq \left(\sum_{i=1}^{n} a_i b_i \right)^2$.

1.2. Proof of Cauchy's Inequality

When $a_1 = a_2 = a_3 = \ldots = a_n = 0$ or $b_1 = b_2 = b_3 = \ldots = b_n = 0$, the inequality is true.

Let at least one of $a_1, a_2, a_3, \ldots, a_n$ not be zero. Then $a_1^2 + a_2^2 + a_3^2 + \ldots + a_n^2 > 0$.

Consider a quadratic function

$f(x) = (a_1^2 + a_2^2 + a_3^2 + \ldots + a_n^2) x^2 + 2(a_1 b_1 + a_2 b_2 + \ldots + a_n b_n) x + (b_1^2 + b_2^2 + b_3^2 + \ldots + b_n^2).$

For any real x, $f(x) = (a_1 x + b_1)^2 + (a_2 x + b_2)^2 + \ldots + (a_n x + b_n)^2 \geq 0$.

Therefore the discriminant of the quadratic function $f(x)$ is less than or equal to zero. That is,

$4(a_1 b_1 + a_2 b_2 + \ldots + a_n b_n)^2 - 4(a_1^2 + a_2^2 + \ldots + a_n^2) \cdot (b_1^2 + b_2^2 + \ldots + b_n^2) \leq 0$

$\Rightarrow (a_1^2 + a_2^2 + \ldots + a_n^2) \cdot (b_1^2 + b_2^2 + \ldots + b_n^2) \geq (a_1 b_1 + a_2 b_2 + \ldots + a_n b_n)^2.$

Equality occurs if and only if when $f(x) = 0$ has one real root, which is when $\Delta = 0$.

When this happens, there is only one real x such that $a_i x + b_i = 0$, $(i = 1, 2, \ldots, n)$.

If $x = 0$, then $b_1 = b_2 = b_3 = ... = b_n = 0$, and Cauchy's inequality is true. If $x \neq 0$, then we have $a_i = -\frac{1}{x}b_i$. Thus equality occurs if and only if $b_i = 0$ $(i = 1, 2, ..., n)$ or $a_i = kb_i$ $(i = 1, 2, ..., n)$.

1.3. Other Forms of Cauchy's Inequality

1.3.1. If a, b, c, d are real numbers, then $(a^2 + b^2)(c^2 + d^2) \geq (ac + bd)^2$. Equality occurs if and only if $ad = bc$.

Proof:
Method 1:
$(a^2 + c^2)(b^2 + d^2) - (ab + cd)^2 = (ad - bc)^2 \geq 0$.
Thus equality occurs if and only if $a = bk$, $c = dk$, where k is real.

Method 2:
If $a^2 + c^2 = 0$, then above inequality is true.
Now consider the case when $a^2 + c^2 \neq 0$.
We consider the quadratic function
$(ax - b)^2 + (cx - d)^2 = (a^2 + c^2)x^2 - 2(ab + cd)x + (b^2 + d^2) \geq 0$,
which is positive for all real x.
Therefore the discriminant $\Delta = 4(ab + cd)^2 - 4(a^2 + c^2)(b^2 + d^2) \leq 0$.
Thus $(a^2 + b^2)(c^2 + d^2) \geq (ac + bd)^2$.

1.3.2. If a, b, x, y are real numbers and x, y are positive, then $\dfrac{a^2}{x} + \dfrac{b^2}{y} \geq \dfrac{(a+b)^2}{x+y}$. Equality occurs if and only if $\dfrac{a}{x} = \dfrac{b}{y}$.

Proof:
Since x, y are positive, the inequality can be written as
$a^2 y(x + y) + b^2 x(x + y) \geq (a + b)^2 xy$.
$a^2xy + a^2y^2 + b^2x^2 + b^2xy \geq a^2xy + 2abxy + b^2xy \quad \Rightarrow \quad a^2y^2 + b^2x^2 \geq 2abxy \quad \Rightarrow$

$(ay - bx)^2 \geq 0$ which is true.

Equality occurs if and only if $ay - bx = 0$ or $\dfrac{a}{x} = \dfrac{b}{y}$.

1.3.3. If a, b, x, y are real numbers and x, y are positive, then $\dfrac{a^2}{x} + \dfrac{b^2}{y} + \dfrac{c^2}{z} \geq \dfrac{(a+b+c)^2}{x+y+z}$.

Equality occurs if and only if $\dfrac{a}{x} = \dfrac{b}{y} = \dfrac{c}{z}$.

1.3.4. Let $a_i \in R$, $b_i > 0$ ($i = 1, 2, \ldots, n$). Then $\dfrac{a_1^2}{b_1} + \dfrac{a_2^2}{b_2} + \ldots + \dfrac{a_n^2}{b_n} \geq \dfrac{(a_1 + a_2 + \ldots + a_n)^2}{b_1 + b_2 + \ldots + b_n}$.

Equality occurs if and only if $\dfrac{a_1}{b_1} = \dfrac{a_2}{b_2} = \cdots = \dfrac{a_n}{b_n}$.

1.3.5. Let a_i and b_i ($i = 1, 2$) be nonzero real numbers that have the same sign, then

$\dfrac{a_1}{b_1} + \dfrac{a_2}{b_2} \geq \dfrac{(a_1 + a_2)^2}{a_1 b_1 + a_2 b_2}$. Equality occurs if and only if $b_1 = b_2$.

Proof:
Method 1:

Since a_1, a_2, b_1, and b_2 have the same sign, we have: $(a_1 b_1 + a_2 b_2)\left(\dfrac{a_1}{b_1} + \dfrac{a_2}{b_2}\right) \geq (a_1 + a_2)^2$, or

$a_1^2 + \dfrac{a_1 a_2 b_2}{b_1} + \dfrac{a_1 a_2 b_1}{b_2} + a_2^2 \geq a_1^2 + 2a_1 a_2 + a_2^2 \Rightarrow \dfrac{a_1 a_2 b_2}{b_1} + \dfrac{a_1 a_2 b_1}{b_2} \geq 2a_1 a_2 \Rightarrow$

$\dfrac{a_1 a_2 b_2}{b_1} + \dfrac{a_1 a_2 b_1}{b_2} - 2a_1 a_2 \geq 0 \Rightarrow \left(\dfrac{b_1^2 - 2b_1 b_2 + b_2^2}{b_1 b_2}\right) a_1 a_2 \geq 0 \Rightarrow \dfrac{(b_1 - b_2)^2}{b_1 b_2} a_1 a_2 \geq 0$.

This is true since $a_1 a_2$ and $b_1 b_2$ are positive.
Equality occurs if and only if $b_1 - b_2 = 0$ or $b_1 = b_2$.

Method 2:

Since none of a_1 and a_2 is zero, we have $\dfrac{a_1}{b_1} + \dfrac{a_2}{b_2} = \dfrac{a_1^2}{a_1 b_1} + \dfrac{a_2^2}{a_2 b_2}$.

By **1.3.2**, we have: $\dfrac{a_1}{b_1} + \dfrac{a_2}{b_2} = \dfrac{a_1^2}{a_1 b_1} + \dfrac{a_2^2}{a_2 b_2} \geq \dfrac{(a_1 + a_2)^2}{a_1 b_1 + a_2 b_2}$.

Equality occurs if and only if $\frac{a_1}{a_1b_1} = \frac{a_2}{a_2b_2}$ or $b_1 = b_2$.

1.3.6. If a_i and b_i ($i = 1, 2, 3$) are nonzero and have the same sign, then
$\frac{a_1}{b_1} + \frac{a_2}{b_2} + \frac{a_3}{b_3} \geq \frac{(a_1 + a_2 + a_3)^2}{a_1b_1 + a_2b_2 + a_3b_3}$. Equality occurs if and only if $b_1 = b_2 = b_3$.

1.3.7. If a_i and b_i ($i = 1, 2, ..., n$) are nonzero and have the same sign, then
$\frac{a_1}{b_1} + \frac{a_2}{b_2} + ... + \frac{a_n}{b_n} \geq \frac{(a_1 + a_2 + ... + a_n)^2}{a_1b_1 + a_2b_2 + ... + a_nb_n}$. Equality occurs if and only if $b_1 = b_2 = ... = b_n$.

APPLICATION OF CAUCHY'S INEQUALITY

2.1. Find The Maximum and Minimum Values

Example 1. If $x + 2y + 3z = 4$, then the smallest value of $x^2 + y^2 + z^2$ is a/b, where a and b are positive integers that are relatively prime. Find $a + b$.

Solution: 015.
By Cauchy's 1.3.3,
$$x^2 + y^2 + z^2 = \frac{x^2}{1} + \frac{(2y)^2}{4} + \frac{(3z)^2}{9} \geq \frac{(x + 2y + 3z)^2}{1 + 4 + 9} = \frac{4^2}{14} = \frac{8}{7}.$$
Equality occurs when $x = \frac{2}{7}, y = \frac{4}{7}, z = \frac{6}{7}$. The smallest value is 8/7. The answer is 8 + 7 = 15.

Example 2. The smallest value of $x + y$ for $x, y \in R^+$ can be expressed as $a + b\sqrt{c}$ in simplest radical form. Given that $\frac{19}{x} + \frac{98}{y} = 1$, find $a + b + c$.

Solution: 169.

$$1 = \frac{19}{x} + \frac{98}{y} = \frac{(\sqrt{19})^2}{x} + \frac{(\sqrt{98})^2}{y}.$$

By Cauchy's (1.3.2), we have $1 \geq \dfrac{(\sqrt{19}+\sqrt{98})^2}{x+y} = \dfrac{19+98+14\sqrt{38}}{x+y}$,

Thus $x + y \geq 117 + 14\sqrt{38}$.

Equality occurs when $\dfrac{\sqrt{19}}{x} = \dfrac{\sqrt{98}}{y}$. That is, when $x = 19 + 7\sqrt{38}$, and $y = 98 + 7\sqrt{38}$, $x + y$ has the smallest value of $117 + 14\sqrt{38}$. The answer is $117 + 14 + 38 = 169$.

Example 3. Find the smallest value of $x + \dfrac{y}{2} + \dfrac{z}{3}$ if $\dfrac{1}{x} + \dfrac{2}{y} + \dfrac{3}{z} = 1$, and $x, y, z \in R^+$.

Solution: 009.

$$\frac{1}{x} + \frac{2}{y} + \frac{3}{z} = 1 \Rightarrow \frac{1^2}{x} + \frac{1^2}{\frac{y}{2}} + \frac{1^2}{\frac{z}{3}} = 1 \Rightarrow 1 \geq \frac{(1+1+1)^2}{x + \frac{y}{2} + \frac{z}{3}} \Rightarrow x + \frac{y}{2} + \frac{z}{3} \geq 9.$$

Equality occurs when $\dfrac{1}{x} = \dfrac{1}{\frac{y}{2}} = \dfrac{1}{\frac{z}{3}}$ or $x = 3, y = 6, z = 9$.

So $(x + \dfrac{y}{2} + \dfrac{z}{3})_{min} = 9$.

Example 4. The largest value of $2x - 3y$ can be written as $a + b\sqrt{c}$ in simplest radical form. Find $a + b + c$ if $x^2 + y^2 = 6x - 4y - 9$.

Solution: 027.
Let $2x - 3y = k$.

$x^2 + y^2 = 6x - 4y - 9 \Rightarrow (x-3)^2 + (y+2)^2 = 4 \Rightarrow \dfrac{(2x-6)^2}{4} + \dfrac{(-3y-6)^2}{9} = 4$

By Cauchy's (1.3.3), $4 = \dfrac{(2x-6)^2}{4} + \dfrac{(-3y-6)^2}{9} \geq \dfrac{(2x-6-3y-6)^2}{4+9} = \dfrac{(k-12)^2}{13}$, or

$$\frac{(k-12)^2}{13} \leq 4 \quad \Rightarrow \quad (k-12)^2 \leq 4 \times 13.$$

Since we want to find the largest value of k, we get $k \leq 12 + 2\sqrt{13}$. The largest value is then $k = 12 + 2\sqrt{13}$, which is obtained when $x = 3 + \frac{4\sqrt{13}}{13}$ and $y = -2 - \frac{6\sqrt{13}}{13}$. These values of x and y can be found by solving the system of equations $2x - 3y = 12 + 2\sqrt{13}$ and $\frac{2x-6}{4} = \frac{-3y-6}{9}$. The answer is $12 + 2 + 13 = 27$.

Example 5. Find the smallest value of $(x-3)^2 + (y+2)^2$ if $x + 2y - 4 = 0$.

Solution: 5.

$$(x-3)^2 + (y+2)^2 = \frac{(x-3)^2}{1} + \frac{(2y+4)^2}{4}.$$

By Cauchy's (1.3.3), we have

$$\frac{(x-3)^2}{1} + \frac{(2y+4)^2}{4} \geq \frac{(x-3+2y+4)^2}{1+4} = \frac{(4-3+4)^2}{5} = \frac{(5)^2}{5} = 5.$$

By solving the system of equations:

$$\begin{cases} x + 2y - 4 = 0 \\ \dfrac{x-3}{1} = \dfrac{2y+4}{4} \end{cases}$$

We get tht $x = 4$ and $y = 0$. Therefore, the smallest value is 5, which is obtained when $x = 4$ and $y = 0$.

Example 6. The greatest value of $y = 5\sqrt{x-1} + \sqrt{10-2x}$ is $a\sqrt{b}$ in simplest radical form, where both a and b are positive real numbers. Find $a + b$.

Solution: 009.
The domain of the function is $[1, 5]$, and $y > 0$.

$y = 5\sqrt{x-1} + \sqrt{2}\sqrt{5-x} \le \sqrt{5^2 + (\sqrt{2})^2} \cdot \sqrt{(\sqrt{x-1})^2 + (\sqrt{5-x})^2}$, or $y \le 6\sqrt{3}$. Equality occurs when $\sqrt{2} \cdot \sqrt{x-1} = 5 \cdot \sqrt{5-x}$ or $x = \dfrac{127}{27}$.

The greatest value of y is $6\sqrt{3}$. Thus the answer is $6 + 3 = 009$.

Example 7. The greatest value of $\sqrt{\dfrac{a}{x}} + 2\sqrt{\dfrac{b}{y}} + 3\sqrt{\dfrac{c}{z}}$ is $s\sqrt{t}$ in simplest rdical form if $a + 2b + 3c = 4$ and $\dfrac{1}{x} + \dfrac{2}{y} + \dfrac{3}{z} = 8$. $a, b, c, x, y, z \in R^+$. Find $s + t$.

Solution: 006

$a + 2b + 3c = 4 \Rightarrow (\sqrt{a})^2 + (\sqrt{2b})^2 + (\sqrt{3c})^2 = 4$

$\dfrac{1}{x} + \dfrac{2}{y} + \dfrac{3}{z} = 8 \Rightarrow \left(\sqrt{\dfrac{1}{x}}\right)^2 + \left(\sqrt{\dfrac{2}{y}}\right)^2 + \left(\sqrt{\dfrac{3}{z}}\right)^2 = 8$.

From Cauchy's: $\sqrt{\dfrac{a}{x}} + 2\sqrt{\dfrac{b}{y}} + 3\sqrt{\dfrac{c}{z}} = \sqrt{a} \cdot \sqrt{\dfrac{1}{x}} + \sqrt{2b} \cdot \sqrt{\dfrac{2}{y}} + \sqrt{3c} \cdot \sqrt{\dfrac{3}{z}} \le \sqrt{4 \times 8} = 4\sqrt{2}$,

Equality occurs when $\sqrt{\dfrac{8}{4}}\sqrt{a} = \sqrt{\dfrac{1}{x}}$, $\sqrt{\dfrac{8}{4}}\sqrt{2b} = \sqrt{\dfrac{2}{y}}$, $\sqrt{\dfrac{8}{4}}\sqrt{3c} = \sqrt{\dfrac{3}{z}}$,

or $ax = by = cz = \dfrac{1}{2}$. Thus $\left(\sqrt{\dfrac{a}{x}} + 2\sqrt{\dfrac{b}{y}} + 3\sqrt{\dfrac{c}{z}}\right)_{max} = 4\sqrt{2}$.

The answer is $s + t = 4 + 2 = 6$.

Example 8. (USAMO) The sum of 5 real numbers is 8 and the sum of their squares is 16. What is the largest possible value for one of the numbers?

Solution: $\dfrac{16}{5}$.

Let the five numbers be a, b, c, d, e.

We have $a + b + c + d + e = 8$, and $a^2 + b^2 + c^2 + d^2 + e^2 = 16$.

By Cauchy's Inequality,

$a^2+b^2+c^2+d^2 = \dfrac{a^2}{1}+\dfrac{b^2}{1}+\dfrac{c^2}{1}+\dfrac{d^2}{1} \geq \dfrac{(a+b+c+d)^2}{1+1+1+1}$, or

$(a+b+c+d)^2 \leq 4(a^2+b^2+c^2+d^2)$.

Since $a+b+c+d = 8-e$ and $a^2+b^2+c^2+d^2 = 16-e^2$, we have

$(8-e)^2 \leq 4(16-e^2) \Rightarrow 5e^2 - 16e \leq 0 \Rightarrow 0 \leq e \leq \dfrac{16}{5}$. When $a = b = c = d = \dfrac{6}{5}$,

$e_{max} = \dfrac{16}{5}$.

2.2. Solving Analytic Geometry Problems

Example 9. (2004 China Hope Cup Math Contest) The greatest value of $x+y$ can be written in the form $\sqrt{a} - b$, where a and b are positive real numbers and a is not a perfect square, given that the point $P(x, y)$ is on the ellipse $\dfrac{(x+2)^2}{4} + (y+1)^2 = 1$. Find $a + b$.

Solution: 008.

Method 1 (official solution):

Let $x = -2 + 2\cos\theta$, and $y = -1 + \sin\theta$, where $0 \leq \theta < 2\pi$.

Then, $x + y = -3 + 2\cos\theta + \sin\theta = -3 + \sqrt{5}\sin(\theta + \varphi)$, where $\varphi = \arctan 2$.

The greatest value occurs when $\sin(\theta + \varphi) = 1$. Thus the answer is $5 + 3 = 8$.

Method 2 (our solution):

By Cauchy, we have $\dfrac{(x+2)^2}{4} + \dfrac{(y+1)^2}{1} \geq \dfrac{(x+2+y+1)^2}{4+1} = \dfrac{(x+y+3)^2}{5}$.

Thus $\dfrac{(x+y+3)^2}{5} \leq 1 \Rightarrow (x+y+3)^2 \leq 5 \Rightarrow x+y+3 \leq \sqrt{5} \Rightarrow$

$x+y \leq \sqrt{5} - 3$.

Equality occurs if and only if $\dfrac{x+2}{4} = \dfrac{y+1}{1} \Rightarrow \dfrac{x+2}{4} = y+1$

Substituting $\frac{x+2}{4} = y+1$ into the equation of the ellipse, we obtain that: $x = \frac{4\sqrt{5}}{5} - 2$ and $y = \frac{\sqrt{5}}{5} - 1$. The answer is 5 + 3 = 008.

Example 10. P is a point on the ellipse $\frac{x^2}{4} + \frac{y^2}{7} = 1$ so that the distance from P to the line $l: 3x - 2y - 16 = 0$ is the shortest. Find $a + b + c + d$ if the coordnates of P are $(\frac{a}{b}, -\frac{c}{d})$.

Solution: 16.

The distance from a point on the ellipse to the line is $d = \frac{|3x - 2y - 16|}{\sqrt{3^2 + (-2)^2}} = \frac{|3x - 2y - 16|}{\sqrt{13}}$.

Since we want to find the smallest value of d, we want to find the greatest value of $3x - 2y$ so that the numerator is as small as possible.

We rewrite $\frac{x^2}{4} + \frac{y^2}{7} = 1$ as $\frac{(3x)^2}{4 \times 3^2} + \frac{(-2y)^2}{7 \times 2^2} = 1$.

By Cauchy's Inequality, $\frac{(3x)^2}{4 \times 3^2} + \frac{(-2y)^2}{7 \times 2^2} \geq \frac{(3x - 2y)^2}{36 + 28} = \frac{(3x - 2y)^2}{64}$.

Thus $1 \geq \frac{(3x - 2y)^2}{64}$.

It follows that $(3x - 2y)^2 \leq 64$ $\Rightarrow$ $3x - 2y \leq 8$.

The greatest value of $3x - 2y$ is 8.

Equality occurs when $\frac{3x}{36} = \frac{-2y}{28}$, or $x = \frac{3}{2}$ and $y = -\frac{7}{4}$. The answer is 3 + 2 + 7 + 4 = 016. (The shortest distance is $d = \frac{8}{\sqrt{13}} = \frac{8\sqrt{13}}{13}$).

Example 11. Point (x, y) is on the ellipse $4(x - 2)^2 + y^2 = 4$. The smallest value of y/x can be written as $-\frac{a\sqrt{b}}{c}$ in simplest radical form, where a, b, and c are positive integers. Find $a + b + c$.

Solution: 008.

Let $y/x = k$. We have $y = kx$. The equation $4(x-2)^2 + y^2 = 4$ can be changed into the form of $\dfrac{(kx-2k)^2}{k^2} + \dfrac{(-y)^2}{4} = 1$.

By Cauchy's Inequality, we have $1 = \dfrac{(kx-2k)^2}{k^2} + \dfrac{(-y)^2}{4} \geq \dfrac{(kx-2k-y)^2}{k^2+4} = \dfrac{4k^2}{k^2+4}$.

Thus $1 \geq \dfrac{4k^2}{k^2+4} \Rightarrow k^2 + 4 \geq 4k^2 \Rightarrow k^2 \leq \dfrac{4}{3}$.

Solving, we get $k \leq \dfrac{2\sqrt{3}}{3}$ or $k \geq -\dfrac{2\sqrt{3}}{3}$. The smallest value of y/x is $-\dfrac{2\sqrt{3}}{3}$. This value occurs when $\dfrac{kx-2k}{k^2} = \dfrac{-y}{4}$, or $x = \mp \dfrac{3}{2}$ and $y = \pm\sqrt{3}$. The answer is $2 + 3 + 3 = 008$.

Example 12. (2005 AIME II Problems 15) Let ω_1 and ω_2 denote the circles $x^2 + y^2 + 10x - 24y - 87 = 0$ and $x^2 + y^2 - 10x - 24y + 153 = 0$, respectively. Let m be the smallest positive value of a for which the line $y = ax$ contains the center of a circle that is internally tangent to ω_1 and externally tangent to ω_2. Given that $m^2 = p/q$, where p and q are relatively prime positive integers, find $p + q$.

Solution: 169.

We use the Cauchy inequality to solve the problem.

Complete the squares to obtain $(x+5)^2+(y-12)^2 = 256$ and $(x-5)^2+(y-12)^2 = 16$ for ω_1 and ω_2, respectively.

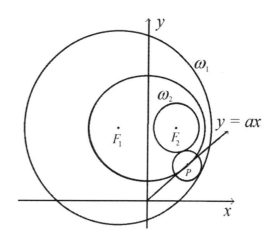

Hence ω_1 is centered at $F_1(-5, 12)$ with radius 16, and ω_1 is centered at $F_2(5, 12)$ with radius 4.

Let P be the center of the third circle, and let r be its radius. Then $PF_1 = 16 - r$ and $PF_2 = 4 + r$. We see that $16 - r + 4 + r = 20$ which is a constant.

Thus P is on the ellipse centered at $(0, 12)$ with foci F_1, F_2 and $PF_1 + PF_2 = 20$. The major axis is 20 and the minor axis is $\sqrt{20^2 - (5-(-5))^2} = 10\sqrt{3}$. Therefore the equation of the ellipse is $\dfrac{x^2}{100} + \dfrac{(y-12)^2}{75} = 1$.

By Cauchy, $1 = \dfrac{(-ax)^2}{100a^2} + \dfrac{(y-12)^2}{75} \geq \dfrac{(y-ax-12)^2}{100a^2 + 75} = \dfrac{(0-12)^2}{100a^2 + 75} = \dfrac{144}{100a^2 + 75}$.

So, we have: $\dfrac{144}{100a^2 + 75} \leq 1 \Rightarrow 100a^2 + 75 \geq 144 \Rightarrow a^2 \geq \dfrac{69}{100}$.

Thus $m^2 = 69/100$, and $p + q = 169$.

2.3. Proving Inequalities

Example 13. Let $a, b, c, d \geq 0$, show that $\dfrac{1}{a} + \dfrac{1}{b} + \dfrac{4}{c} + \dfrac{16}{d} \geq \dfrac{64}{a+b+c+d}$.

Proof:

$$\dfrac{1}{a} + \dfrac{1}{b} + \dfrac{4}{c} + \dfrac{16}{d} = \dfrac{1^2}{a} + \dfrac{1^2}{b} + \dfrac{2^2}{c} + \dfrac{4^2}{d}$$

By Cauchy's (1.3.3): $\dfrac{1^2}{a} + \dfrac{1^2}{b} + \dfrac{2^2}{c} + \dfrac{4^2}{d} \geq \dfrac{(1+1+2+4)^2}{a+b+c+d} = \dfrac{64}{a+b+c+d}$.

Example 14. Show that $\dfrac{a^2}{b+c} + \dfrac{b^2}{c+a} + \dfrac{c^2}{a+b} \geq \dfrac{a+b+c}{2}$ if $a, b, c \in R^+$.

Proof:

By Cauchy's (1.3.3), $\dfrac{a^2}{b+c} + \dfrac{b^2}{c+a} + \dfrac{c^2}{a+b} \geq \dfrac{(a+b+c)^2}{2(a+b+c)} = \dfrac{a+b+c}{2}$.

Example 15. Let a, b, c be positive real numbers. Prove the inequality $\dfrac{a}{b+c} + \dfrac{b}{c+a} + \dfrac{c}{a+b} \geq \dfrac{3}{2}$.

Proof:

By Cauchy's (1.3.3),
$$\frac{a}{b+c}+\frac{b}{c+a}+\frac{c}{a+b}=\frac{a^2}{ab+bc}+\frac{b^2}{ab+bc}+\frac{c^2}{ac+bc}\geq\frac{(a+b+c)^2}{2(ab+bc+ca)}$$

$$=\frac{a^2+b^2+c^2+2(ab+bc+ca)}{2(ab+bc+ca)}\geq\frac{3(ab+bc+ca)}{2(ab+bc+ca)}=\frac{3}{2}.$$

Note we used the following well-known inequality: $a^2+b^2+c^2\geq ab+bc+ca$.

Example 16. Let a, b, x, y, z be positive real numbers. Prove that
$$\frac{x}{ay+bz}+\frac{y}{az+bx}+\frac{z}{ax+by}\geq\frac{3}{a+b}.$$

Solution:

We have $\dfrac{x}{ay+bz}+\dfrac{y}{az+bx}+\dfrac{z}{ax+by}=\dfrac{x^2}{axy+bxz}+\dfrac{y^2}{ayz+bxy}+\dfrac{z^2}{axz+byz}.$

By Cauchy's (1.3.3),
$$\frac{x}{ay+bz}+\frac{y}{az+bx}+\frac{z}{ax+by}\geq\frac{(x+y+z)^2}{(a+b)(xy+xz+yz)}\geq\frac{3}{a+b}.$$

Example 17. a, b, c are positive numbers. $a+b+c=1$. Prove: $\left(a+\dfrac{1}{a}\right)^2+\left(b+\dfrac{1}{b}\right)^2+\left(c+\dfrac{1}{c}\right)^2\geq\dfrac{100}{3}.$

Solution:
By Cauchy's (1.3.3), we have
$$\left(a+\frac{1}{a}\right)^2+\left(b+\frac{1}{b}\right)^2+\left(c+\frac{1}{c}\right)^2\geq\frac{(a+\frac{1}{a}+b+\frac{1}{b}+c+\frac{1}{c})^2}{1+1+1}=\frac{(1+\frac{1}{a}+\frac{1}{b}+\frac{1}{c})^2}{3}\quad(1)$$

By Cauchy's (1.3.3), we have $\dfrac{1}{a}+\dfrac{1}{b}+\dfrac{1}{c}\geq\dfrac{(1+1+1)^2}{a+b+c}=9 \quad (2)$

Substituting (2) into (1): $\left(a+\dfrac{1}{a}\right)^2 + \left(b+\dfrac{1}{b}\right)^2 + \left(c+\dfrac{1}{c}\right)^2 \geq \dfrac{(1+9)^2}{3} = \dfrac{100}{3}$.

Example 18. x, y, and z are positive numbers. $x^2 + y^2 + z^2 = 1$. Prove:
$\dfrac{1}{x^2} + \dfrac{1}{y^2} + \dfrac{1}{z^2} + \dfrac{2(x^3 + y^3 + z^3)}{xyz} \geq 15$.

Solution:

$\dfrac{1}{x^2} + \dfrac{1}{y^2} + \dfrac{1}{z^2} + \dfrac{2(x^3 + y^3 + z^3)}{xyz} = \dfrac{1}{x^2} + \dfrac{1}{y^2} + \dfrac{1}{z^2} + \left(\dfrac{2x^3}{xyz} + \dfrac{2y^3}{xyz} + \dfrac{2z^3}{xyz}\right)$

$= \dfrac{1}{x^2} + \dfrac{1}{y^2} + \dfrac{1}{z^2} + 2\left(\dfrac{x^2}{yz} + \dfrac{y^2}{xz} + \dfrac{z^2}{xy}\right)$.

By Cauchy 1.3.3, $\dfrac{1}{x^2} + \dfrac{1}{y^2} + \dfrac{1}{z^2} \geq \dfrac{(1+1+1)^2}{x^2 + y^2 + z^2} = 9$ \hfill (1)

By Cauchy 1.3.3, $\dfrac{x^2}{yz} + \dfrac{y^2}{xz} + \dfrac{z^2}{xy} \geq \dfrac{(x+y+z)^2}{xy+yz+zx} = \dfrac{x^2+y^2+z^2+2(xy+yz+zx)}{xy+yz+zx}$

$\geq \dfrac{xy+yz+zx+2(xy+yz+zx)}{xy+yz+zx} = 3$.

So $\quad 2\left(\dfrac{x^2}{yz} + \dfrac{y^2}{xz} + \dfrac{z^2}{xy}\right) \geq 6$ \hfill (2)

(1) + (2): $\dfrac{1}{x^2} + \dfrac{1}{y^2} + \dfrac{1}{z^2} + \dfrac{2(x^3+y^3+z^3)}{xyz} \geq 15$.

Example 19. (IMO) Let a, b, c be positive numbers such that $abc = 1$. Prove that
$\dfrac{1}{a^3(b+c)} + \dfrac{1}{b^3(a+c)} + \dfrac{1}{c^3(a+b)} \geq \dfrac{3}{2}$.

Solution:
Method 1:

We see that $\dfrac{1}{a^3(b+c)}+\dfrac{1}{b^3(a+c)}+\dfrac{1}{c^3(a+b)}=\dfrac{\frac{1}{a^2}}{ab+ac}+\dfrac{\frac{1}{b^2}}{ab+bc}+\dfrac{\frac{1}{c^2}}{ac+bc}$.

By Cauchy's (1.3.3), $\dfrac{\frac{1}{a^2}}{ab+ac}+\dfrac{\frac{1}{b^2}}{ab+bc}+\dfrac{\frac{1}{c^2}}{ac+bc} \geq \dfrac{(\frac{1}{a}+\frac{1}{b}+\frac{1}{c})^2}{2(ab+bc+ac)}$.

We know that $abc = 1$, so $\left(\dfrac{1}{a}+\dfrac{1}{b}+\dfrac{1}{c}\right)^2 = \dfrac{(ab+bc+ca)^2}{(abc)^2} = (ab+bc+ca)^2$.

Therefore $\dfrac{1}{a^3(b+c)}+\dfrac{1}{b^3(a+c)}+\dfrac{1}{c^3(a+b)} \geq \dfrac{(ab+bc+ca)}{2} \geq \dfrac{3\sqrt[3]{(abc)^2}}{2}=\dfrac{3}{2}$.

Method 2:
$\dfrac{1}{a^3(b+c)}+\dfrac{1}{b^3(a+c)}+\dfrac{1}{c^3(a+b)}=\dfrac{(bc)^2}{ab+ac}+\dfrac{(ac)^2}{bc+ba}+\dfrac{(ab)^2}{ac+bc}$.

By Cauchy's (1.3.3), we have
$\dfrac{(bc)^2}{ab+ac}+\dfrac{(ac)^2}{bc+ba}+\dfrac{(ab)^2}{ac+bc} \geq \dfrac{(bc+ac+ab)^2}{ab+ac+bc+ba+ac+bc}=\dfrac{1}{2}(ab+bc+ca)$

By AM-GM, we know that $bc+ca+ab \geq 3\sqrt[3]{(abc)^2}=3$. So
$\dfrac{(bc)^2}{ab+ac}+\dfrac{(ac)^2}{bc+ba}+\dfrac{(ab)^2}{ac+bc} \geq \dfrac{1}{2}(ab+bc+ca) \geq \dfrac{1}{2}\cdot 3\sqrt[3]{(abc)^2}=\dfrac{3}{2}$.

Example 20. (ARML) If $a, b, c > 0$ and $a + b + c = 6$, show that
$(a+\dfrac{1}{b})^2+(b+\dfrac{1}{c})^2+(c+\dfrac{1}{a})^2 \geq \dfrac{75}{4}$.

Solution:

$(a+\dfrac{1}{b})^2+(b+\dfrac{1}{c})^2+(c+\dfrac{1}{a})^2 \geq \dfrac{(a+\dfrac{1}{b}+b+\dfrac{1}{c}+c+\dfrac{1}{a})^2}{1+1+1}=\dfrac{(6+\dfrac{1}{a}+\dfrac{1}{b}+\dfrac{1}{c})^2}{3}$ (1)

By Cauchy's (1.3.3), we have $\dfrac{1}{a}+\dfrac{1}{b}+\dfrac{1}{c}\geq=\dfrac{(1+1+1)^2}{a+b+c}=\dfrac{9}{6}=\dfrac{3}{2}$ \hfill (2)

Substituting (2) into (1): $(a+\dfrac{1}{b})^2+(b+\dfrac{1}{c})^2+(c+\dfrac{1}{a})^2\geq\dfrac{(6+\dfrac{3}{2})^2}{3}=\dfrac{75}{4}.$

50 AIME Lectures — Chapter 10 Cauchy's Inequalities

PROBLEMS

Problem 1. The smallest value of $3x^2 + 2y^2 + 5z^2$ can be expressed as $\dfrac{m}{n}$, where m and n are positive integers relatively prime. Find $m + n$ if $3x + 4y + 5z = 1$. ($x, y, z \in R$).

Problem 2 The smallest value of $x^2 + y^2 + z^2$ can be expressed as $\dfrac{m}{n}$, where m and n are positive integers relatively prime. Find $m + n$ if $2x + y + z = 9$. x, y, z are real.

Problem 3. Find the smallest value of $(p + 1)^2 + (q - 3)^2$ if $2p + 3q + 6 = 0$. $p, q \in R$.

Problem 4. The greatest value of $\sqrt{3a+1} + \sqrt{3b+1} + \sqrt{3c+1}$ can be expressed as $m\sqrt{n}$ in simplest radical form. Find $m + n$ if $a + b + c = 1$.

Problem 5. Find the greatest possible value for a if $\dfrac{1}{x^2} + \dfrac{1}{(a-x)^2} \geq 2$ is always true when $0 < x < a$.

Problem 6. (China Hope Cup) Find the range of $a^2 + b^2 + c^2$ if $a + b + c = 2$, $0 < a, b, c < 1$.

(A) $[\dfrac{4}{3}, +\infty)$.   (B) $[\dfrac{4}{3}, 2]$.   (C) $[\dfrac{4}{3}, 2)$.   (D) $(\dfrac{4}{3}, 2)$.

Problem 7. (2000 China Fujian High School Math Contest) $a, b \in R^+$. $a + b = 1$.
Prove: $(a + \dfrac{1}{a})^2 + (b + \dfrac{1}{b})^2 \geq \dfrac{25}{2}$.

Problem 8. Show that $(a-1)^2 + (b-1)^2 \geq \dfrac{9}{2}$ if $a+b+1=0$.

Problem 9. Let $x, y, z > 0$. Prove that $\dfrac{2}{x+y} + \dfrac{2}{y+z} + \dfrac{2}{z+x} \geq \dfrac{9}{x+y+z}$.

Problem 10. Let $a, b, c > 0$. Prove that $\dfrac{a^2+b^2}{a+b} + \dfrac{b^2+c^2}{b+c} + \dfrac{a^2+c^2}{a+c} \geq a+b+c$.

Problem 11. Let $x, y, z > 0$. Prove that $\dfrac{x}{x+2y+3z} + \dfrac{y}{y+2z+3x} + \dfrac{z}{z+2x+3y} \geq \dfrac{1}{2}$.

Problem 12. Problem 8. Let $x, y, z > 0$. Prove that
$$\dfrac{x^2}{(x+y)(x+z)} + \dfrac{y^2}{(y+z)(y+x)} + \dfrac{z^2}{(z+x)(z+y)} \geq \dfrac{3}{4}.$$

Problem 13. The smallest value of $\dfrac{1}{\alpha^2} + \dfrac{1}{\beta^2} + \dfrac{1}{\gamma^2}$ can be expressed as $\dfrac{m}{\pi^2}$, where if $\alpha, \beta,$ and γ are three angles in radians of a triangle, and m is a positive integer. What is m?

Problem 14. (ARML) a, b, c, x, y, z are real numbers. $a^2 + b^2 + c^2 = 25$, $x^2 + y^2 + z^2 = 36$, and $ax + by + cz = 30$. $\dfrac{a+b+c}{x+y+z}$ can be expressed as $\dfrac{m}{n}$, where m and n are positive integers relatively prime. Find $m + n$.

Problem 15. (AMC) Given that $x^2 + y^2 = 14x + 6y + 6$, what is the largest possible value that $3x + 4y$ can have?

Problem 16. The equation of a plane is $5x - 2y - z - 20 = 0$. P in the plane is the foot of the perpendicular from the origin to the plane. The x-coordinate of P can be written as $\dfrac{m}{n}$, where m and n are positive integers relatively prime. Find $m + n$.

Problem 17. (China Hope Cup Math Contest Training) Line $l: y = x + 5$ meet x-axis at A and y-axis at B. C is a point on the ellipse $\dfrac{x^2}{16} + \dfrac{y^2}{9} = 1$. What is the greatest possible area of $\triangle ABC$?

Problem 18. The shortest distance from a point on the hyperbola $\dfrac{x^2}{25} - \dfrac{y^2}{9} = 1$ to the line $l: x - y - 3 = 0$ can be written as $\dfrac{\sqrt{m}}{n}$ in simplest radical form. Find $m + n$.

Problem 19. P is a point on the ellipse $\dfrac{x^2}{25} + \dfrac{y^2}{16} = 1$ such that the distance from P to the line $l: 4x + 5y - 40 = 0$ is the shortest. The x-coordinate of P can be written as $\dfrac{s\sqrt{m}}{n}$ in simplest radical from. Find $s + m + n$.

Problem 20. (2002 USAMO) Let ABC be a triangle such that
$$\left(\cot\dfrac{A}{2}\right)^2 + \left(2\cot\dfrac{B}{2}\right)^2 + \left(3\cot\dfrac{C}{2}\right)^2 = \left(\dfrac{6s}{7r}\right)^2,$$
where s and r denote its semiperimeter and its inradius, respectively. Prove that triangle ABC is similar to a triangle T whose side lengths are all positive integers with no common divisor and determine these integers.

Problem 21. (ARML) If $a, b, c,$ and d are each positive, $a+b+c+d=8$, $a^2+b^2+c^2+d^2=25$, and $c = d$, compute the greatest value that c can have.

SOLUTIONS:

Problem 1. Solution: 017.
By Cauchy's 1.3.3,
$$3x^2 + 2y^2 + 5z^2 = \frac{(3x)^2}{3} + \frac{(4y)^2}{8} + \frac{(5z)^2}{5} \geq \frac{(3x+4y+5z)^2}{3+8+5} = \frac{1}{16}.$$
Equality occurs when $x = \frac{y}{2} = z = \frac{1}{16}$. So the smallest value is $\frac{1}{16}$ and $m + n = 17$.

Problem 2. Solution: 029.
By Cauchy's Inequality 1.3.3:
$$x^2 + y^2 + z^2 = \frac{(2x)^2}{4} + y^2 + z^2 \geq \frac{(2x+y+z)^2}{4+1+1} = \frac{27}{2}.$$ The smallest value is $\frac{27}{2}$ and $m + n = 29$.

Equality occurs when $\frac{2x}{4} = \frac{y}{1} = \frac{z}{1}$ or $x = 3$, $y = 3/2$ and $z = 3/2$.

Problem 3. Solution: 013.
$$(p+1)^2 + (q-3)^2 = \frac{(2p+2)^2}{4} + \frac{(3q-9)^2}{9}.$$

By Cauchy's (1.3.3), we have
$$\frac{(2p+2)^2}{4} + \frac{(3q-9)^2}{9} \geq \frac{(2p+2+3q-9)^2}{4+9} = \frac{(-6+2-9)^2}{4+9} = \frac{(-13)^2}{13} = 13.$$

$$\begin{cases} 2p + 3q + 6 = 0 \\ \dfrac{2p+2}{4} = \dfrac{3q-9}{9} \end{cases}$$

Solving the system of equations, we get $p = -3$, and $q = 0$.
Therefore the smallest value is 13 when $p = -3$, and $q = 0$.

Problem 4. Solution: 005.
By Cauchy's Inequality,
$(a_1^2 + a_2^2 + ... + a_n^2) \cdot (b_1^2 + b_2^2 + ... + b_n^2) \geq (a_1 b_1 + a_2 b_2 + ... + a_n b_n)^2$, we have
$(\sqrt{3a+1} \cdot 1 + \sqrt{3b+1} \cdot 1 + \sqrt{3c+1} \cdot 1)^2 \leq [(3a+1) + (3b+1) + (3c+1)] \cdot (1^2 + 1^2 + 1^2) = 18$.

Equality occurs when $a = b = c = \dfrac{1}{3}$.

The greatest value of $\sqrt{3a+1} + \sqrt{3b+1} + \sqrt{3c+1}$ is $3\sqrt{2}$. $m + n = 5$.

Problem 5. Solution: 002.

By Cauchy's inequality 1.3.2: $\dfrac{x_1^2}{y_1} + \dfrac{x_2^2}{y_2} \geq \dfrac{(x_1+x_2)^2}{y_1+y_2}$, we have

$$\frac{1}{x} + \frac{1}{a-x} \geq \frac{4}{a} \qquad (1)$$

Squaring both sides of (1): $(\dfrac{1}{x} + \dfrac{1}{a-x})^2 \geq (\dfrac{4}{a})^2$

$$\Rightarrow \frac{1}{x^2} + \frac{1}{(a-x)^2} + 2 \cdot \frac{1}{x(a-x)} \geq (\frac{4}{a})^2 \qquad (2)$$

We know that by AM-GM: $\dfrac{1}{x^2} + \dfrac{1}{(a-x)^2} \geq 2 \cdot \sqrt{\dfrac{1}{x^2 \cdot (a-x)^2}} = 2 \dfrac{1}{x} \cdot \dfrac{1}{a-x}$.

If we replace $2 \cdot \dfrac{1}{x(a-x)}$ by $\dfrac{1}{x^2} + \dfrac{1}{(a-x)^2}$, the inequality is still true.

Thus, (2) becomes $2(\dfrac{1}{x^2} + \dfrac{1}{(a-x)^2}) \geq (\dfrac{4}{a})^2 \Rightarrow \dfrac{1}{x^2} + \dfrac{1}{(a-x)^2} \geq \dfrac{8}{a^2}$

Equality occurs when $x = \dfrac{a}{2}$.

From $\dfrac{8}{a^2} \geq 2$, we get $0 < a \leq 2$. $\quad \therefore a_{\max} = 2$. The greatest possible value for a is 2.

Problem 6. Solution: (C).

By Cauchy's (1.3.3): $a^2 + b^2 + c^2 \geq \dfrac{(a+b+c)^2}{1+1+1} = \dfrac{4}{3}$.

So $a^2 + b^2 + c^2 \geq \dfrac{4}{3}$.

We also know that $0 < a, b, c < 1$.
We can have $(1-a)(1-b)(1-c) > 0 \Rightarrow \quad 1 - (a+b+c) + (ab+bc+ca) - abc > 0$.
So $ab + bc + ca > 1$.

Thus $a^2 + b^2 + c^2 = (a+b+c)^2 - 2(ab+bc+ca) = 4 - 2(ab+bc+ca) < 4 - 2 = 2$.

The answer is $\frac{4}{3} \leq a^2 + b^2 + c^2 < 2$.

Problem 7. Solution:
By Cauchy's Inequality, we have
$$(a+\frac{1}{a})^2 + (b+\frac{1}{b})^2 \geq \frac{1}{2}[(a+\frac{1}{a})+(b+\frac{1}{b})]^2 = \frac{1}{2}[1+(\frac{1}{a}+\frac{1}{b})]^2$$

but $\frac{1}{a}+\frac{1}{b} = (a+b)(\frac{1}{a}+\frac{1}{b}) \geq 2\sqrt{ab} \cdot 2\sqrt{\frac{1}{a} \cdot \frac{1}{b}} = 4$.

Therefore $(a+\frac{1}{a})^2 + (b+\frac{1}{b})^2 \geq \frac{1}{2}(1+4)^2 = \frac{25}{2}$.

Problem 8. Solution:

By Cauchy's (1.3.3), $(a-1)^2 + (b-1)^2 \geq \frac{(a-1+b-1)^2}{2} = \frac{(a+b-2)^2}{2} = \frac{(-1-2)^2}{2}$, or

$(a-1)^2 + (b-1)^2 \geq \frac{9}{2}$.

Problem 9. Solution:

Writing the left-hand side as $\frac{(\sqrt{2})^2}{x+y} + \frac{(\sqrt{2})^2}{y+z} + \frac{(\sqrt{2})^2}{z+x}$.

By Cauchy's (1.3.3), $\frac{(\sqrt{2})^2}{x+y} + \frac{(\sqrt{2})^2}{y+z} + \frac{(\sqrt{2})^2}{z+x} \geq \frac{(3\sqrt{2})^2}{2(x+y+z)} = \frac{9}{x+y+z}$.

Equality occurs when $x = y = z$.

Problem 10. Solution:
We write the left-hand side as
$$\frac{a^2}{a+b} + \frac{b^2}{b+c} + \frac{c^2}{a+c} + \frac{b^2}{a+b} + \frac{c^2}{b+c} + \frac{a^2}{a+c}.$$

By Cauchy's (1.3.3), $\frac{a^2+b^2}{a+b} + \frac{b^2+c^2}{b+c} + \frac{a^2+c^2}{a+c} \geq \frac{(2a+2b+2c)^2}{4(a+b+c)} = a+b+c$.

Problem 11. Solution:
We write the left-hand side as
$$\frac{x^2}{x^2+2xy+3xz}+\frac{y^2}{y^2+2yz+3xy}+\frac{z^2}{z^2+2xz+3yz}$$

By Cauchy's (1.3.3), we have
$$\frac{x}{x+2y+3z}+\frac{y}{y+2z+3x}+\frac{z}{z+2x+3y}\geq\frac{(x+y+z)^2}{x^2+y^2+z^2+5(xy+xz+yz)}.$$

We know that $x^2+y^2+z^2 \geq xy+xz+yz$.

It follows that
$$\frac{(x+y+z)^2}{x^2+y^2+z^2+5(xy+xz+yz)}\geq\frac{1}{2}, \text{ and } \frac{x}{x+2y+3z}+\frac{y}{y+2z+3x}+\frac{z}{z+2x+3y}\geq\frac{1}{2}.$$

Problem 12. Solution:
By Cauchy's (1.3.3), we have
$$\frac{x^2}{(x+y)(x+z)}+\frac{y^2}{(y+z)(y+x)}+\frac{z^2}{(z+x)(z+y)}\geq\frac{(x+y+z)^2}{x^2+y^2+z^2+3(xy+xz+yz)}.$$

We know that $x^2+y^2+z^2 \geq xy+xz+yz$.

It follows that $\dfrac{(x+y+z)^2}{x^2+y^2+z^2+3(xy+xz+yz)}\geq\dfrac{3}{4}$, or

$$\frac{x^2}{(x+y)(x+z)}+\frac{y^2}{(y+z)(y+x)}+\frac{z^2}{(z+x)(z+y)}\geq\frac{3}{4}.$$

Problem 13. Solution: 027.
We know that $x^2+y^2+z^2 \geq xy+yz+zx$

If we let $\dfrac{1}{\alpha}=x$, $\dfrac{1}{\beta}=y$, and $\dfrac{1}{\gamma}=z$, we will be able to above inequality to get:

$$\frac{1}{\alpha^2}+\frac{1}{\beta^2}+\frac{1}{\gamma^2}\geq\frac{1}{\alpha\beta}+\frac{1}{\beta\gamma}+\frac{1}{\gamma\alpha} \tag{1}$$

By Cauchy's (1.3.3): $\dfrac{1}{\alpha\beta}+\dfrac{1}{\beta\gamma}+\dfrac{1}{\gamma\alpha}\geq\dfrac{(1+1+1)^2}{\alpha\beta+\beta\gamma+\gamma\alpha}$ (2)

We know that $(\alpha+\beta+\gamma)^2 = \alpha^2+\beta^2+\gamma^2+2(\alpha\beta+\beta\gamma+\gamma\alpha)\geq 3(\alpha\beta+\beta\gamma+\gamma\alpha)$.

$$\dfrac{(\alpha+\beta+\gamma)^2}{3}\geq \alpha\beta+\beta\gamma+\gamma\alpha \quad (3)$$

Substituting (3) into (2), we get: $\dfrac{1}{\alpha\beta}+\dfrac{1}{\beta\gamma}+\dfrac{1}{\gamma\alpha}\geq\dfrac{(1+1+1)^2}{\dfrac{(\alpha+\beta+\gamma)^2}{3}}=\dfrac{27}{\pi^2}$.

Equality occurs when $\alpha+\beta+\gamma=\dfrac{\pi}{3}$. The smallest value of $\dfrac{1}{\alpha^2}+\dfrac{1}{\beta^2}+\dfrac{1}{\gamma^2}$ is $\dfrac{27}{\pi^2}$. So $m = 27$.

Problem 14. Solution: 011.

By Cauchy's, $(a^2+b^2+c^2)(x^2+y^2+z^2)\geq (ax+by+z)^2$. Plugging in the given values in the problem, this inequality becomes $25\times 36 \geq 30^2$, which is true.

Equality occurs when $\dfrac{a}{x}=\dfrac{b}{y}=\dfrac{c}{z}=k \Rightarrow a=kx, b=ky, c=kz$.

$a^2+b^2+c^2 = k^2(x^2+y^2+z^2) \Rightarrow k^2 = \dfrac{25}{36}$ (ignoring the negative value).

Therefore $\dfrac{a+b+c}{x+y+z}=k=\dfrac{5}{6}$. $m + n = 11$.

Problem 15. Solution: 073.

(1996 AMC problem #25). There are two official solutions to this problem. Here we provide a third solution of our own.

The equation $x^2 + y^2 = 14x + 6y + 6$ can be written as $(x-7)^2 + (y-3)^2 = 8^2$. (1)

We can further write the equation in the form of

$$\dfrac{(3x-21)^2}{3^2}+\dfrac{(4y-12)^2}{4^2}=8^2 \quad (2)$$

Applying Cauchy's (1.3.2) to the left hand side of (2):
$$\frac{(3x-21)^2}{3^2}+\frac{(4x-12)^2}{4^2}\geq \frac{(3x-21+4y-12)^2}{3^2+4^2}=\frac{(3x+4y-33)^2}{5^2}.$$

So we have $8^2 \geq \dfrac{(3x+4y-33)^2}{5^2}\quad \Rightarrow \quad 5^2\cdot 8^2 \geq (3x+4y-33)^2$.

Since we want the largest value of $3x + 4y$, we can take the square root of both sides of the above inequality and obtain

$5\cdot 8 \geq 3x+4y-33 \quad \Rightarrow \quad 73\geq 3x+4y$.

Equality occurs when $\dfrac{3x-21}{3^2}=\dfrac{4y-12}{4^2} \quad \Rightarrow \quad \dfrac{x-7}{3}=\dfrac{y-3}{4} \quad \Rightarrow \quad x-7=\dfrac{3}{4}(y-3)$

(3)

Substituting (3) into (1), we have

$\dfrac{4^2(y-3)^2}{3^2}+(y-3)^2=8^2 \quad \Rightarrow \quad \dfrac{5^2(y-3)^2}{3^2}=8^2 \quad \Rightarrow \quad y=\dfrac{47}{5}$, and $x=\dfrac{59}{5}$.

It follows that the largest value of $3x + 4y$ is 73.

Problem 16. Solution: 013.

Let the coordinates of P be (x, y, z).

The distance from the origin to the plane is $d=\sqrt{x^2+y^2+z^2}$.

By Cauchy, $x^2+y^2+z^2=\dfrac{(5x)^2}{25}+\dfrac{(-2y)^2}{4}+\dfrac{(-z)^2}{1}\geq \dfrac{(5x-2y-z)^2}{25+4+1}=\dfrac{20^2}{30}=\dfrac{40}{3}$.

Equality holds when $\dfrac{5x}{25}=\dfrac{-2y}{4}=\dfrac{-z}{1} \quad \Rightarrow \quad x=-5z$ and $y=2z$.

So $5x-2y-z-20=0 \quad \Rightarrow \quad 5(-5z)-2(2z)-z=20$

$z=-\dfrac{2}{3}$, $y=-\dfrac{4}{3}$, and $x=\dfrac{10}{3}$. $m+n=13$.

Note that the distance from the point (x_1, y_1, z_1) to the plane $ax + by + cz + d = 0$ can also be calculated by $\dfrac{|ax_1+by_1+cz_1+d|}{\sqrt{a^2+b^2+c^2}}$.

Problem 17. Solution: 25.
Method 1 (official solution):
Let the coordinate of C be $C(4\cos\theta, 3\sin\theta)$.

The distance from C to l: $d = \dfrac{|5\cos(\theta+\varphi)+5|}{\sqrt{2}}$. The greatest

value of d is $\dfrac{10}{\sqrt{2}}$ when $\cos(\theta+\varphi)=1$.

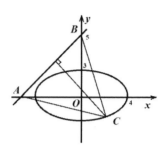

Applying Pythagorean Theorem in right triangle AOB we get: $|AB|=5\sqrt{2}$. We know that $S_{\triangle ABC} = \dfrac{1}{2}|AB|d$. Therefore $(S_{\triangle ABC})_{\max} = \dfrac{1}{2}\times 5\sqrt{2}\times\dfrac{10}{\sqrt{2}} = 25$.

Method 2 (our solution):
We want to find the greatest area of $\triangle ABC$. The length of AB is constant. So we want to have the greatest value for the height (the distance from C to the line AB).

$d = \dfrac{|x-y+5|}{\sqrt{1^2+(-1)^2}} = \dfrac{|x-y+5|}{\sqrt{2}}$.

We want to find the greatest value of $x-y$.

By Cauchy, $1 = \dfrac{x^2}{16} + \dfrac{y^2}{9} = \dfrac{x^2}{16} + \dfrac{(-y)^2}{9} \geq \dfrac{(x-y)^2}{16+9} = \dfrac{(x-y)^2}{25}$.

So $(x-y)^2 \leq 25 \quad\Rightarrow\quad x-y \leq 5$.

The greatest value of $x-y$ is 5. Equality occurs when $\dfrac{x}{16} = \dfrac{-y}{9}$, or $x = \dfrac{16}{5}$ and $y = -\dfrac{9}{5}$.

So the greatest value of d is $\dfrac{10}{\sqrt{2}}$. Therefore $(S_{\triangle ABC})_{\max} = \dfrac{1}{2}\times 5\sqrt{2}\times\dfrac{10}{\sqrt{2}} = 25$.

Problem 18. Solution: 004.
Method 1:
When l: $x-y-3=0$ is sliding right to be tangent to the hyperbola, the distance from a point to the line l is the smallest, which is the distance between two parallel lines.

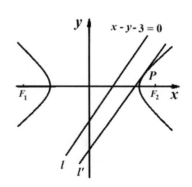

Let l': $x-y-m=0$, then $l'// l$.
Substituting $y = x-m$ into the hyperbola, we get

$16x^2 - 50mx + 25m^2 + 225 = 0$.
So $\Delta = (50m)^2 - 4 \times 16 \times (25m^2 + 225) = 0$.
Solving, we get $m = 4$, and $m = -4$ (we can ignore this value).
Thus $l': x - y - 4 = 0$.

The distance between two lines is $\dfrac{|-3+4|}{\sqrt{2}} = \dfrac{\sqrt{2}}{2}$, so the shortest distance is $\dfrac{\sqrt{2}}{2}$. $m + n = 4$.

Method 2 (our solution):

The distance from a point on the hyperbola to the line is $d = \dfrac{|x-y-3|}{\sqrt{1^2 + (-1)^2}} = \dfrac{|x-y-3|}{\sqrt{2}}$.

The smallest distance d is obtained when $x - y$ is as close to 3 as possible.

$$1 = \frac{x^2}{25} - \frac{y^2}{9} = \frac{x^2}{25} + \frac{(-y)^2}{-9} \geq \frac{(x-y)^2}{25-9} = \frac{(x-y)^2}{16} \quad \Rightarrow \quad 16 \geq (x-y)^2.$$

The closest possible value of $x - y$ is 4, which is achieved when $\dfrac{x}{25} = \dfrac{-y}{-9}$.

Solving the system of equations:
$$\begin{cases} 9x = 25y \\ x - y = 4 \end{cases}$$
we get $x = 25/4$ and $y = 9/4$.

$d = \dfrac{|x-y-3|}{\sqrt{1^2+(-1)^2}} = \dfrac{|x-y-3|}{\sqrt{2}} = \dfrac{|4-3|}{\sqrt{2}} = \dfrac{1}{\sqrt{2}} = \dfrac{\sqrt{2}}{2}$. $m + n = 4$.

Problem 19. Solution: 009.

The distance from a point on the ellipse to the line is $d = \dfrac{|4x+5y-40|}{\sqrt{4^2+5^2}} = \dfrac{|4x+5y-40|}{\sqrt{41}}$.

We want to find the smallest value of d. So we want to find the greatest value of $4x + 5y$ so the numerator could be the smallest.

We rewrite $\dfrac{x^2}{25} + \dfrac{y^2}{16} = 1$ as $\dfrac{(4x)^2}{25 \times 4^2} + \dfrac{(5y)^2}{16 \times 5^2} = 1$.

By Cauchy, $\dfrac{(4x)^2}{25 \times 4^2} + \dfrac{(5y)^2}{16 \times 5^2} \geq \dfrac{(4x+5y)^2}{25 \cdot 16 + 16 \cdot 25} = \dfrac{(4x+5y)^2}{800}$.

253

Thus $1 \geq \dfrac{(4x+5y)^2}{800}$. So $(4x+5y)^2 \leq 800 \Rightarrow 4x+5y \leq 20\sqrt{2}$.

The greatest value of $4x + 5y$ is $20\sqrt{2}$.

Equality occurs when $\dfrac{4x}{400} = \dfrac{5y}{400}$, or $x = \dfrac{5}{2}\sqrt{2}$ and $y = 2\sqrt{2}$. So $s + m + n = 5 + 2 + 2 = 9$.

Note that the shortest distance is $d = \dfrac{20\sqrt{2} - 40}{\sqrt{41}}$.

Problem 20. Solution:

We know that $\cot\dfrac{A}{2} = \dfrac{s-a}{r}$, $\cot\dfrac{B}{2} = \dfrac{s-b}{r}$, $\cot\dfrac{C}{2} = \dfrac{s-c}{r}$.

So $(\cot\dfrac{A}{2})^2 + (2\cot\dfrac{B}{2})^2 + (3\cot\dfrac{C}{2})^2 = (\dfrac{6s}{7r})^2$ can be written as

$$(s-a)^2 + 2^2(s-b)^2 + 3^2(s-c)^2 = (\dfrac{6s}{7})^2 \qquad (1)$$

From the following we see that (1) is the case of Cauchy inequality when the equality holds.

$$\dfrac{(s-a)^2}{1} + \dfrac{(s-b)^2}{\frac{1}{4}} + \dfrac{(s-c)^2}{\frac{1}{9}} \geq \dfrac{(s-a+s-b+s-c)^2}{1+\frac{1}{4}+\frac{1}{9}} = (\dfrac{6s}{7})^2$$

$$\dfrac{(s-a)}{1} = \dfrac{(s-b)}{\frac{1}{4}} = \dfrac{(s-c)}{\frac{1}{9}} = \dfrac{(3s-a-b-c)}{1+\frac{1}{4}+\frac{1}{9}} = \dfrac{36s}{49} \Rightarrow \dfrac{a}{13} = \dfrac{b}{40} = \dfrac{c}{45}.$$

So triangle ABC is similar to a triangle with side lengths 13, 40, 45.

Problem 21. Solution: $\dfrac{7}{2}$.

Let the four numbers be a, b, c, d.

We have $a + b = 8 - 2c$, and $a^2 + b^2 = 25 - 2c^2$.

By Cauchy's Inequality,

$$a^2 + b^2 = \frac{a^2}{1} + \frac{b^2}{1} \geq \frac{(a+b)^2}{1+1}, \text{ or } (a+b)^2 \leq 2(a^2+b^2).$$

Since $a+b = 8-2c$ and $a^2+b^2 = 25-2c^2$, we have

$(8-2c)^2 \leq 2(25-2c^2) \Rightarrow 8c^2 - 32c + 14 \leq 0 \Rightarrow \quad 4c^2 - 16c + 7 \leq 0 \Rightarrow \quad \frac{1}{2} \leq c \leq \frac{7}{2}$。

The greatest value of c is $\frac{7}{2}$ when $a = b = \frac{1}{2}$.

A

acute angle, 64
acute triangle, 55, 60, 106
angle, 11, 23, 30, 31, 36, 43, 64, 116, 134, 135, 139, 144, 153
area, 2, 3, 4, 5, 6, 9, 10, 12, 14, 17, 18, 19, 20, 21, 22, 23, 29, 30, 31, 33, 37, 38, 50, 66, 67, 77, 80, 84, 100, 101, 102, 103, 104, 107, 108, 112, 113, 114, 115, 116, 117, 118, 119, 120, 124, 130, 132, 136, 137, 142, 143, 144, 149, 167, 171, 245, 252
arithmetic sequence, 193

B

base, 2, 3, 5, 10, 11, 12, 14, 15, 18, 19, 28, 29, 30, 49, 52, 60, 62, 95, 179, 197, 199
base 10, 179
bisect, 74, 89

C

Cauchy inequality, 237, 254
center, 6, 19, 31, 55, 61, 109, 135, 237
circle, 20, 83, 94, 105, 114, 120, 136, 138, 143, 237
collinear, 43, 44, 45, 54, 55, 56, 61, 62, 111, 112, 128, 135, 139, 143, 144, 149, 153
common divisor, 245
congruent, 1, 26, 28, 64, 125
constant, 238, 252
Converse, 128, 130
convex, 44, 47, 48, 49, 54, 55, 57, 83, 96, 97, 115, 124, 141
coplanar, 51, 63
corresponding angles, 64
cube, 2, 3, 4, 5, 6, 7, 8, 9, 11, 12, 13, 16, 46, 47, 49, 50, 52, 54, 55, 60, 61, 62, 63

D

data, 140
denominator, 164
diagonal, 2, 4, 9, 11, 12, 13, 17, 39, 49, 50, 54, 61, 63, 69, 80, 97, 113
diameter, 114, 120, 136, 138
difference, 193, 220
divisor, 189

E

edge, 2, 11, 14, 19, 23, 24, 31, 32, 37, 43, 47, 48, 49, 51, 52, 53, 55, 58, 59, 60, 61, 62
ellipse, 236, 238, 245, 253
endpoint, 50
equation, 108, 109, 125, 163, 174, 175, 181, 182, 184, 185, 186, 187, 189, 190, 192, 194, 195, 196, 198, 199, 204, 206, 207, 208, 209, 210, 211, 212, 213, 214, 216, 217, 218, 220, 221, 222, 223, 224, 225, 226, 236, 238, 245, 250
equilateral, 3, 5, 6, 12, 16, 19, 20, 22, 23, 24, 28, 30, 37, 38, 48, 49, 50, 54, 60, 145
equilateral triangle, 3, 5, 6, 12, 16, 19, 20, 22, 23, 24, 28, 30, 37, 38, 48, 49, 54, 60, 145
even number, 130
exponent, 179
expression, 168, 181, 194, 196, 197, 228

F

face, 4, 20, 43, 47, 48, 49, 50, 52, 53, 54, 55, 57, 59, 61, 62, 63
factor, 32, 163, 168, 175, 184, 185
formula, 38, 43, 44, 46, 47, 48, 53, 55, 57, 58, 59, 63, 163, 175, 183, 188, 197, 198, 226
fraction, 29
function, 228, 229, 233

G

geometric sequence, 188, 193

H

hexagon, 4, 7, 9, 14, 47, 48, 83, 111, 143
hypotenuse, 64, 105, 133

Index

I

inequality, 162, 228, 229, 238, 247, 249, 250, 251
integer, 65, 155, 156, 158, 159, 165, 167, 172, 176, 183, 188, 189, 193, 194, 195, 196, 201, 244
integers, 3, 4, 9, 49, 50, 51, 58, 59, 67, 72, 76, 77, 80, 81, 82, 103, 112, 115, 131, 137, 142, 143, 145, 157, 158, 162, 163, 164, 167, 168, 169, 172, 185, 188, 189, 191, 192, 193, 206, 209, 210, 213, 216, 217, 218, 231, 236, 237, 243, 244, 245
intersecting lines, 44, 45, 56
intersection, 2, 18, 45, 46, 60, 66, 70, 71, 77, 78, 82, 83, 124, 132, 133, 134, 135, 137, 138, 142, 143, 144
isosceles, 21, 28, 31, 39, 83, 148
isosceles triangle, 21, 28, 31, 83

L

lateral edge, 1, 19, 22, 30, 53, 63
lateral surface area, 12
line, 44, 45, 54, 56, 61, 65, 69, 71, 77, 78, 81, 88, 126, 128, 131, 132, 133, 134, 138, 139, 145, 146, 150, 151, 152, 236, 237, 245, 252, 253
line segment, 44, 45, 54, 61, 71, 88

M

mean, 185, 205
median, 15, 19, 21, 36, 38, 41, 72, 82, 141, 142
midpoint, 11, 21, 22, 25, 26, 28, 33, 34, 39, 51, 52, 62, 65, 70, 72, 82, 101, 107, 108, 113, 116, 134, 140, 141, 145, 154

N

negative number, 179
numerator, 52, 164, 236, 253

O

octagon, 47, 48
octahedron, 6, 59
odd number, 54
ordered pair, 185, 186, 192, 196
origin, 245, 251

P

parallel, 1, 2, 43, 44, 45, 54, 56, 65, 66, 67, 68, 71, 77, 78, 80, 81, 106, 125, 148, 152, 252
parallelogram, 1, 69, 70, 71, 74, 81, 82, 85, 97, 101, 113, 115, 124, 125, 134, 142, 143
pentagon, 115, 124
perpendicular, 1, 2, 22, 30, 32, 34, 42, 65, 105, 109, 116, 152, 245
plane, 1, 2, 4, 5, 6, 9, 14, 15, 19, 20, 21, 23, 25, 26, 27, 28, 33, 34, 35, 36, 37, 39, 40, 43, 45, 46, 47, 50, 51, 55, 56, 61, 62, 128, 245, 251
point, 5, 11, 19, 29, 36, 45, 51, 52, 56, 60, 61, 62, 66, 67, 68, 69, 70, 71, 73, 77, 80, 81, 82, 97, 102, 105, 106, 110, 113, 114, 115, 124, 128, 132, 133, 134, 135, 136, 138, 140, 142, 143, 144, 145, 146, 236, 245, 251, 252, 253
polygon, 43, 49, 54, 58
polyhedron, 1, 7, 8, 19, 43, 44, 47, 48, 49, 54, 55, 57, 58, 59
positive number, 163, 190, 193, 211, 212, 239, 240
prism, 1, 2, 3, 6, 9, 10, 11, 13, 16, 28, 29, 55, 61
probability, 51, 52
product, 2, 5, 80, 114, 132, 185, 189, 192, 213, 214
proportion, 64
pyramid, 53, 55, 63
Pythagorean Theorem, 20, 21, 23, 33, 35, 36, 40, 252

Q

quadrilateral, 57, 80, 96, 97, 100, 103, 104, 112, 113, 114, 118, 130, 133, 136, 137, 141, 142, 144, 149, 150

R

radius, 20, 94, 105, 109, 120, 237
range, 233, 243
ratio, 3, 9, 13, 14, 19, 24, 25, 31, 38, 65, 66, 77, 78, 95, 96, 101, 108, 114, 123
real number, 84, 157, 162, 164, 165, 167, 168, 169, 175, 179, 183, 193, 196, 205, 206, 207, 216, 218, 221, 227, 228, 229, 230, 234, 238, 239, 244
real numbers, 157, 164, 165, 167, 168, 169, 175, 179, 183, 193, 205, 206, 207, 216, 218, 221, 227, 228, 229, 230, 234, 238, 239, 244

rectangle, 6, 15, 16, 18, 31, 65, 80
regular polygon, 1
relatively prime, 4, 9, 11, 24, 25, 30, 31, 51, 67, 72, 76, 77, 80, 81, 82, 103, 112, 115, 131, 137, 142, 143, 145, 162, 164, 167, 168, 169, 189, 191, 193, 206, 216, 218, 231, 237, 243, 244, 245
right angle, 105
right triangle, 14, 16, 18, 20, 23, 33, 36, 60, 61, 64, 84, 105, 120, 252
root, 228

S

sequence, 193
set, 197
similar, 24, 25, 37, 53, 64, 65, 67, 71, 78, 84, 96, 108, 117, 149, 245, 254
solution, 17, 63, 67, 69, 70, 71, 76, 77, 78, 79, 100, 101, 102, 103, 105, 106, 107, 108, 120, 124, 125, 132, 135, 149, 158, 172, 184, 185, 186, 187, 192, 194, 195, 196, 197, 201, 202, 205, 209, 210, 211, 212, 213, 214, 217, 218, 221, 222, 224, 225, 235, 250, 252, 253
sphere, 20
square, 3, 7, 9, 10, 15, 28, 29, 31, 44, 47, 57, 66, 81, 101, 104, 108, 114, 136, 155, 177, 188, 189, 220, 226, 237, 251
square root, 251
sum, 2, 3, 4, 9, 11, 14, 22, 23, 32, 43, 49, 50, 54, 59, 81, 155, 158, 192, 199, 217, 223, 225, 234
surface area, 3, 6, 9, 10, 13, 16, 20, 24, 25, 32

T

tetrahedron, 3, 5, 8, 9, 10, 12, 14, 16, 19, 20, 21, 22, 23, 24, 25, 26, 28, 29, 30, 31, 32, 33, 34, 36, 37, 38, 39, 41, 49, 51, 52, 55, 60, 62, 63
transversal, 126, 128, 129, 131, 132, 133, 134, 135, 136, 137, 138, 139, 140, 146, 147, 149, 151, 152, 153, 154
trapezoid, 39, 83, 98, 124
triangle, 7, 9, 14, 15, 17, 19, 21, 22, 30, 31, 33, 34, 37, 39, 49, 50, 60, 64, 65, 66, 67, 72, 74, 77, 82, 94, 97, 98, 100, 101, 102, 103, 105, 107, 108, 109, 110, 113, 115, 116, 117, 118, 122, 123, 126, 127, 128, 129, 130, 132, 135, 137, 140, 141, 142, 143, 145, 146, 148, 149, 150, 244, 245, 254
trisect, 6, 72, 112

V

vertex, 9, 19, 41, 43, 47, 48, 49, 50, 53, 54, 55, 58, 60, 123, 128, 135
volume, 2, 3, 4, 6, 7, 8, 10, 11, 14, 18, 20, 21, 22, 23, 24, 28, 29, 30, 31, 32, 33, 36, 37, 39, 41, 42

X

x-axis, 245
x-coordinate, 245
x-intercept, 179

Y

y-axis, 245

Z

zero, 184, 197, 228, 230

Made in the USA
Middletown, DE
12 February 2016